AVALANCHE

Heretical Reflections on the Dark and the Light

W. BRUGH JOY, M.D.

BALLANTINE BOOKS · NEW YORK

Copyright © 1990 by W. Brugh Joy, M.D.

All rights reserved under International and Pan-American Copyright Conventions. Published in the United States by Ballantine Books, a division of Random House, Inc., New York, and simultaneously in Canada by Random House of Canada Limited, Toronto.

Scripture taken from the Holy Bible, New International Version. Copyright © 1973, 1978, 1984 International Bible Society. Used by permission of Zondervan Bible Publishers.

Library of Congress Catalog Card Number: 91-93088

ISBN: 0-345-36722-7

Cover design by Sheryl Kagen
Text design by Holly Johnson

Manufactured in the United States of America

First Trade Paperback Edition: July 1992

10 9 8 7 6 5 4 3 2 1

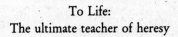

To Life:
The ultimate teacher of heresy

ACKNOWLEDGMENT

I am pleased to acknowledge the work of John S. Niendorff, who edited the manuscript of *Avalanche*. He contributed significantly to the clarity with which this material is presented.

———

Have you ever suspected that unseen, almost mystical, forces are moving a project? I swear such forces lie behind the writing and the publication of this work. Part of these forces flowed from a group of individuals I term "The Women." Signe Quinn Taff, Cheryl Woodruff, Susan Petersen, and Liz Williams . . . thank you!

CONTENTS

AVALANCHE

**Heretical Reflections on
the Dark and the Light**

PROLOGUE

A decade has passed since I wrote *Joy's Way—A Map for the Transformational Journey*. In that book I discussed the many experiences, thoughts, feelings, and insights that moved me from the practice of traditional medicine, as an internist specializing in diagnostics and pulmonary diseases, into the rich and varied world of the Life Teacher. In that latter capacity, I was to work with and teach such things as awakening expanded ranges of human awareness, self-healing, the meaning and interpretation of dreams, the use of the Tarot, human energy fields associated with the chakra system, inner Teachers and outer Teachers, and the extraordinary power of Unconditional Love and the Heart Chakra state of consciousness.

Joy's Way was a distillation of those teachings—teachings that I presented in my two-week residential Conferences, and that had moved and inspired people from all walks of life over the preceding five years. That book had to be written so I might capture the power and significance of the first major change of my professional life . . . from the traditional, ordinary, and orthodox to the nontraditional, the transordinary, and the unorthodox. At the end of *Joy's Way*, I also indicated that I felt another major change was about to occur in me. Now, eleven years later, I can finally articulate what did occur and how powerfully my viewpoints have shifted and matured.

However, I shall not lead the reader through the material in a linear fashion, as though I were presenting a chronicle. Rather, I offer subjective impressions, revealing how I recall and appreciate experiences that deeply moved me. Thus, *Avalanche* is not only about the external events of the past decade. It is also about the insights, revelations, and creative perspectives that have further enriched my experience of the Mystery of Being. From life-changing dreams to innovative perspectives on old stories and old forms, I offer the reader a view of my consciousness as it reflects my nature both as a Teacher of Life and as a Student of Life, with all the shifting psychological values and viewpoints that these two perspectives entail. Where I can, I attempt to credit the many teachers and other people whose contributions have influenced this material, but much of the time I do not actually recall specific sources. Moreover, because most of the text has arisen intuitively and spontaneously within me, there is simply no external source to credit.

Should one be familiar with *Joy's Way* in order to benefit from *Avalanche*? Not necessarily. An awareness of what I shared in *Joy's Way* would primarily be helpful for purposes of comparison—allowing the reader to appreciate the changes I have undergone and to understand the full spectrum of my life's journey. But even with the background from *Joy's Way*, much of this new material is so challenging and creative by itself that little or no reference to the earlier material is necessary.

To me, the past decade seems as though it contains the experiences of several lifetimes. Or, to put it into the context of this book, the experiences of several different selves incarnating into the same body. The material is deeper, richer, and more mature than what I presented in *Joy's Way*. For me, it is threatening and soul-stretching, filled with the kinds of creative insight and revelation that give life a sense of profound value and mystery. I must point out clearly, however, that while I present this material as truth—as truth which can be contemplated and also engaged experientially—I don't represent it as *the* truth. It is only *a* truth or *a* perspective among many that can lead to individual awakening.

Most readers will find this material renovative and stimulating, perhaps even alarming in its various implications. I will purposefully explore very menacing and controversial viewpoints, to crack the consciousness so it can experience a more substantial reality, one beyond the perspectives of the ordinary. This birthing into creative experiences with a freshness of perspective is, for me, what awakening at this staging of my own life is all about.

I experienced such a birthing in 1981, during a sunrise meditation in Egypt, atop the Great Pyramid of Cheops.

The preparation and the actual climb to the top of the Great Pyramid is always an exciting experience no matter how many times one has done it. The ritual contains, for me, elements of fear, danger, and the unknown. As climbing the pyramid is forbidden, an early morning ascent (between 3:00 and 4:00 A.M.) is necessary to avoid the police and most, but not all, of the extremely enterprising Egyptians who haunt the pyramid complex day and night. Taking these Egyptians into consideration is important, for they are a part of the total experience of a series of negotiations that results in a potentially peak meditative experience on top of the pyramid, or the even more exciting peak experience of spending the night in the pyramid . . . alone.

The ascent of 450-plus feet is not easy for most people. Paying some money to one of the "guardians" of the pyramid to show the way to the top and to help when a particularly difficult part of the climb is encountered is well worth the expenditure, as many who have traveled to Egypt with me have reported. Never mind the almost constant renegotiations over amounts of money or the frequent sexual groping by the ever-aggressive Egyptian men of both males and females. At the most important moments, the "guides" respect silence and nontouch.

For this particular climb I had arisen at 2:30 in the morning, ritually bathed, dressed, and carefully packed a knapsack with four large crystals I was intending to gift. I also took a flashlight, which is essential on a moonless night, as the top is uneven and has several layers of stone-block. I headed for the northwest corner of the pyramid and quickly began the ascent without disturbance.

No matter how many times I have climbed the pyramid, I invariably reach a place about two-thirds of the way up where I deal with panic. Fear of heights mingles with a strange compulsion to fling myself off the face of the pyramid, or I sense a repelling force and fear being thrown off. I have to lean into the giant structure and take each huge block layer one at a time until I reach the summit. Covering the top one-third takes me longer than climbing the first two-thirds. Once I am on top, though, the feeling completely subsides. It does not recur on the descent.

Seven or eight other people were on top that morning . . . several Americans, with the rest apparently from various parts of Europe and Asia . . . along with the ubiquitous "guides." I positioned myself at the eastern edge so I could face the approaching sunrise, then carefully laid out the large crystals on a purple velvet cloth and entered a preparatory meditation.

I wanted the first rays of the sun to strike the crystals, which were already exposed to the plume of energy that is emitted from the apex of the pyramid. I would then cover the crystals just before the descent. All was in accord.

A few minutes before sunrise, as I watched the crystals gathering the early morning light and the glow of the sun just before it appeared, I was in a wonderful state. I was approaching the mystery of the sun and the sunrise . . . not from the perspective of the intellect but rather from the perspective of the intuition, which sees the Spiritual Sun, the symbol of awakening and illumination. I was inspired, excited, anticipatory, and expanded.

Then, without warning, I experienced the onset of a quaking within my body. It is a subjective shaking, as my physical body doesn't appear to be moving when it happens. Similar feelings had occurred in me before in other parts of the world, and they usually signaled major changes in my life. Often they forecasted the collapse of social or spiritual values. I thought, "Oh God, not again!"

This time, the quaking was particularly powerful. And within four minutes, everything I held as sacred collapsed into one large heap! Gone was the inspiration of Christ. Gone was the sense of Compassion of the Buddha. Gone were the senses of spiritual uplift-ment, induction, and specialness I invariably experienced when I con-templated aspects of Tibetan Buddhism, Native American Indian beliefs, Zen, Shamanism, and Judaism; or such places as Jerusalem and Machu Picchu; or Egyptian temples, cathedrals, and mosques. Until one experiences it personally, understanding how pervasive, immediate, and devastatingly complete such an internal collapse can be is impossible. The pain of the vacuum was unbearable, and I involuntarily cried out.

My first instinct was to fill this meaningless, painful void with something ... anything ... even if I had to make it up—then an impression arose from deep within me. It was not the same as the inner voice that spoke to me in 1974 announcing the end of my career as a physician. It was a thought-impression, more like a feeling, and it counseled me thus: "Don't fill this painful place with yet another spiritual viewpoint. Let Life teach you what Spirit is!"

I was shocked into ecstasy. In that timeless moment, the spiritual filters through which I had appreciated, evaluated, accepted, and rejected parts of myself and of the world as spiritual and not spiritual crumbled, giving me, for the first time, the realization that spiritual viewpoints *are* filters and *do* incline toward exclusivity and often *do* contain an intrinsic rejection of most of what is Self and what is the world. The experience was totally and completely renovative, birthing what for me was a creative "new" reality. I felt liberated and peculiarly unburdened. The mystery of the Mystery was again nascent. I could once again apprentice myself to Life and feel the wholeness of its manifestations.

Thus began my experience on the path of inclusiveness in all areas, including that of Spirit. A simple shift in perspective and the world miraculously changed!

Much to my surprise, some of the "sacred" viewpoints I had held to be Truth reversed or collapsed under the impact of the new way I perceived the world. For instance, I now no longer embrace the view that personal continuity follows death, nor do I embrace reincarnational perspectives, although each was a huge and significant foundation stone in my own earlier staging. Even more astonishing is the fact that, although I no longer hold to many of the tenets I once believed, I can find parts of myself that still *do* believe that material and that still find it germane to certain important and essential stages of teaching. This seeming paradox is part of the remarkable transformation of thought and Being that is currently flowing through my life.

In 1973 a forbidden thought entered my awareness. Can disease be felt as fields of energy radiating from the body? And my perception of the physical world was permanently transformed. In 1974 a voice spoke to me during a morning meditation and my life was irrevocably changed in course and content. In 1979 a nightmarish dream ruptured my comfortable world of Spirit and matter, plunging me into the awesome and vastly challenging material I shall present in this book.

Thus, prepare yourself. Just as with my Conference work, one cannot contact this material deeply without being permanently influenced by it. It is definitely not for beginners, nor for those who base their understanding of spiritual development just on Love, Light, and Harmony or on other New Age viewpoints advocating only the virtue of the positive or the power of peace. It requires that the ability to center in the Heart Chakra, with its attributes of Unconditional Love and Compassion, be experientially well established. The capacity for creative thought and for appreciation of the Mystery are also requisite. In short, what is required is the capacity to be inclusive . . . to allow the masculine principle of exclusivity to die as the dominant path in spiritual Unfoldment.

My intention, therefore, is not only to share ideas and feelings but also to generate psychological tension in you, the reader, through offering heretical viewpoints that can stimulate you to encounter Life with a fresh perspective.

Many artistic works produce this same result, whether intentionally or not. Some of Chekhov's plays, for example, present certain themes in such a confrontive and anxiety-producing manner that members of the audience are thrown into personal crisis and, upon leaving the performance, are forced to resolve the tension through introducing greater spontaneity and creativity into their lives. Through this book I hope to accomplish a similar result, except, as we shall come to understand, the resolution of that tension is not brought about by your conscious mind but by the vast individual and collective Unconscious forces on which your conscious mind rests.

Welcome then to an avalanche of the psychospiritual dimension, one in which my frozen spiritual values finally broke free. Welcome to a Mystery Play ... which begins with a dream.

PART I

THE DARK AWAKENING

CHAPTER ONE

THE DREAMER AND THE
DREAM ARE INDIVISIBLE

The quality and overall pattern of the first major phase of my psychospiritual development were announced to me at the age of nine by a wondrous dream. The end of that phase and the beginning of the next were announced exactly three decades later, by a nightmare.

The dream. Age nine, Los Angeles, California.

I am running home to tell my mother that Christ has come and I am going to follow him. It is a beautiful, sunlit day. I enter what is our home in the dream—a pure white adobe building, rectangular in shape, with a large wooden plank front door and wooden plank floors. With all the excitement and wonder a nine-year-old boy can express, I make this announcement and beg my mother, my twin brother, and my older brother to follow, but they are not interested in what I have to say. I realize that I will leave home alone and follow this great Being.

When I awoke, I was overwhelmed simultaneously with ecstatic joy and profound grief.

I told no one of the dream. Needless to say, I liked it, for I had a rich, warm feeling whenever I happened to recall it. But it seemed almost foreign to my sense of who I was at that time. The adobe house was nothing like any of our homes had been, and neither I nor my family were religious in the traditional sense. The dream had to wait thirty years before I could appreciate how prophetic it had been.

The nightmare. Age thirty-nine, Lucerne Valley, California. This was an encounter with a very different aspect of God.

It is night. With the fuel gauge indicating empty, I am driving into a well-lighted service station to get some gasoline for my car, an arctic white 1939 Plymouth with a louvered hood. (Such a vehicle was in fact the first car I ever owned.) I am alone in the car. I notice in the shadows, just outside the station, a gang of Hell's Angels types revving up their motorcycles. I don't feel they will be a threat, as the station is very well lighted. I park beside a gas pump and get out of my car to talk to an old man who is inside a glass enclosure twenty or thirty feet away from the pumps. He is a friendly old man. I decide he is the owner and ask him to pump some gas for me, which he agrees to do.

When I turn to walk back to my car, I feel an evil presence behind me. I think immediately of the Hell's Angels gang. When I turn to confront what I feel, I am terrified to see that it is not just an evil presence. It is Evil Incarnate, Himself, stalking me.

I run to my car, jump in, slam the door, and frantically roll up the window and manage to lock the door with my elbow. I am letting out a sigh of relief when I look into the rearview mirror and see that Evil Incarnate is sitting in the backseat of my car, locking eyes with me in the mirror. My hair stands straight up on end . . . I let out a scream and awake screaming.

It was months before I could even begin my analysis of this dream, and five years before I told anyone about it. It was a dream that initiated the slow-motion destruction of every one of my childhood, adolescent, and young-adult values, both spiritual and temporal. It raped my innocence and left a wound that cannot be healed in a portion of my psyche. I did not realize, nor was I ready to accept if I had known, what had been announced through the dream . . . that my life, which had been markedly influenced at conscious and unconscious levels by the pattern of the positive polarity of Christ's life, had reached a turning point. The Spiritual Fall was to begin.

Approaching the Analysis of Dreams

To convey a sense of the meaning I felt in these dreams, I will present some of my beliefs about dreams as well as preliminary material about how I approach dreams and their interpretation.

• Dreams reflect actual forces at work in our larger Beingness, no matter what our outer awareness is thinking or experiencing or in what time reference our outer mind is framing things. The outer mind lives in a world mostly of its own making and has little if any idea of how tenuous and illusory that world actually is. For this reason alone, as I continually repeat, the outer mind, the outer awareness, is 99.99999 percent comatose!

• Dreams are reflections of fundamental psychic forces reflected as patterns interacting in the form of images and feelings . . . patterns that are contained in the very nature and mystery of matter itself.

• Dreams are our greatest and truest teachers, as they reflect our basic aspects in constantly creative variations. At times, they are direct and candid beyond our personal ability to tolerate.

• The meaning of dream-reality symbols is the same as the meaning of waking-reality symbols. This is the key connection between dreamscapes and the outer life. Neither the sense of self in the dream nor the sense of self in the outer life ordinarily has access to the implication of the symbols.

• The various states of the dream experience occur in dimensions not confined by outer reality. I believe dreams are more closely aligned with dimensions that are relatively independent of time and space as we usually perceive time and space.

• Dreams not only reflect an individual's personal unconscious material (physical, psychological, and spiritual), but they also reflect each individual's relationship to larger and larger human collectives (physical, psychological, and spiritual), from the individual's family to universal humanity and its relationship to the earth—in the past, in the present, and in the future. Therefore, some of our dreams may be of collective import and speak of our relationship to a larger whole, with little relevance to our individual sense of self with its values, mores, and sense of spirituality.

• There is good reason to take the view that all possible experiences of the individual—including those of dreams, visions, fantasies, daydreams, hypnosis, deliriums, and drug states, as well as experiences of ordinary reality—are interrelating aspects of the individual's vaster Self. Purely outer senses of wholeness can never be complete and can only reflect a temporary stage of development. One approaches Wholeness by integrating all conscious experiences with all unconscious experiences—made conscious. This "new" state of consciousness is not solely based in the ego.

To me, dreams are profoundly significant and sacred. I believe they reveal and illuminate material about oneself, others, and Life itself in a way the outer self—the more ordinary states of awareness— cannot. To me, dreams are a privileged experience in which the individual is made aware of the interrelationships of the mysterious forces of Life, forces that are often overwhelming to the outer awareness. Dreams reflect forces that are in tension and at work in one's life, regardless of what the outer awareness, the ordinary consciousness, is thinking or experiencing, and regardless of the time-reference with which the outer mind is working. Dreams are at the threshold of immense unconscious dimensions of one's Beingness.

Dreams: The Doorway to the Awesome Mystery

Chapter 8 covers my approach to dream analysis in considerable depth. Here at the outset, however, I want to present a few general indications of how I work with dreams.

The technique I use differs from the more common ways of trying to understand dreams. It does not involve memorizing the supposed meaning of dream symbols and then applying those meanings to dream content, as if the symbols were independent of the dreamer. It involves directly and intuitively perceiving the underlying intention of the pattern of the dream, as that pattern relates to the dreamer. This technique is learned through an induction process, wherein someone who has the ability to work intuitively with dream symbols and their relationship to the dreamer directly stimulates a similar potential in a student. This induction process occurs while the teacher is actually interpreting dreams.

For example, Eunice Hurt, the Spiritual Teacher who initiated me into heightened states of consciousness in the early 1970s, would interpret dreams using her augmented awareness—her expanded or intuitive awareness. As a consequence of my spending time with her when she did this, I began also to experience the augmented state of consciousness she entered. Soon I discovered that I too was able to discern the deeper meanings of dreams, as were others in her classes.

This approach to interpretation accesses a vast state of consciousness that has information about the dream and the dreamer not known to the outer awareness of either the dreamer or the person interpreting the dream. This heightened consciousness (which I call the Dream Interpreter self) discerns the underlying patterns in a dream. These patterns form the basis of the language of the vast individual Unconscious as it blends imperceptibly with the even more vast collective Unconscious, the arena whose existence was proposed by Carl G. Jung, M.D., the great pioneering Swiss investigator of the unconscious aspects of the human psyche. These personal and collective unconscious patterns, in my opinion, control every detail of the conscious experience of all individuals, at both the personal and the group level. When these fundamental patterns are disclosed in a dream and then brought to awareness, the areas in the dreamer's life that are influenced by them become apparent and predictable.

This approach also acknowledges that both individual and collective reality are determined by the patterned forces of the Unconscious and that these patterns therefore directly influence both the dream life and the waking life of the individual. For this reason, when people do not have a dream to present in group discussion, I may simply ask them to relate the events of the day, and to do so as if the events had occurred in a dream. I then use the same state of heightened awareness to interpret the patterns behind those events as I would if a dream had been presented. The results are exactly the same.

Dream material has even deeper and richer meaning for me when I move to a state of consciousness where an awareness of Life's ultimate grace and mystery is rekindled ... the grace and the mystery of existence itself. The fact that I exist at all is a miracle beyond anything I can understand or even contemplate meaningfully. When I reexperience this most awesome perspective, I am brought to the fundamental realization that all of life is an astonishing and awesome Mystery. I feel an immediate and profound reprioritizing of my values and concerns. Suddenly concepts about the world are only concepts about the world, and I recognize that what's real is something unknown, something far greater than anything our concepts might reveal. Trees are not just trees. Butterflies are not just butterflies. Cats are not just cats. Christ is not just Christ, and Evil Incarnate is not just Evil Incarnate. Each becomes an aspect of something unfathomable. The experience of Life as being seamless begins!

Such a fresh relationship with the Mystery, which I find so invaluable in breaking mind-sets about Life and Spirit, was now bringing me to new and more difficult levels of appreciation, through my having to acknowledge that, whatever spiritual forces are, they have a dark side ... that while there may only be one God, God has many faces. Christ and Lucifer are twin rays ... Cain and Abel are two aspects of the same energy ... and I had very dark aspects that were not yet in my conscious awareness. Even worse, because these dark elements were not consciously known to me, I had no way of seeing them as part of myself.

I recognized that I had been experiencing what I termed spirituality exclusively through positive filters. God is the Great Good; God is Love; there is no darkness . . . only ignorance; the Supreme Deity is invariably masculine, a Good Father; the path to God is through perfection of self to Self; I am a single soul exploring and experiencing the world; God loves me personally; a soul evolves through many lifetimes; Life follows death. These were the kinds of ideas I had believed in with a sense of comfort and security at various times during the first thirty-nine years of my life. Now, however, something radically different was being presented to me.

I was certainly not the first to have grappled with the realization that God has a dark side. I am reminded of the epic twenty-five-hundred-year-old Hindu poem, the *Bhagavad Gita*. In it, Arjuna, a leader and warrior representing what is good and of value in humanity, is arguing with Krishna—God—about going into battle against his kinsmen. At one point in the poem, Arjuna recognizes that he is experiencing only the beatific appearance of God. Arjuna knows Krishna has a demonic side and asks Krishna if he would show him that. Krishna dismisses the request several times before he finally gives in and suddenly changes from a radiant, handsome, youthful male into a terrifying creature in front of whom Arjuna cringes, begging that Krishna reappear in his beatific form. Krishna changes back . . . much to the relief of Arjuna. Now, even as they did thousands of years ago, I was realizing that not only did God have both aspects but also that there was a general preference to see only the good side of God. Despite that preference, however, the destructive and chaotic side does exist and can be experienced in myriad ways when one allows that perspective to come forth.

As I slowly grasped the symbols and dynamics of the Evil Incarnate dream, I was forced to begin acknowledging certain aspects of God, myself, and the world that I had previously denied. I recognized the necessity that I not discount or disown these aspects. I was aware that when such material is ignored, it tends to take form in one's life, often in dramatic ways. The changes experienced by Jim Jones that led to the Jonestown tragedy were vividly in my awareness. The only way I knew to deal appropriately with the dark material without setting up unconscious defenses, and therefore unconsciously participating in its potentially destructive eruption, was to allow this dark material into consciousness and to appreciate it as being simply part of the "suchness," the "is-ness" of Life, rather than something I would push out of view because my personal preferences reacted violently against it. As a result of my not trying to avoid the conflict but rather finding ways to embrace it, I felt deep inner stirrings which informed me intuitively that my decision in favor of inclusivity was correct.

Having realized that other viewpoints regarding God were now possible, I suddenly recognized that all my feelings, statements, and thoughts about God and the world during the initial phase of my spiritual development had been what I *preferred* to feel, say, or think about God and the world. I was now being asked to experience Life more directly and more honestly. I was being born into a dimension of consciousness that could reveal to me aspects of my own unconscious . . . and through my own unconscious, our Unconscious.

The Unconscious! When we first become aware that totally unconscious aspects of ourselves exist—having greater intelligence and operating in vaster dimensions than does the outer self—we are struck to the very foundation of what we hold to be true about ourselves. We are further shocked to realize that the Unconscious is not simply a wastebasket of unresolved material, of personal information and feelings ready to be recalled by our outer awareness. It is limitless, definable in terms similar to those we often use for God, in relation to which our sense of a personal self is as a dinghy floating on a vast ocean.

I find that approaching the Unconscious as if it has various levels is extremely helpful. For the human being there is the personal unconscious, which reflects one's unconscious personal material, including the disowned aspects that are unacceptable or inappropriate to the outer sense of self. There is the family or clan unconscious, which includes collective values and patterns related to the particular family or clan background. There is the ethnic or cultural unconscious, related to tribal, social, and religious groupings. Finally, there is the universal collective unconscious that relates to humanity as a whole.

Each aspect of the Unconscious can influence the conscious level differently, often dramatically. For instance, the destructive elements of the personal unconscious can have a certain impact in the life of an individual, but destructive elements of the universal collective unconscious have far greater consequences when they are erupting through that same individual. As an example, one might contrast the personal unconscious destructive elements of Adolf Hitler and the collective unconscious destructive elements that manifested *through* Adolf Hitler.

Because the Unconscious represents the fullness of our Beingness, a fullness far beyond what we regard as self at the outer conscious levels, no true sense of who and what we are can be appreciated until we have the courage to acknowledge and integrate as much of the Unconscious as is possible. Without at least a rudimentary understanding of the Unconscious, there can be no sense of Wholeness . . . which is the fruit of genuine spiritual Unfoldment.

Over the fifteen years I have studied individuals' dreams, I have come to appreciate a difficult perspective . . . that not only is there a direct relationship between what is transpiring in a person's dreams and what is transpiring in the individual's outer life, but also that the unconscious dynamics or forces present in dreams reflect the actual forces that are causing events and relationships in the outer life of the individual, from the fetal stage to death. When the unconscious aspects of ourselves are taken into consideration, the idea that infants are blank tablets to be molded primarily by the environment, parents, and contemporary society becomes tenuous, and these external influences are seen as clearly secondary to the unconscious forces. As all mothers in every culture of the world know, each newborn is different and has very distinct patterns of behavior and personality that distinguish it from all the other children that mother has borne.

From the perspective that unconscious forces regulate health, disease, and events in the life of the individual, we can readily appreciate that the conscious or cognitive mind is not the important causal consciousness, the primary consciousness, of any individual at any stage, from conception to death. This realization should help to soften some of the objections put forth by those who insist that the fetus, infant, and child are not developed enough to be responsible for events that occur in their lives. The fetus, infant, and child are not innocent of the circumstances that transpire around them, although their outer cognitive minds (or what has, to that point, developed as their outer cognitive minds) may perceive such events to be unconnected to themselves. The Unconscious of an infant is as fully developed as the Unconscious of the Elder. The fetus, infant, and child simply have fewer tools than do the later stages of development with which to be conscious of the expression of the Unconscious.

From the foregoing, it should be plain that what I am addressing in regard to the Unconscious involves far more than the instinctual aspects of biological life. The Unconscious includes the instinctual patterns, but the instinctual patterns do not include most of the unconscious patterns to which I am referring.

Dreams and Disease

A Dream of Death.

As one explores the Unconscious more deeply, including its foreshadowings of forthcoming events, one recognizes that even the outcome of illness can be recognized in dreams . . . if one has the courage to bring such difficult material to consciousness. Let me give you some examples of how dreams can relate to disease in this fashion. The following dream was presented to me by a nineteen-year-old girl—and I say *girl* because, psychologically, she was premenstrual, somewhere around the age of twelve. She had a widespread cancer, a lymphoma.

> I am with my girlfriends. We are attempting to cross a concrete spillway for a river at the point where it empties into the ocean. There is no water in the river. The crossing point is high above the seashore area. All my girlfriends are able to cross, but when I get halfway, I fall into the sand below. I am not hurt. The dream ends.

When I heard the dream, I knew this nineteen-year-old would die. The dream said so. The dream stated that she was at a crossing point in her life, from adolescence into young womanhood. Her girlfriends were going to make this transition successfully, but she was not. The dream stated, in fact, that her life force had run out, which was reflected by the image of the dried-up riverbed. The concrete spillway reflected the rigidity of her fixation with childhood as well as the barrenness of her outlook about the future. It also reflected that her life was controlled by the values of her father and by father figures. The seashore indicated that she was close to death, as the approach of death is often reflected symbolically by a river or a riverbed joining the sea. One's Beingness is preparing to be absorbed back into the greater Mystery. (I caution the reader at this point that, as I will discuss later, dream symbols do not have fixed meanings. The same or similar symbols may have very different meanings in different people's dreams, or even in different dreams by the same people. Thus, the symbol of the river reaching the seashore may not always reflect mortal death but may indicate, for example, a period of time when the psyche will enter the depths of the Unconscious for renewal, healing, or psychological transformation.)

She had just finished high school. Her father completely adored her, as did her uncle, who had accompanied her for this interview with me. When I questioned her as to what she thought about getting older or about the possibility of having boyfriends, of sexuality, relationships, or of pregnancy, she scrunched up her face and said she wanted nothing to do with any of those things. She loved her childhood and the stage she was completing, and had a "mortal fear" of the next stage.

She had no positive images of mature women. In fact, when I probed her deeper aspects, I detected nothing that would carry her into the next stage of development. She had, so to speak, lived her life, and nothing in her sought to sustain itself beyond this staging. She did indeed talk about not wanting to die, about trying to get better, but this was her outer mind talking, not the forces in her that controlled her destiny. She died in six weeks, despite intensive chemotherapy and psychotherapy.

To me, this was an example of an individual who had incarnated with patterns that could only sustain her through the virginal youth aspects of the Feminine. It reminded me of myths of the young virgin who sacrifices herself to heaven to be with the Father (God). As shocking as it sounds, there really are powerful unconscious patterns that cause certain individuals to withdraw from life at very early ages—even while in the womb.

You may be thinking that this girl was going to die anyway, as the disease was so widespread, and perhaps the dream was just confirming what anybody would have concluded without the dream symbols. Then let me tell you about some other dreams.

A Dream of Transformation.

A thirty-six-year-old male with both a neurological evaluation and brain scans revealing what was tentatively diagnosed as a rapidly progressive brain tumor came to the island of Kauai to seek counsel from me.

His health had been generally excellent except for viral meningitis, which occurred just after he married for the first time two years earlier. For most of his life he had great difficulty expressing his feelings and usually avoided emotional content by escaping into his mental, conceptual levels. He tended to be critical and judgmental, often viewing the world in terms of black-and-white values. He was compulsive and perfectionistic in his work as the manager of an art gallery. He had recently been under great pressure at work. He smoked cigarettes and was concerned that they might be damaging his health.

I asked him about any recent dreams. He told me he had dreamed the night before coming to see me. He was amazed, as he had remembered only a few dreams since experiencing a recurring nightmare around the age of seven or eight. This was his recent dream:

> I am in a house walking down a long hallway. I am opening doors and peering into many rooms. There seem to be more rooms than I expect to find. In one of the rooms is a large TV set, which has an electrical malfunction. Although the set is not turned on, it is smoking. Men are working on this television set. I feel they are going to be able to repair the set. There is a large social gathering of some sort in the living room. I join this social gathering. The dream ends.

Here was a dream announcing that no matter what the medical diagnosis was or what the probability of death might be ... death was not going to occur, at least not from anything in the head area at this time in the dreamer's life. Whatever the problem was in his brain, it was being repaired, as represented by the men repairing the television set. (The television is a good modern way to represent the head, since it provides us with the same experience we have when we look through our eyes to see the world.) The smoke coming from the set reflected some kind of deep-seated inner conflict that was not evident in this dream, although it might have been partly related to his use of cigarettes. The fact that the television set was smoldering, though not turned on, reflected that the inner conflict was outside his conscious awareness and control.

A house, even if unfamiliar, generally is symbolic of self/Self. In this case he was a stranger to the parts of his interior self he was now seeing symbolically and he was compartmentalized in his thinking, which was represented by his opening the doors to many rooms in a strange house. The discovery of more rooms than he expected meant the dream was revealing that he was to grow in his sense of self ... that there were parts and aspects of himself he was yet to encounter in his outer sense of self. The large social gathering in "the living room" indicated that a large part of himself was directed toward living.

At this point I could have looked like a true saint. All I would have needed to do was to touch him and declare that he was cured, since he had no idea that the dream indicated he was going to get well anyway! I told him we could afford to observe and to wait before instituting any radical intervention via the traditional medical approach. If his symptoms progressed, we could reevaluate. Thereafter, he sought no traditional treatment. He worked with his diet, quit smoking at the suggestion of a naturopathic physician, and commenced daily meditation for relaxation and well-being. His symptoms completely subsided.

Four months later he joined me and a group of eleven other men for a journey into Tibet. While in Tibet, he had the first numinous dream he could ever recall and the only dream he could recall during the previous four months. The dream:

I am in a very crowded tent with open sides—like a revival meeting tent. I am with my wife. I am concerned that we will be crushed. A shamanlike figure is standing in the center of an elevated platform, like a boxing ring. He is wearing a long black robe with big sleeves—like the vestment sleeves of nuns. From one of the sleeves the shaman pulls out a pure white adult Angora cat. I know he is going to sacrifice this cat by skinning it alive with a long knife, which he also pulls from his sleeve. There is a surge of excitement in the audience. I am overwhelmed and panicked and try to get out of the tent. It is very difficult to escape, as the audience is becoming more excited about the sacrifice. The dream ends.

We now have an opportunity to see some of the interior conflicts that caused the emotional blunting and the mental defense of compartmentalization.

The shaman in the crowded tent, about to use a long knife to skin alive the pure white Angora cat, reflected this man's earlier struggle with phallic awakening, represented by the long knife itself and by the sacrifice of the untouched or unblemished instinctual Feminine, represented by the pure white adult Angora cat. We can assume that the cat is a symbol of his mother, as the primary encounter an infant and child has with the Feminine is with the mother. Cats are associated with the Feminine, and the fact that it is an adult and has long, soft hair further supports the association with the mother. We can now appreciate that the main underlying conflict is sexual and most likely centered in the area of an unconscious incestuous relationship with the mother.

To be skinned alive is commonly threatened as punishment when an extremely serious transgression has occurred. Something in this man's psyche is seeking to punish the instinctual or animal Feminine . . . to skin it alive . . . to get rid of the Feminine for some unconsciously experienced or perceived wrongdoing. In this case, the unconscious childhood incestuous relationship with the mother, with its associated guilt and punishment, were most likely the source of the interior conflict. We also see that the shaman is, in the eyes of the dreamer, a dark and overwhelmingly dangerous, larger-than-life figure—a trickster, pulling things out of his sleeves—whose intention is the destruction of the cat. This suggests that his childhood sense of self is afraid of some sort of evil adult interior self lurking behind the scenes, one that is destructive and devious and that might overwhelm him and cause him to commit some heinous act with the mother or any mother-equivalent.

The religious undertones were clearly evident in the image of the revival tent and of the long robe with the big sleeves worn by the shaman. This was actually a blended image, as, on later questioning, the dreamer revealed that the robe reminded him of the vestments of Catholic priests, but the big sleeves reminded him of the vestments of nuns, where he felt they hid their hankies. The hiding of hankies can be associated with the hiding of the feelings. It could also be related to tissue that he used to conceal ejaculate produced by masturbation around the time of his conscious phallic awakening. Tied into his Catholic background, then, must be associations involving the Devil, sexuality, mother, punishment, and his powerful, unconscious attraction into, and impulses toward, violent and destructive sexuality. This would account for this man's outer conscious abhorrence of war, violence, and pain.

The crowded tent reflected the pressure of his interior conflict. His difficulty in escaping the conflict was emphasized by the trouble he had getting out of the tent with his wife. The wife in this case actually represented the mother, with whom he first came into the unconscious destructive sexual conflict and whom the dreamer was attempting to protect from the forbidden sexual excitement of the crowd. (The crowd was reflecting his own sexual excitement and attraction to a forbidden form of sexual encounter with the mother.) The compulsion to get out of the tent was produced by the fear that knowledge of his early, primitive, and forbidden sexual feelings—feelings that included very destructive elements—would erupt into his conscious awareness. The immense guilt, the fear of reprisals, and the dreamer's destructive phallic relationship with the mother, all at an unconscious level, set the stage for him to close off from his emotions and feelings, relegating them to an unconscious existence until he had enough maturity of consciousness to integrate them.

The intensity of the unconscious, interior conflict can easily be seen as sufficient for it to be a nidus for whatever is happening in his central nervous system. It certainly accounts for the blunting of his emotional development, causing him great difficulty in relating at any depth to women, including his wife. Relating to art forms, any art forms, was a safe way for him to handle a relationship with the Feminine, as opposed to his dealing with the actual human feminine. (I first appreciated this realization through the writing of Anaïs Nin.) The defense against the destructive sexual and emotional aspects of his Unconscious would then cause him to prefer the mental and abstracted realms of the mind rather than the physical, emotional, and sexual realms when dealing with the Feminine.

In further pursuit of the deeper unconscious material, this man revealed on subsequent interrogation that he had been attached to his mother until he was seven or eight years old, when he started to have a frequently recurring nightmare which terrorized him for many years. The nightmare, which was always the same, was as follows:

Just as I fall asleep, a two-foot-square opening appears on the wall above my head, and a small, supine mummy, wrapped in black strips of cotton, floats out.

He would awaken terrified. The man also remembered an episode that occurred at about this age when his mother said to him, "What happened to the happy, outgoing little boy you used to be?" We now know that the unconscious conflict was activated around the time of the initial nightmare, as the initial nightmare and the change in the relationship with his mother occurred at about the same time.

My interpretation of this dream is that the mummy (closely related to the word "mommy") represents the revealing of evidence of some terrible crime that was, at an unconscious level, committed against the mother by an aspect of the child's psyche. Some sinister, destructive, demonic, evil, totally unacceptable aspect of his unconscious sense of self is attempting to be birthed into the conscious awareness, and there is no mature vehicle to handle the integration of the disowned aspect. Being bonded to the mother is reflected by the black cotton wrapping strips. That it is interpreted by the dreamer as a nightmare implies that he did not, and perhaps still does not, have enough ego strength to handle the darker forces of his unconscious nature. When we have to imagine an object of attraction as evil, dark, and demonic, we do so to be able to have some control over it, to help us break the power of its attraction. When I inquired as to whether he had any conscious thoughts of wishing his mother dead, he responded immediately that he had had no such thought but that he had been upset with a sibling who stated he wished the mother were dead. His all too rapid denial of having had any destructive thoughts directed toward the mother strongly supports the working hypothesis that this man's primary unconscious conflict is a childhood incestuous relationship with the mother.

It became apparent to me from his history that, following the nightmare and the outer, affective change in the relationship with his mother, he symbolically continued the attachment to her in the form of devotion to the Catholic Church.

At age eleven, he experienced extremely painful guilt over the fact that he masturbated. He thought it was bad and evil until a priest explained to him that it was a sin only because it represented the selfish experience of a pleasure that was intended for the sacrament of marriage. This assuaged his conscious guilt.

He remained devoted to the Church until he was thirteen or fourteen, when adolescent rebellion replaced devotion. He became contentious with the priests, his grades fell, he felt like he was from another planet, and he regarded people who believed in the Church as superficial and unthinking. All of these actions were further defenses against the unconscious relationship to his mother and to the larger mother energetics of his Unconscious.

With this historical perspective having been presented, we can jump forward to when he was in his late thirties. This is several years after the initial episode of the brain mass, and it occurred while he and I, along with sixteen other people, were on a river-rafting trip down the Colorado River. He told me of a then recent dream he thought might interest me:

> I am approaching a large, old prospector's shack. The terrain is similar to that of the high desert area of Southern California. I become aware that there is a very dangerous black or dark-colored monster in a large cellar under the floor of the shack. A trapdoor in the floor of the shack leads to the cellar. I am both fearful and yet also calm, for I know the monster is not going to try to get out and I have no intention of opening the trapdoor. The monster is aware of me and I am aware of it.

Here, the dream has announced that the inner conflict that is predisposing him to the central nervous system pathology—including recurrent tension headaches, meningitis, and a space-occupying mass in the head—is contained in his Unconscious . . . the cellar. He indicates in telling the dream that it is a large cellar and that the monster has enough room. This indicates that, at the time of the dream, the source of the conflict was not creating any pressure or symptoms.

Although he fears the monster, he feels that as long as he doesn't disturb it, he will be safe. This was reflected by the monster's being in the cellar—the Unconscious—and by the fact that the dreamer had no intention of opening the trapdoor. The prospecting aspect of the dream is also suggesting that he, at the unconscious level, is exploring and searching for the underlying cause of his physical and emotional dilemmas but that the source of the conflict is still too overpowering to engage. It also warns me not to push too hard into his unconscious material at this time. The reference to the high desert may reflect his escape into the more arid, barren mental arenas of consciousness and also his associations with coming to me for help, as I then conducted my residential Conferences in the high desert of Southern California.

Some of his neurological symptoms returned three years later, after he again had been under major pressure at work. He also inhaled high concentrations of volcanic gases on the island of Hawaii the day the symptoms erupted, symptoms that included short-term memory loss, headaches, and the inability to differentiate between dream states and outer reality.

Since he couldn't remember a dream that might be helpful in appreciating what his Unconscious was intending, and since the entire neurological workup by his physician, including a spinal tap, was inconclusive, I was left with only his symptoms to observe and to guide me in regard to counseling him. As his symptoms were improving, I recommended observation.

When I saw him several months later at a healing Conference to which I had suggested that he and his wife come for further understanding of the forces involved in his circumstances, he was continuing to show improvement in the neurological symptoms. He also openly cried while listening to a recording by Enya called "Watermark." It reminded him of the innocence of a young mother. Of course, he was also out of the rat race of compulsive perfectionism in his work, and that certainly contributed to his well-being. He also mentioned that because he didn't like the volcanic aspect of the island of Hawaii, where he lived at the time, he was thinking of moving to the island of Kauai. From my perspective, this attitude was a commentary on his pent-up destructive emotions, which he is still not able to express. He promised to call if he had a dream. This man's unconscious dark material is still not integrated and continues to pose a physical and emotional threat to him.

Accepting the Unconscious through Dreams

An example of unconscious aspects being accepted and integrated is contained in one of the most powerful stories about people and dreams I ever read. It appears in Carl Jung's *The Structure and Dynamics of the Psyche*. Dr. Jung cites "an interesting report in the ethnological literature" about a Native American warrior chief "to whom in middle life the Great Spirit appeared in a dream. The spirit announced to him that from then on he must sit among the women and children, wear women's clothes, and eat the food of women. He obeyed the dream without suffering a loss of prestige."

What a remarkable man the chief was! He had realized that—as is true for all males who engage in principally masculine pursuits for most of their lives—the natural forces that supported those pursuits had run their course. He further realized that to bring about balance and an even greater life experience, he should actively participate in the solution offered by the dream.

We have a real privilege if we pay attention . . . to witness the Mystery of the larger life as it dances through us. Few of us have a dream where the literal interpretation is the same as the symbolic interpretation, as was that of the Native American warrior chief, yet all of our dreams reflect the creative process of Life as it seeks to balance, to heal, and to harmonize. We must also remember that because the Unconscious is impersonal to the outer levels of awareness, the resolution it presents may not be ego-enhancing. Finally, we must be especially careful of literal interpretations, for, in my experience, most dream images and circumstances are symbolic of inner transformation and healing, and will only secondarily be represented in the outer reality.

Before we take up the interpretation of my two spiritual dreams, I want to make one more important point. I strongly recommend that one not use *any* psychological technique to change dream content. In a dream, we are privileged to see the workings of the Unconscious, which has a far greater understanding of Life and of Beingness than our outer awareness could possibly have. Changing a dream—meddling with the Unconscious—would be like a subatomic quark in an atom in a molecule in a cell in a hair on the tail of a dog . . . wagging the dog!

The Dream and the Nightmare

Let us now return to my own two dreams, viewing them in the context we have discussed. See if you can catch their significance and how they interrelate to each other.

The dream. Age nine, Los Angeles, California.

I am running home to tell my mother that Christ has come and I am going to follow him. It is a beautiful, sunlit day. I enter what is our home in the dream—a pure white adobe building, rectangular in shape, with a large wooden plank front door and wooden plank floors. With all the excitement and wonder a nine-year-old boy can express, I make this announcement and beg my mother, my twin brother, and my older brother to follow, but they are not interested in what I have to say. I realize that I will leave home alone and follow this great Being.

When I awoke, I was overwhelmed simultaneously with ecstatic joy and profound grief.

The nightmare. Age thirty-nine, Lucerne Valley, California.

It is night. With the fuel gauge indicating empty, I am driving into a well-lighted service station to get some gasoline for my car, an arctic white 1939 Plymouth with a louvered hood. (Such a vehicle was in fact the first car I ever owned.) I am alone in the car. I notice in the shadows, just outside the station, a gang of Hell's Angels types revving up their motorcycles. I don't feel they will be a threat, as the station is very well lighted. I park beside a gas pump and get out of my car to talk to an old man who is inside a glass enclosure twenty or thirty feet away from the pumps. He is a friendly old man. I decide he is the owner and ask him to pump some gas for me, which he agrees to do.

When I turn to walk back to my car, I feel an evil presence behind me. I think immediately of the Hell's Angels gang. When I turn to confront what I feel, I am terrified to see that it is not just an evil presence. It is Evil Incarnate, Himself, stalking me.

I run to my car, jump in, slam the door, and frantically roll up the window and manage to lock the door with my elbow. I am letting out a sigh of relief when I look into the rearview mirror and see that Evil Incarnate is sitting in the backseat of my car, locking eyes with me in the mirror. My hair stands straight up on end . . . I let out a scream and awake screaming.

In the first dream, Christ represents an aspect of the vast Self. He is often interpreted as representing the first fully human state of consciousness beyond the animal nature on the path of development into full Beinghood. Esoterically, he represents the awakened Heart Chakra or fourth state of consciousness in the chakra system cosmology of the East. Thus, even when I am at that early age, the deep psyche is announcing I will approach the deeper awakening into Beinghood via an illumined Heart Center. The Christed patterning as teacher, healer, and priest will pervade the unfolding sequence.

The dream indicates the special bonding between mother and son . . . an announcement of the pattern of the Divine Child and the Divine Mother. The purity and simplicity of the adobe house elaborate the ancient theme of being born to simple and humble surroundings. It also compensates for and conceals an unconscious drive to power and wealth.

The day is beautiful and sunlit, which further plays on the theme of conscious spiritual awakening.

The father is absent, meaning the main emphasis is to come from the mother. The rectangular, white adobe house is also a reference to the purity, innocence, and divinity of the temple of the mother, whether this be the outer relationship between us, the inner unconscious relationship between us, or the experience in her womb. The breaking of the bonds of family is revealed by the fact that no one will come with me to follow Christ. The New Testament refers to this in Luke 14:26 (New International Version): *If anyone comes to me and does not hate [i.e., be totally detached from] his father and mother, his wife and children,*

his brothers and sisters—yes, even his own life—he cannot be my disciple.
A person must enter alone . . . free from the usual patterns that bind
most people to ordinary states of awareness.

For thirty years the pattern disclosed in that dream had unfolded
in my life. But . . . a basic principle of unconscious dynamics is that
whenever a polarity has been overlived, without having been balanced by its counterpart, an eruption of the counterpart can be expected. This was evident in the dream of the Native American chief
and it was evident in my Evil Incarnate dream.

The Evil Incarnate dream begins at night . . . which represents
the feminine principle, the Unconscious. The life force that was animating my experience up to that time was nearly exhausted, as was
reflected by my driving on empty. My persona, or mask, was reflected by the arctic white 1939 Plymouth with the louvered hood.
This was the mask of purity and simplicity referred to in the first
dream, with the addition of an adolescent touch . . . the louvered
hood. Since my first car actually was a 1939 Plymouth, which I
painted arctic white when I purchased it at the age of 16, I was, at
that time, unconsciously creating an extension into the material world
of the persona of purity and innocence which was earlier reflected in
the dream about Christ.

My being alone in the car is connected to the first dream, which
indicated that I would have to proceed alone in my desire to experience spiritual awakening. That there were shadows, and in those
shadows were Hell's Angels types, now begins to announce which
elements have been disowned . . . raw masculine energy, sexual energy (as reflected by the motorcycles), and the company of men. I
had ignored all of these elements, or had engaged them solely in
moments when I could escape the roles of physician/healer or spiritual teacher/healer . . . moments only rarely available to me. Even
when such moments were available, I would engage these aspects only
briefly, as though I were on a sortie, then quietly and quickly withdraw back into the world of the Saint and Inspirer, moving toward
greater and greater inner heights of mind and Spirit. But psychologically moving to greater and greater heights without also engaging
the body is disastrous and is exactly what causes the eruption of the
balancing counterparts.

The old man signals the real significance of the dream. He is a representation of the Divine Father or God (the Supplier) and is in a glass enclosure, which refers back to a dream I described in *Joy's Way*. That dream occurred after I had been traveling in India. In it, I was in the center, on the second floor, of a crystal two-story house where I could see into all the rooms, as all the walls and floors were transparent. In the present dream, the old man in the glass enclosure can see both the white element (me, as I had regarded myself until the time I had the dream) and the dark elements (my disowned aspects). When I turn my back on the old man—that is, expose my unconscious side—the Good Father/God becomes its counterpart . . . Evil Incarnate!

I am horrified and run back to my 1939 arctic white Plymouth . . . meaning that I am not prepared to face the dark and destructive side of my own nature, of the nature of Life itself. My getting into the car is like getting back into a womb, protected and safe.

The open window shows me the key to my awakening: *vulnerability*. A closed window is safe and secure. and nothing new can enter. An open window is an access to infinite possibility. I close the window, but, as Ovid stated, "too late, I grasp my shield." The counterforce to everything I had represented and celebrated as spiritual and as Spirit itself was inside me . . . represented by Evil Incarnate being in the backseat of the car. Seeing something in a mirror suggests "mirroring back" what one is. Thus, I was going to see and to experience my dark side regardless of personal preference.

The psychic tension of being confronted with unadulterated Evil is always too much for the outer awareness. Waking up to such larger aspects of Spirit is painful and frightening, forcing an initiation into a vehicle of awareness that can handle the "new" truths. In the Judaic tradition, the dark side of God—in the form of jealousy, retribution, destruction of the enemy's firstborn sons, floods, plagues, tests of faith (as in the case of Job), and directing people to and supporting the acquiring of territory through war (as in the taking of the land of "milk and honey")—is appreciated and accepted. In the Christian tradition, however, the dark side of God is all but forgotten, as Jesus and his attributes supersede the Judaic image of God. One doesn't see the major dark side of Christ until the book of Revelation, when

Christ, as he goes forth to eliminate the forces of Evil, takes up not just one sword but two! From an even deeper psychological viewpoint, the dark side of Christ erupts in the form of Lucifer, the enslaver of humankind. And from a larger psychospiritual viewpoint, Christianity simply contained the dark side of God in Lucifer and presented the positive or constructive aspects of God in Christ.

Indeed it was a frightening dream, but horrific dreams, as with horrific outer events, contain the energy of great transformation. This nightmare, though it crushed my innocence and initiated me into the Fall from Grace, was the prelude to a period of extraordinary personal expansion and increasing maturity.

CHAPTER TWO

THE FALL FROM GRACE

The Fall confronts us with one of the most powerful and painful experiences on the path of psychological and spiritual maturation. In Western religious terms, it refers to the fall from God's grace and/or from the grace of the Church due to major transgressions wherein one has deviated from what is considered to be right or proper. It leads to ostracism, excommunication, and/or damnation. Psychologically, a fall from grace occurs whenever an individual significantly deviates from any image held to be normal or acceptable by a perceived authority figure. The punishment is one of exclusion from the benefits and protections of the ruling forces, whether of a deity, a ruling mass, or parents. Fundamentally, this involves abandonment and/or rejection . . . two of the strongest forces a family or a society can invoke to maintain equilibrium or the status quo.

To appreciate the power of these sanctions, I find it helpful to enter the more primary aspects of my psyche to feel what such sanctions might mean to an individual who is part of a tribe or clan. Through this experience, I can cause these primitive, instinctual patterns of abandonment and rejection to become more full to me . . . more real, less conceptual. Another way to engage a richer experience of the fear of abandonment and rejection is to enter the infantile stages of awareness, wherein vulnerability and complete dependency are fully present. In both of these situations, the primitive and the infantile, we find a threshold to an experience of instinctual forces that have a powerful controlling influence throughout our lives. Further, we must realize that whether one is aware of these forces or not, they and their attendant fears and anxieties are always operating psychologically and physiologically.

As long as one's sense of self or well-being is identified with an external object, individual, or group, one is vulnerable to the forces associated with it/them for self-esteem and well-being. One cannot deviate significantly, even creatively, without incurring interior guilt and anxiety as well as exterior disapproval, which is, in a sense, a form of threatened abandonment. Thus, in most esoteric spiritual training, when a transcendental value system is to replace earlier values, any attachment to the outer object, individual, or group must be broken. The person is trained to base himself or herself in a strictly interior sense of self/Self and in mature aspects of Beinghood beyond the infantile, the childish, the adolescent, and the young adult.

In an inner Fall, exactly the same dynamics occur as with an outer Fall, except that the source of well-being is now strictly in relationship to an internal aspect. The individual is struggling with some inner portion of self that deviates from what is considered acceptable, proper, or right by some other inner portion of self. This other aspect has the power to punish or to reward, just as the outer levels do. The individual may not be conscious of the inner material and only experience the symptoms of the conflict without knowing why the symptoms exist.

The Fall can lead to deeper personal development and greater spiritual maturation, but more often it leads to self-hatred, humiliation, collapse into negativity, or, worse still, frantic reinforcement of the masks of positiveness and goodness. The fall from power of Richard Nixon, the kind of fall from "spiritual purity" exemplified by some evangelists, nuns, priests, and rabbis; and even more generally, the fall from parental grace—from protection and support when an adolescent or young adult has deviated from the sense of right held by one or both parents—are easily recognizable examples.

The Body and the Fall

How might we understand more about the Fall? As a physician, I like to be instructed by the wisdom of the body when I am struggling to understand mythic material or spiritual teachings, dogmas, and mysteries. I have come to realize that most of what is regarded as divine truth or direct revelation from God is intrinsically rooted in the anatomy and the physiology of the body. My making note of this insight is not meant to detract from the awesome nature of the Mystery. I simply want to point out that the study of the body and of nature in general can reveal profound truths that are often regarded as having an otherworldly source. I was fascinated to hear Joseph Campbell, in his superb video series with Bill Moyers called "The Power of Myth," make this point so directly when he stated that all archetypes and patternings of the deep psyche are, in effect, only the organs of the body interacting with one another. That is a powerful statement, which requires extensive contemplation for its profundity to be fully appreciated.

Where, then, in the awesomely mysterious arenas of human physiology can one discover the equivalents of the phenomenon we are examining? Where do empowerment and protection exist when normal or desired behavior is manifested, and ostracism, exclusion, and even death exist when unacceptable behavior is manifested? They are found, of all places, in the body's immune system.

A broad, general way of describing the function of the immune system is to say that it maintains and protects the physical sense of self. The sense of self is always unique and exclusive to an individual. Anything entering the body that is not perceived as self is destroyed, walled off, neutralized, or extruded. The immune system is merciless when it performs this function. It doesn't ask questions or grant compassion or offer forgiveness when another life form that may disrupt the integrity of self enters the body. It destroys or eliminates the intruder. It may need time to build its defenses or destructive forces, but its intent is clear from the outset: seek out and destroy the perceived enemy.

When considering the fact of the body's automatic, ongoing action against invaders, I am struck by the unconscious irony of individuals who profess a belief in the sacredness of all life, with its implicit, accompanying sanction against doing harm to any life form. This is especially evident in the actions of those people who use peacock feathers to remove ants from their path, so no living thing will be accidentally killed as they pass, thus to prevent them from incurring guilt or karmic debt. As this is going on, however, there is a daily process of destruction under way in their own bodies in which bacteria by the hundreds of millions, if not billions, are killed. Even simple acts of common hygiene destroy billions of bacteria living on their body surfaces. (And, by the way, these hygienic processes, no matter how carefully they may be carried out, leave billions more bacteria still alive and well on the skin.) Just because one can't see life forms doesn't make them insignificant, especially if a pathogenic bacterium is around! Bacteria, for example, come from single cells just as we humans do, and have a basic physiology and biochemistry, just as do most of the cells that make up our own bodies. The Mystery, thus, must be appreciated from a larger perspective than just one of life as opposed to death, and that appreciation must include life forms other than those of which we are conscious. The Mystery includes death, as life feeds on life.

In the very early stages of fetal development the immune system has not yet developed. This allows the new product of the sperm and egg—the conceptus, or fetus—to come into existence with unique individuality. If the conceptus simply inherited the immune mechanism of the mother or the father, nothing unique could arise without being immediately destroyed. Prior to conception, the female's immune system treats the sperm like invaders . . . foreign objects to be destroyed. One of the reasons why so many sperm must be delivered into the vagina during coitus is so the female's vaginal immune system can be overcome by sheer numbers of sperm (in the range of two to three hundred million at a time). Interestingly, the sperm are also considered by the male's body to be foreign objects, and an elaborate system of protection for the sperm must be maintained while they are still in the male's testicles and seminal vesicles. The fact that both male and female bodies react to the sperm as foreign objects to be resisted and destroyed if possible, while the ovum is accepted by the female body, presents some interesting possibilities as to the basis of unconscious psychosexual dynamics between the sexes.

These considerations of the very foundations of human development and sexuality can give immense insight into the complex, unconscious fears men and women have of one another. The male's fear of being absorbed into the Feminine is not unrelated to the process in which the sperm penetrates the egg and dies, whereby the male's genetic contribution survives but the sperm does not. The female's unconscious rejection of the Masculine is manifested through her immune system and the acidity of the vagina, both of which destroy sperm by the millions upon millions. For a review of the fundamental forces at play between the sexes at the biological level, I highly recommend the "Nova" videocassette *The Miracle of Life*.

Then, at a critical stage, the immune system of the fetus develops the physical or biological image of self, so anything contained within the fetus at that time is appreciated as "the physical self" and is not rejected. Most foreign tissue or objects placed into the fetus after the immune system has developed are sensed as not-self and will either be destroyed or isolated and extruded from the body.

The dynamics of self/not-self biologically displayed in the immune system are so similar to the psychological dynamics of self/not-self that there is good reason to suspect they both may be based in some transcendent pattern or quality innate to matter itself. Thus, just as the body has its immune mechanism, so, too, does the individual psyche ... as do families, clans, villages, towns, cities, brotherhoods/sisterhoods, societies, corporations, religions, and nations. I often warn people who study with me that society will tolerate only so much "deviant" behavior before it activates its immune mechanism to incarcerate, make over, rehabilitate, burn, kill, extrude, or otherwise eliminate the perceived threat. As long as the mask of relative normality is worn, there is no problem. Woe, however, to the individual or individuals who deviate from the perceived preferred sense of collective "self."

This collective sense of self is not consciously organized and determined, either at the individual level or at the collective level. It is based in the individual and the collective *unconscious*, and therein lies its vast power. Salman Rushdie, author of the book called *The Satanic Verses*, learned something about it when he had to go into hiding after the Muslim world reacted violently to his thinly disguised criticism of the Islamic religion. Death squads were sent out and $2.5 million was offered to any Iranian who would kill him. Here was clearly an example of a society's immune system activating. Other societies and other religious groupings whose images were not threatened by his writings activated no collective immune reaction.

The principles that underlie the immune system of the body also underlie our legal system, our systems of religion, our written and unwritten laws of socialization, our collective senses of self, and our experiences of discrimination (such as racism, religious intolerance, bigotry, apartheid, sexual discrimination, and, in fact, prejudice in any form).

No legislation can possibly influence this most fundamental and instinctive principle of our nature. It has nothing to do with the mind and how the mind thinks things ought to be. It is not based in outer moral values (which change from time to time) or in religious ethics (which so often defend against fundamental forces of our Beingness that can be so humiliating to the spiritually sophisticated and evolved). I don't feel the underlying aspects of prejudice and bigotry have been influenced in the slightest by all of the legislation and marches ... by all the attempts to desegregate and by all the films and writings attempting to influence mass opinion. Surface appearances or social masks are neither honest nor long-term solutions to innate and difficult aspects of life. The sense of what is self and what is not-self is simply too deep within the human psyche (of which we know so little!) for these maneuvers to be effective.

Current legislation serves to conceal or to deny prejudice. It is superficial at best and anxiety- and guilt-producing at worst. A far more honest position would be to accept the prejudices and begin to work from that standpoint toward a possible relationship with what is perceived as not-self. Instead, we hammer away at children, telling them that prejudice is bad and wrong, when its basis is established at the very foundation of our physical existence. To change prejudice would be like having someone influence and alter the instinct to survive. Appreciation, not denial, is the way to integrate prejudice.

The irony is that our society will send out its immune cells to destroy another society because that society is engaging in an activity that is not perceived as "self" by our society, though our society has hardly resolved its own unconscious aspects of exactly the same issue—as, for example, in regard to apartheid. I am always amazed when I observe individuals who, in their virtually absolute unconsciousness, are so blatant as to accuse others of what they themselves are unconscious of in their own personal lives.

We are unconscious when we react to something outside ourselves and are unaware that the reactivity is really in defense of unconsciously held ideas of forces within us. The enemy is not "out there." As we appreciate the unconscious aspects of our own being, we soon discover that those who react the most to bigotry and prejudice carry heavy doses of bigotry and prejudice at the personal, unexposed areas of their consciousness and/or in the unconscious areas of their being. The awakening into Self-Realization can be very humiliating to such individuals as peace marchers, social reformers, utopians, environmentalists, and missionaries (of all sorts). I will cover projection of unconscious attitudes, beliefs, and activities more thoroughly in a later chapter, but in the context of fundamental forces of the body and psyche, the introduction of such a powerfully reactive area is certainly appropriate here.

A Journey into Darkness: Self and Not-Self Collide

In this regard, I will share the story of a six-week trip I took with three other white men into East and Central Africa in September 1986.

Africa, of course, is called the dark continent. This doesn't just refer to the dark-skinned peoples there, for it is also symbolic of the disowned animal and primitive aspects in all of us, aspects that are overlaid by thin veneers of civilization, socialization, and religious dogma.

I had been preparing for years to be able to enter Africa, and to do so at an experiential level, not merely as a tourist or an uninvolved witness to its rich, wild, natural environment. As a consequence of a series of deep daily meditations, when I arrived in Nairobi, Kenya, I was experiencing the instinctual levels of my Beingness to a degree far outside the ranges of my ordinary consciousness. The Hunter and Gatherer were close to my awareness. The instincts to kill and to defend from being killed were also close to the surface. Even my way of walking, my sense of sight, my sense of smell, the quality of my sleep, and the content and form of my conversations with others were being influenced. I was awake and alive in a much different way than I ordinarily am.

For this trip I had specifically requested that a black African be our guide. I wanted to experience someone who had been raised in the wilds of Africa, where death and disease go hand in hand with celebration and life. I wanted someone who could lend me new eyes and ears and a new nose in order that I might more fully appreciate the parts of Africa we were entering. Most important, I wanted someone who was older and wise . . . respected by his people for his integrity and leadership. Such a guide was Ben Ouko.

I first saw Ben as he came loping through the lobby of the Norfolk Hotel in Nairobi. He was tall, powerfully well built, and very black, with long legs and arms. He had graying, short, tightly curled, receding hair. I mostly saw white teeth and white eyeballs and waving arms as he approached.

I was stunned by the handsomeness of his chiseled face, which reminded me of some of the Pharaonic statuary in the Egyptian Museum in Cairo, where faces with large lips, high cheekbones, and angular features can be seen today. Ben, I realized, didn't need haircuts or razors. His scalp hair grew no longer than the short, tightly curled hair he was born with, nor was major beard growth possible for him. (Egyptian guides often talk about the ancient Egyptians as having been beardless, as having had little or no natural facial hair, suggesting this as the reason for the false beards worn by the Pharaohs. That tends to reinforce the feeling I have had since I first entered Egypt in 1975 that at least one of the ancient Pharaonic lines was black.)

As it turned out, Ben was a Nilot, a member of a tribe that had, in the distant past, migrated up the Nile river to the Lake Victoria region, where the tribe remains today. Nilots are noted for being teachers. As I also learned, his tribe has oral traditions that include its having once been powerful and great in the land of the lower Nile.

Ben approached the four of us with almost a boyish camaraderie, ready to greet us with handclasps and robust, shoulder-slapping good will. His first comment was, "This is going to be a wonderful trip . . . brothers traveling together. After all, we are all the same under skin, aren't we?"

I looked at him intently, then with a slow delivery of the feelings I was having, I said, "I don't feel that way at all. Something inside me instinctively fears you. You are not me. You are much more powerful than I. You are also very black. I don't trust the white-washing of your feelings about us in that kind of greeting!" His mouth slammed shut. Now I could only see white eyeballs several inches above mine.

It was the most honest, most vulnerable level at which I had ever encountered another human being. I wanted to know, to feel, the truth of the forces between us. I wanted to acknowledge my fears, my concerns, my reactivities, in order to prepare the way for the possibility of a deeper relationship. I wanted nothing to do with pabulum or social masks. My life was being placed in the hands of this man. My years of preparation to enter Africa and the encounter with black Africans were too meaningful to my psychological/spiritual development to squander on niceties.

The ground rules had been struck. No masks. And the honest presentation of feelings was being called for.

Ben gave me a long, deep look, then stood tall and mature. He quietly told us to be ready to leave on safari early the next morning. It was several days before Ben approached me on a level other than that of a guide. His statement was direct. "Of course, you know . . . I feel the same way about you." We could now begin to learn about each other and to unmask . . . to be really vulnerable and therefore alive to each other.

My sensitivities in the psi area—knowing about places, people, and objects without having acquired the information in the usual manner—had been gradually developing over the years. I was only too painfully aware of what Ben really thought about whites and the struggle the blacks were having, not just with the whites but with intertribal conflict and warfare throughout all of Africa. I was now in a three-dimensional reality of huge forces of self versus not-self, in a setting where one could easily be killed—not necessarily by wild animals (although that was a possibility) but by someone who was being danced by a collective immune mechanism. A Japanese tourist had been killed because he took a photograph of a tribesman without the tribesman's permission. The tribesman went up to the tourist and, without warning, speared him in the neck. No legal or retaliatory action was taken, as the custom in certain parts of Africa is that you don't take pictures without negotiation and permission.

Later during our trip, while on a remote and rarely traveled road in northern Kenya, one of the three men traveling with me innocently took some pictures of what appeared to be children and women as we stepped out of the safari vehicles to stretch. Immediately after he took the pictures, our guides became nervous. They saw tribesmen, seemingly coming out of nowhere, with spears in hand, though they were not yet in an attack posture. The children and women and then the men were asking a large sum of money because the pictures had been taken.

The man who took the pictures thought this was simply a bargaining ploy and was trying to get the tribespeople's price down, but they would have nothing to do with bargaining. Our guides motioned to us to slowly move away as they tried to defuse the situation with small jokes about the whites. The guides paid the price asked.

As it turned out, we were in the tribespeople's territory, isolated from the usual safari camps. The guides were only too familiar with other occurrences when an entire party had been killed and the vehicle simply disappeared. Amazing, isn't it, about self and not-self, the immune instincts, and how rapidly the destructive aspects can be activated.

Ben was a master teacher when it came to spotting and locating game. His eyes were seeing what mine could not yet see. His ears were hearing what mine could not yet hear. It was astonishing to be around someone with such heightened sensory abilities. Because I was trained as a physician, my senses of sight, sound, smell, and touch are more highly developed than those of most people, yet here was a being who had taken these senses to levels far beyond mine. It was exciting to be initiated . . . again.

As I got to know Ben better, he revealed the name used by his people in referring, in a derogatory manner, to whites. We were called *mazoogoos* (a word I never saw spelled and which I render into English here in its phonetic form). It is akin to the word *nigger*, when a nonblack speaks derogatorily about a black, or, better yet, the Hawaiian word *haole* . . . a highly derogatory word for whites, which means "without life or breath." In other words, "dead . . . lacking life and vitality." Mazoogoo is never said in front of white people but is used frequently when referring to them.

One morning when we were entering a village where Ben was not known, I suddenly called out to some blacks that Ben and his mazoogoo friends were in need of supplies. The blacks were initially very nervous each time I repeated the statement, then suddenly broke into laughter when they saw the humor of the situation. Here I was, a white, announcing that I was a mazoogoo, perfectly well understanding its derogatory meaning and even enjoying the experience—as were the other three white men and, particularly, Ben. In this moment of our not resisting or masking, but joining with what ordinarily would have been a call to crisis, masks cracked and new possibilities of relationship and experience became possible.

The richness and depth of our encounters with Ben developed over the six weeks of our intimacy and travel together. We shared with each other our nighttime dreams, our visions and fantasies, our sensitivities, our vulnerabilities, our weaknesses . . . as well as our strengths and our humor. Finally, at the age of forty-seven, in relating to a person who was viewed by my unconscious and the instinctual forces in me as not-self, I felt as if I was getting below surface appearances and the surface interactions that most day-to-day relationships involve. The process is by no means complete, but I am very excited to begin living life and experiencing relationships more directly and more vulnerably . . . despite the uncomfortable and sometimes painful moments such honesty can generate.

Vegetarians, Carnivores, and Cannibals:
Eating and Consciousness

In further examining how biological principles are reflected into wider areas of life, we can consider two other major physiological dynamics and their psychological equivalents, recognizing how they operate as we seek to understand the unconscious, underlying forces in a Fall.

The first is the principle of *homeostasis*, or balance, which is expressed so powerfully by the body and by the psyche. The second is the principle of the *attraction to opposites*, which introduces the theme of duality or complementary parts. Although both of these dynamics ultimately involve far more complexity than I will present here, the following material does introduce certain basic principles and include simple examples.

Homeostasis is the word used in the field of medicine to refer to the process by which forces maintain equilibrium in the body, whether in regard to temperature, the acid/base balance, endocrine cycles, sleep/wake rhythms, or just a single breathing cycle. Homeostasis involves maintaining the status quo, the stability of a system. The instant the stability is disturbed, counterforces are activated to return the system to its original point of stability.

Whether physiologically or psychologically, if we are at a point of calm or balance, we are usually unaware of the forces constantly interacting to maintain that state of balance. We simply sense our condition as being one that is effortlessly maintained. Such is not the case, however, as we find out if we move from the point of balance toward either extreme. If that happens, we experience ever-increasing forces that seek to move us back to the center point. The forces are gentle when we have only moved a small distance from the center, but when we approach the extremes, extreme counterforces are set into motion to return us to the balance point. Often there also may be overcompensation, and, like a pendulum swinging back and forth past the center point until its motion ceases, we may experience back-and-forth swings.

The principle of homeostasis not only operates in the body and in the psyche of an individual, but its dynamics can also be seen in collectives such as families, communities, and nations. Here also lies one of the fundamental reasons for resistance to change everywhere, whether in the body, in the mind, or in the spirit.

Physical health, then, can be appreciated as the result of homeostatic processes within the body. In simple words ... health is achieved through balance.

If a new cell, new tissue, or new blood is to be built, a supply of materials must be obtained, broken down into its constituent parts, and assimilated appropriately by the body. This mystery of building up and tearing down is what maintains each of us in life. The physical body can maintain itself only when the forces of construction and destruction are in ongoing harmony and equilibrium. If anything goes wrong with the processes that cause breakdown and destruction or with those which cause construction and rebuilding ... we die.

Although many dying cells and dead cells are reabsorbed into our bodies during the cycle of regeneration and can be reused, we are unable to renew ourselves only from our own recycled material. In addition, many of our body cells, fluids, and proteins are completely lost to the body through perspiration, the sloughing of dead skin cells, hair, and fingernails, or through the sloughing of cells and fluids into the urinary tract or the gastrointestinal tract. Thus, without the capacity to capture, destroy, ingest, digest, and assimilate new materials for physical survival, we would soon fall prey to other life forms that are seeking our constituents for *their* maintenance!

The destructive processes involved in capturing and killing the life forms we ordinarily use for our personal continuity in life are usually not acknowledged or discussed. It is, for instance, considered in bad taste to raise the issue of how food actually gets from its original environment to our mouths (an excellent example of an aspect of everyday reality that is disowned by our society). Also, just because something is a plant rather than an animal doesn't minimize the awesome responsibility that is involved in our consuming parts of it or the entirety of it, for it is still another life form. To appreciate that we are actually eating another life form and thus gaining its mana, its particular power to manifest itself in life, and simultaneously transforming that life force into another complex living form— ourselves—is what actually redeems the death of the plant or the animal.

In the transubstantiation of bread and wine into the body and blood of Christ, objects are miraculously transformed into a living psychospiritual presence of Christ. The ritual of the Mass, if performed well, makes the transformation a psychological truth. The eating of Christ is what redeems the death of Jesus. Jesus dies and the mystery of the Christ is born anew. But to reach the state that can redeem, we must experience, acknowledge, and accept each of the stages of the ritual of transubstantiation, including the sacrifice of livingness in one form for livingness in another form.

The mystery of the cycles that create a new balance (homeostasis) of a higher order—cycles of disturbance, sacrifice, death, and birth into a new dimension of being, with the resulting redemption of the life that was sacrificed—is fundamental to the religious experiences of all peoples, in all times and places. It is fundamental to biological development, since, at each subsequent physical stage, a sacrifice of the previous physical form occurs. Its constituents are absorbed and integrated into the next physical stage, thus physically redeeming the previous stage.

When I was on Easter Island in 1981, I was entranced by stories of the Birdman. The Birdman was a deified mortal who proved his physical prowess in competition with all the other young men on the island by obtaining an egg from a bird's nest located on a small, rocky outcropping in very treacherous waters, then climbing up a sheer cliff to where the priests of the island tribes were waiting. The Birdman was granted absolute power over life and death, marriages, the settlement of disputes, and religious rituals for one year. He would be active in the communities for the first six months, then would retire into seclusion for the remaining six months, after which his term would expire.

If one of the clans whose male youth did not win the competition was unhappy with the individual who did win this godlike power, that clan could claim the power for one of its own if the Birdman could be captured and eaten, with the new Birdman eating his heart. Here, the mana, the power, was regarded as actually being in the Birdman and not in the priests nor in some intellectual concept or abstraction. The Birdman was the physical and spiritual incarnation of the deified Presence. One could experience a partial encounter with the Presence by being around the Birdman or by coming into contact with his garments, utensils, or other personal effects. But eating the heart of the Birdman was the only way to come into full empowerment.

Is this not similar to the sacrifice of Jesus and the mystery of Holy Communion? In this most sacred ritual, the capacity to actually induct the state of consciousness that brings the priest and the members of the church into the psychospiritual experience of the living Christ is contingent on two major factors. The first is the capability of the priest to enter the heightened state of consciousness that can evoke the experience of Holy Communion. The second is the ritual format. However, it is not the form of the ritual that brings about psychospiritual transformation. The ritual is only a structure for the psyche to help guide the transformation of consciousness. Therefore, simply because the ritual form is conducted does not guarantee the desired psychospiritual induction into the corporate body of Christ. The ritual pattern is actually dispensable, but the heightened state of consciousness that psychospiritually transubstantiates the bread and the wine into the body and the blood of the living Christ is not. I have observed many Masses, and only a few priests, in my opinion, are capable of bringing themselves and the attending church members into the Mystery of the Mass.

Foods of Plant and Animal Origin

While I am considering states of consciousness and the process of ingesting food for psychological and/or biological energy, I would like to share some impressions in regard to eating food derived from animals and food derived from plants.

Although there are many different opinions regarding which foods promote which states of consciousness, I do feel as though all matter is conscious and that this basic consciousness is enriched by life forms in proportion to the degree to which those life forms have physically evolved. (From a religious viewpoint, the body and blood of Christ are psychologically far superior to the body and blood of a beet!)

Through patterns of increasing complexity, beginning with the material level, matter is configured in such a way as to generate bio-logical consciousness and—eventually—the cognitive, reflective con-sciousness of the human being. There is no question in my mind that animals, for instance, are more highly evolved and more complex than plants. Because of this, and because I believe the state of con-sciousness of any life form is a function of the structure and com-position of its matter and that the nuclei of the cells making up the life form contain the "intelligence" of that life form, I strongly rec-ommend eating higher forms of animals as part of a "vibrationally balanced" life-essence diet, which would also include plants and plant products, minerals, and even insects.

Although I personally do not condone cannibalism, I gather from the little information available on the subject that most groupings that practice cannibalism consider human flesh to be the most sacred and the most evolved, reserving the consumption of a human being for sacramental feasts. Nor is this basic viewpoint limited to areas we regard as "primitive." Our preservation of the bones and organs of saints and the quest for the Holy Grail allude to the psychological understanding that the physical matter associated with special people is different from the physical matter associated with ordinary people. The psychological appreciation of the heightened vibrational nature of special people is further demonstrated in the drive to touch or be touched by them as well as to seek clothing and personal objects they have worn or with which they have been associated.

An example of this phenomenon, only reversed from the usual form, was in evidence when the kahuna reigned all-powerful on the islands of Hawaii. A commoner would be put to instant death if his or her shadow fell on the high priest.

Primitive medicine takes powerful advantage of these psycholog-ical perspectives through the use of animal or plant totems during ritual healing.

Perhaps someday we will actually be able to produce scientific evi-dence that a protein molecule from a fish is not the same as an apparently identical protein molecule from a cat. For now, however, we must un-derstand that the energetic differences between the various food sources are psychologically important and can even override the "factual" or scientific perspective on what is good or what is bad for us.

Sex and Consciousness: A Multiplicity of Selves

Intimately related to the principle of homeostasis is the principle of the attraction of opposites, which involves the forces of sexuality expressing in matter. The patterns of these forces form the basis of human sexuality as it is experienced in the body, in the mind, and in the spirit. Thus, while homeostasis can be viewed as the phenomenon by which opposite interacting forces come into equilibrium, the actual forces that are interacting can be viewed in terms of the principle of the attraction of opposites.

Every schoolchild is familiar with the attracting and repelling forces of magnets. These forces, as basic as they are, remain awesome to me. The positive pole (whatever that really means) of one magnet is attracted to the negative pole (whatever that really means) of another. The opposite poles seek each other out and want to be together. That is really a powerful mystery. Of course, I realize how this is explained from an intellectual standpoint, in terms of current scientific theories. But beneath this veneer of concepts and its accompanying illusions of authority and control lies the dimension I am addressing . . . and the very mystery of the existence of matter itself.

From a procreative perspective, for example, we can easily appreciate what is implied by the example of the interaction of magnets in terms of the attraction of opposite sexes. From a deeper psychological perspective, the example has even greater impact, as an awareness of the attraction of opposites prepares us to recognize many life experiences that are far beyond mere genital, sexual forces.

For instance, such is the nature of basic psychodynamics that all of a male's female aspects are usually held in his unconscious. The male does not know that his female psychological counterparts are actually there or that these counterparts are unconsciously projected onto external screens—other people—who approximate the inner counterparts. He only realizes that he falls in love with or is attracted to particular women . . . or that he does not like or is repelled by other women. In actuality, the outer females—whether liked or unliked—are only substitutes for those interior females the male is unconsciously seeking or rejecting. Women experience the same psychodynamics, except that the aspects held in the unconscious are masculine, and they are likewise projected out onto individuals who approximate the interiorly held images or patterns.

And therein lies one of the great difficulties in human relationships. Neither partner is actually fully satisfying the primary forces of attraction in the other, for the outer partner is actually a substitute for an unconsciously sought interior relationship. In the mystical traditions, however, the attraction of the masculine to the feminine and of the feminine to the masculine does occur as a primary internal experience, which eventuates in the hermetic marriage and paves the way for the androgyne, the androgynous states of consciousness.

My experience indicates that the androgyne, a blended and sexually neutralized aspect of the Self, is the first state of consciousness from which most awakening individuals can begin to express Unconditional Love, "that transpersonal form of impersonal love that relates all things together . . . the glue of the universe," as Eunice Hurt, the Teacher who ignited my spiritual Unfoldment in my early thirties, used to say. Unconditional Love as a concept seems fairly easy to grasp but turns out to be one of the more difficult transitions to achieve, as it means leaving the identification with any personal sense of self, and identifying with an impersonal, nondual state of consciousness. The experience of Unconditional Love involves a huge stretch for most people, a giant leap in consciousness, yet it is essential for anyone approaching the more expanded and mature levels of Beingness. The androgyne, as one of many nondual pattern levels of consciousness that can operate in either space/time or non-space/nontime, is eminently capable of expressing Unconditional Love and entering into selfless service to humanity as a whole.

I was first made aware of the multiplicity of masculine and feminine parts and the androgyne through the work of Bella Karish and her spiritual partner, Wayne Guthrie, who head the Fellowship of Universal Guidance, which they founded over twenty-five years ago, and which is now located in Glendale, California. Their insights, plus my own experience and that of many others who have attended my workshops, have caused me to understand that there are usually several stages of identification with one or more masculine and feminine aspects before one becomes consciously identified with the androgyne. First comes a basic recognition of the pairs of sexual opposites existing in one's own Unconscious, followed by an awareness that various unconscious relationships can exist among them. These include relationships in which opposites don't get along with each other and those in which the opposites are totally supportive of each other. There may also be a doubling of the male aspect or of the female aspect with no countergender present, as well as partial blendings of several kinds (called hermaphrodites)—or the fully blended form, the androgyne. As we can see even from this brief overview, matters of psychological gender and of psychosexual relationship in the human being are complex and can only very, very rarely be perceived in terms of a single-gender aspect of the Self.

Thus, the first major shock comes when we realize that the unconscious countergender selves have an existence all their own and can act autonomously and independently of our conscious outer gender. So a biological male with a conscious sense of self that is male will find he is sexually attracted to women, and usually to a particular woman, who fulfills the unconscious drive for homeostasis and balance. But the unconscious female aspects within this very same man will be attracted to men, and usually each to a particular type of man. This attraction is ordinarily not conscious in the male but is experienced in terms of homoerotic and homosensual feelings, the kind that can be experienced in the various ways that males customarily engage one another, particularly through sports.

In homosexual relationships, the conscious and unconcious psychological selves, which are not necessarily the same as the physical gender, may be either male or female in either partner, but the general principle of the attraction of opposites will still hold true most of the time. For this reason, relationships which are physically homosexual are nevertheless not psychologically homosexual in the vast majority of cases. They involve the same attractive forces that are experienced in heterosexual relationships. What must be remembered is that the gender the outer mind identifies with and regards as being the gender of self may not be the same gender that is unconsciously driving the relationship. For example, a biological male who is consciously, psychologically male can be attracted to the psychologically feminine aspect of another biological male. A most remarkable situation occurs in relationships between individuals of the same physical sex when both of them have consciously identified with their own opposite psychological gender, and each is therefore attracted to their same physical gender in their partner. In other words, in the case of two men, both have identified with their feminine psychological aspect and each is attracted to the masculine physical aspect of the other.

There can be a very complex relationship in which the biological gender, the conscious psychological gender, and the gender of the unconscious psychological self that is most active in the attraction are all the same in both partners. In a situation like this, I believe the principle of the attraction of opposites is still active but it has now been converted from opposite-gender attraction to attraction between relative differences in the same gender.

We should not forget that the possible shadings of maleness and femaleness in combination with a person's different conscious and unconscious selves create an inner landscape that is infinitely complex. None of this, therefore, should be regarded as a simplistic formula for evaluating the subtleties of attraction between people.

The attraction of opposites is easily recognized when it is pleasurable and powerful, as it is in sexuality. But the principle holds true whether there is pleasure or displeasure. The independent, powerful individual is unconsciously attracted to the dependent individual, the Saint is attracted to the Sinner, the Great Good is attracted to the Great Evil, peace is attracted to war, and life is attracted to death. Of course, the contrary is also true in each case. The list of opposites is as long as the number of polarities one can think of. The real mystery in the attraction of opposites, however, lies in the dynamics between nonduality and duality and not in the subjective attitudes one may hold about any particular pair of opposites.

The Dance of Wholeness: Duality and Nonduality

Whatever causes time and space to exist calls duality into existence, while nontime and nonspace manifest nonduality or unity. From this perspective, duality and nonduality are themselves polarities, and they function like polarities. They attract each other and generate each other. Therein lies a profound realization. There is no special preference of the deep psyche for either dual or nondual aspects. Both are necessary for Wholeness. What bridges duality and nonduality are, of all things, those patterns capable of existing in nontime and nonspace as well as in time and space. This insight, as we shall see later when we take up pattern-level reality, is fundamental. Consciousness is dual and nondual, sequentially and simultaneously!

The moment one's awareness enters states of duality, of time and space—*this* as distinct from *that*, male as distinct from female, good as distinct from evil, mine as distinct from yours—the psyche is fractured and seeks to reestablish its connection to unity and wholeness, that wholeness which the greater part of our Beingness experiences. *But nonduality seeks duality also*, which is a point most spiritual paths ignore.

One way the psyche may experience wholeness, other than by entering nondual states of Being, is for the dualistic states of consciousness to experience *relative* wholeness and balance through cycles and rhythms. By taking a vantage point that permits us to embrace relatively long periods of time in our awareness, we can often sense a wholeness and balance that, from the perspective of any particular moment, would seem quite out of balance.

One of the mysteries behind the Judaic creation story of Adam and Eve is the process that leads from unity (represented by the Garden of Eden) into duality (represented by the world). Contrary to popular Western religious teachings, the Fall—entry into the world, into time and space, into duality—is neither a mistake nor a sin. It represents symbolically, among other things, the initial phase of a profound cycling of consciousness, moving from unity to duality and back to unity. We do it when we move from the womb into the world. There has even been some talk in scientific circles that perhaps the constituent parts of the atoms that make up our bodies and the whole physical universe do it billions of times per second. Most of the time, these particles may be nonexistent! And something drives this being/not-being oscillation, the duality/unity dance. Though we do not know what forces cause the process, we might describe the interrelationship as a "yearning" of the opposite for its counterpart. Thus, contained in the unity principle is a "yearning" for duality, and contained in the duality principle is a "yearning" for unity.

From a psychological viewpoint, the desire for duality or separated existence is what the Fall is all about. In the literal interpretation of the biblical account of Adam and Eve in the Garden of Eden, a typical Fall story unfolds. Paradise is offered and maintained as long as the inhabitants of the Garden remain under the influence and control of the ruling, sustaining deity. When Adam and Eve disobey the one rule of the Garden by eating the fruit of the tree of the knowledge of good and evil, they become godlike. This so upsets God that he casts them out of paradise and forces them to live in the world and to undergo the painful experiences of worldly life.

The infantile psyche perceives this as rejection and abandonment by the parent and feels guilt-ridden and filled with shame. It then sets out on a path to be redeemed in the eyes of the parent. The maturing psyche, however, accepts the challenge of the new situation and calls upon inherent, untapped resources within its own sense of self that were previously supplied by the parental aspect on which it was dependent. Initiation into greater Beinghood occurs, therefore, *because* of the Fall!

The all-too-common feminist attitude regarding the story of Adam and Eve is that the Feminine and Her sexuality are demeaned by the Masculine. Not only does Eve have her origin through Adam and not come into being in her own right, but she is also accused of being weak, since she is seduced by the Serpent. In Chapter 11 I will take up the story of Adam and Eve from the perspective of dream interpretation to reveal a much different, richer, and quite surprising point of view. Meanwhile, to men I say: Wake up! Our feelings of superiority are based in a defense against the unconscious power of the Feminine. Let us remember that the shadow side of the Feminine—vulnerability and chaos—is fundamental to change and to Unfoldment. To women I say: Wake up! Your feelings of powerlessness are contained in your own unconscious rejection of the Feminine and in your unconscious deification of the Masculine. It's not men who have enslaved you. It's your own incapacity to contain the full power, vulnerability, and chaos the feminine principle represents. This causes women to stampede to the Masculine for protection and support—even when that masculine protection and support are, at the unconscious level, in the woman herself.

The Fall . . . chaos and change! I am reminded of the work of the Belgian Nobel prize laureate Ilya Prigogine on dissipative structures, which shows that when any organized system collapses (this can be a physical system in matter or, in terms of an extension of his work, a psychological system, a social system, etc.), it will reorganize into a new and more complex form. And chaos theory, which is right at the leading edge of speculation about complex physical systems, demonstrates an order lurking in the dynamics of that which was thought to be orderless. Chaos and the principles of destruction and collapse are somehow integral to new and greater potentials, whether they be psychological, social, spiritual, or cosmic.

With these viewpoints in mind, we can now appreciate the Fall with more understanding.

When the Fall from Grace occurs, the previous stage or sense of self must be sacrificed in order for one to embrace the next possibility, which has new resources that can handle the greater responsibilities of livingness. But if one is totally dependent on the external for a sense of well-being or has established no inner center that can allow the death of less mature aspects that are still dependent on parental values, the sacrifice cannot be made and one returns to the Garden repentant . . . the initiation aborted.

However, if one has experienced an inner awakening into innate spiritual states and into values that have no need to defend against anything . . . if one has established a relationship with the Mystery and with the unconscious aspects of self that attune to the deepest Beinghood, which is the Self, then the sacrifice of the previous values and senses of self can be successfully accomplished and the vulnerability of a new potential embraced.

We can pass through a Fall unconsciously or consciously, with immaturity or with maturity. The major difference in terms of our relationship to it is whether we experience the pain and the ecstasy as defeat and humiliation or as Unfoldment and liberation.

CHAPTER THREE

ONE BODY—MANY SELVES

*The eyes and ears that serve the outer
consciousness serve also the myriad
unconscious selves in service to the Self.*

Changing perspectives and breaking mind-sets are both fundamental to the Awakening process ... the process of growing out of ordinary states of awareness into vaster, more mature resources of consciousness. When such an Awakening process is undertaken, all traditional viewpoints about life, the self, spirituality, sexuality, and even reality itself are subject to dramatic, unexpected, and sudden change.

For me, such fundamental changes in perspective often occur when an unthinkable thought breaks through into my awareness. For example, one of the most powerful renovations of my consciousness occurred when I entertained the almost taboo consideration that there simply may be no such thing as a single self, a single soul in a single body. The realization went on to include the possibility that the basis of the human psyche ... both the conscious and the unconscious aspects ... may be a collective of selves, independent and autonomous yet interrelating with one another, and mostly unknown to the outer awareness. Just as the body is a collective of well-defined patterns of energy identified as organ systems, the psyche, I realized, is a collective of well-defined patterns of forces discerned as selves. Each self has degrees of access to and control over the body. Each may seize not only the body but the consciousness as well, perhaps displacing the ordinary awareness of self or perhaps influencing the ordinary awareness to various degrees without overshadowing or displacing it.

The idea that, unknown to the outer mind, many selves utilize the same eyes and the same ears in each body is an awesome creative thought that has profoundly changed how I perceive myself and others.

Thus, as one engages larger and larger arenas of awareness, the *multiplicity of Beingness* begins to be recognized and appreciated. One's larger Beingness is understood to be many-faceted, composed of well-defined and highly compartmentalized selves which may include both genders as well as being asexual, and which may range from the fetal and infantile levels through all intermediate stages and finally to those of Elderhood and Enlightenment.

Just ask any elderly person to allow his or her internal little boy or little girl out to play, and watch that person undergo a most amazing transformation! Memory, resources, and movements are instantly changed. Depending on which child is accessed, the experience may involve the expression of fun and well-being, unhappiness with feelings of abandonment and rejection, or any of numerous other potentials.

What is important to understand is that I am not talking about the person's simply replaying adult memories of childhood. I am talking about the activation in consciousness of a child who has existed in consciousness and who has continued to exist unconsciously as a child within the deeper individual psyche. Its function is to be a specific kind of a child. It will never grow up, nor is it intended to grow up. Its awareness of all things, including spiritual matters, is that of a child.

When exploring people's deeper aspects, I am always struck by how *many* children exist in any one individual. They range from the infantile to the adolescent, and they all can and do influence the conscious reality of that person to varying degrees. Some may still be at the fetal level of development, and most are in the preverbal stages. The ones that dominated the conscious awareness during certain stages of development are the ones that can be accessed most easily. There are also others of which no conscious recall is available.

They exist solely as unconscious selves, but may occasionally be seen manifesting through dreams.

A partial list of the types of children I have encountered in my work with individuals includes: the Abandoned Child, the Wounded Child, the Alien Child, the Adult Child, the Sickly Child, the Good Child, the Humiliated Child, the Unworthy Child, the Helpless Child, the Evil Child, the Angelic Child, the Devouring Child, the Victim Child, the Ugly Child, the Divine Child, the Magical Child, the Gifted Child, the Unlovable Child, the Mischievous Child, the Baby Child, the Bully Child, the Innocent Child, the Bad Child, the Beautiful Child, the Special Child, the Rejected Child, the Angry Child, the Shy Child, the Frightened Child, and the Nature Child.

As you read through the list you are sure to find at least one and perhaps several that describe your own childhood senses of selves. Again, those that can be easily recalled are the dominant, conscious child-patterns from earlier stages of life. Of course, there are others that may not be easily recalled and that may only exist at the unconscious level yet still be very influential in the adult or later life stages. As certain of my own children were uncovered in the course of my psychological awakening, I began to realize that each one has a very different sense of what the parents were like and what childhood was like, and all were contained in the same person—me! I also began to realize that one's inner children are often associated in complementary pairs, such as the Sexual Child and the Abused Child; the Angelic Child and the Evil Child; the Sickly Child and the Special Child. Although I feel that recognizing the combinations of children in any particular individual is of immense importance in understanding that individual's life patternings, I am only in the early stages of correlating those important combinations with later adult development.

I have further come to believe—and this is another difficult concept in terms of ordinary perspectives—that all of these children represent immortal patterns in the human psyche. All of these patterns incarnate to varying degrees and in varying combinations in each individual in every generation. The developing conscious awareness becomes attached to one or more of the immortal child patternings and defines its own Child self through those classic patterns. There may be a tendency for particular classic patterns to manifest in a certain family from generation to generation. Theoretically, any of the basic patterns should be able to incarnate in any single individual, yet there are certain trends in family groupings. I don't believe anyone actually knows how or why this happens, nor how the patterns manifest nor why. I do know that the child-rearing behavior of parents and the social environment have only the most superficial influence on which of the child patterns comes into existence in any specific human being. Circumstances that do seem to have a great influence are birth order and the number of other siblings.

To appreciate the degree to which inner children can be different, I would like to present a few of the senses of self that are a part of me, personally. One of my inner children, for instance, still prays and thinks in terms of angels and heaven. He is a little boy about four years old. He is sweet, angelic, and pure. He can be easily frightened by anger or violence and never understands when someone doesn't like him. He is very shy and sensitive and can be easily hurt if someone makes the slightest critical remark. There is another inner little boy, about age seven, who is fat, feels he is unlovable, is inept in sports, loves to dance, feels humiliated around intelligent people, fears father figures, and loves to please mother figures. There is a male mulatto child who was birthed into my awareness through a series of dreams. Although I briefly felt the interior presence of this child in those dreams a decade ago, he has not reappeared and I have no conscious recall of him as a sense of self in the way I usually know myself. Others exist, but these three illustrate the point that there is not just one child or one male or one female inside. There is a large community of selves in each one of us.

We all need to pay particular attention to the inner children since, as my experience has indicated to me, they are the forces lying behind most illness and most inappropriate behavior in all stages of life except childhood itself. One of the reasons I feel the child has such great influence in regard to disease patterns is her/his instinctual, undifferentiated relationship to the emotions and to sexuality, with little capacity to handle such powerful forces. Another reason, which will be elaborated on in the chapter on induction and initiations, is the lack of family and societal rites of passage that would ordinarily help prevent an individual from regressing to infantile patternings under stress.

Who Gets Sick: Selves in Action

I have never encountered a patient in whom a mature Adult self is in charge of a disease process at the unconscious level. Usually the self in charge is a young, vulnerable, and often very unhappy child whose solution to life's conflicts is disease and/or death. The example of the nineteen-year-old girl I cited in Chapter 1 disclosed that the self in charge was a child about ten or twelve years old who would rather die than enter womanhood.

It is important to note that a Child self may not be the only self that seeks illness and/or death in order to resolve conflicts. Arrested development at any stage has the potential to act as the force for disease and death. Some mothers, when their last child is leaving home, develop a life-threatening illness because the Mother self, which has been in charge of the psyche for many years, can't imagine life without a family around which to center its attention. Such women have no sense of a self to carry them on into the rich phases of the menopausal woman and eventually into the mystery of the feminine Elderhood, and no way to uncover those potentials. The same is true of some men who face retirement, with its concomitant loss of power. I and other physicians have observed that there is a tendency for spouses to die within a two-year period following the death of a husband or wife. In such cases the surviving partner is unable to engage a sense of self that can sustain life without the other person.

A sudden, dramatic change in one's sense of purpose (which may be reflecting a change in an interior-self pattern) can impact the physical body and the course of disease. For example, a young woman with widespread lymphoma which occurred following a difficult divorce made up her mind that she would live until her only child—a son—graduated from high school four years later. Without any medical treatment, the lymphoma completely disappeared from her body except in one area in the lower abdomen, where it stayed localized, without treatment, until six months before her son was due to graduate, at which time it again became aggressive. She died the day he graduated. Here we see the superimposition of a more mature self, which instituted the change in the body's response to the disease for a specified time period. In my opinion, the self that sought death as the resolution to her conflicts was overridden for a substantial period of time. It is truly remarkable when we pause to consider that a change in consciousness can effect a change in the course of a disease.

Our relationships with authority figures or with persons we admire and hold in high esteem may cause us to be seized momentarily by much younger, often very infantile, selves, producing unexpected and frequently even humiliating responses. For example, many individuals will tend unconsciously to see physicians as father figures. This usually elicits an unconscious Child self within the patient, one who has all the resources and value systems of that particular Child self. The other resources of the patient are lost the moment this unconscious child is called forth. Since the outcome of the therapeutic process is strongly influenced by whichever unconscious aspect of the patient is actually present, if the person's parent/child dynamics were harmonious, the outcome of the therapy is usually enhanced (although positive parent/child dynamics can also potentiate the illness if certain secondary gains related to attention getting and victim-consciousness are activated). If the unconscious child evoked in the patient experienced negative parent/child dynamics, all sorts of unconscious sabotaging can take place during what appears, at the conscious level, to be two adults working through a medical problem.

A well-known situation in medical practice is that which often occurs when the wives of some physicians are ill. The unconscious dynamics that bring a woman to marry any man are always powerfully based in father/daughter patternings. In the case of the woman who marries a physician, the father/daughter pattern can be highly magnified, since the physician is a bigger-than-life father figure, no matter what he is like at the personality level. Compounding this underlying pattern is the devotion to the care of the ill that the life of a physician entails. The Infant self of the wife can perceive this devotion by the husband to his practice as though it were involvement with a competing woman, just as in childhood a little girl may perceive her mother as a competing force for the father's love.

When a physician's wife of this type is ill, she has so much un-conscious anger tied into the transference of the father/daughter bonding, as well as secondary gain through attention she gets from the illness, that strong tendencies exist in her to thwart any action or recommendation given by any authority figure, but in this case, particularly by any male physician. All of these dynamics are at the unconscious level and reside completely in a child aspect of the wom-an. Unfortunately, these components can conspire to create the most horrendous complications during treatment. There isn't a nurse or a physician of either gender who doesn't know about the difficult prob-lems that are encountered with such women.

On several occasions I have encountered particularly powerful experiences involving the unconscious activation of parent-child pat-terns, when either men or women, as patients or students, were strug-gling with powerful unconscious rage against the father. Initially they would tend to deify their relationship with me and experience dra-matic, unexpected changes in consciousness and great improvement in the symptoms that brought them to me in the first place. Before I understood the dynamics of this process, I would be seduced into inflated evaluations of my own capabilities, not realizing that this was the hook that set the stage for the humiliation that was soon to follow.

The second stage was an apparent lack of response in the individ-ual to the same approach that was successfully used initially. This soon progressed to the third stage, where nothing worked for the individual and where any of my recommendations were rationalized as being either unworkable or doomed to failure. The final stage was the verbal abuse the individual would shower on me. This effectively crushes the authority figure by making any recommendation or ac-tion by that authority figure a failure. Astonishingly, all of these dynamics take place at unconscious levels in both of the players, and only rarely does the individual who is playing the role of father figure consciously grasp what dynamics are operating in the people he or she encounters.

The solution to this deep psychological pattern is for the author-ity figure, as soon as the dynamics are perceived, to immediately announce that he or she can do nothing for the individual. The threatened abandonment by the authority figure is enough to cause the patient/student to reverse his or her course of action and to be open again to treatment and/or counsel. Of course, he or she may also leave the interaction to find more fertile territory in which to satisfy the rage pattern of the unconscious Child self.

The Multiplicity of Selves

The child-selves must be distinguished from those adult-selves that manifest resources of simplicity. For example, the self I usually identify with I call Simple Brugh. This aspect is uncomplex, couldn't care less about spiritual teachings, doesn't recall what was said in a seminar or in a lecture, likes to take long walks in the desert or in the mountains, likes to cook, likes to be alone, loves television, doesn't want to write books, thinks he is asexual, enjoys sunrises and sunsets, and engages in simple appreciation for what he has and for the amount of life he experiences. As 90 to 95 percent of our lives occur in troughs where nothing of great moment is happening—that is, nothing other than the usual miracle of Life—the ability to engage one's Simple Self is truly a great gift, for the Simple Self has no desire to do more than it can do with the resources available to it. This part is grounded, unpretentious, and very ordinary.

Simple Brugh is resourceless when it comes to expanded awareness or the capacity to effect healing, to interpret dreams, to write, to be a sensitive lover, or to handle business affairs, to name only a few areas of his incompetence. But he is very likable, enjoyable, and he has a wonderful sense of humor when he isn't threatened by women. Simple Brugh becomes very anxious and upset when I am preparing to speak to a group or to a large audience when he is still in charge of my awareness. I wring my hands, my heart pounds, and I accuse myself of being a sham, since there isn't one great thought or one great skill in Simple Brugh's mind that anyone would be interested in, and he knows it.

After about five minutes of dealing with the upset and anxiety of Simple Brugh, something pops into my awareness and says to Simple Brugh, "Shut up . . . you are not the one giving this talk!"

I can't tell you how relieved he is. Simple Brugh dissolves along with the fear, and a very different part of my Being enters my awareness just as I begin to speak. When this happens, my vocabulary changes, my body language changes, the character of my voice changes, and I am experiencing once again all the richness and resources of a Teacher who is filled with the inspiration of Spirit, of the Mystery . . . with clarity of thought, extended awareness, and the capacities to move individuals into a greater potential. I don't lose consciousness when that happens. I don't feel shoved aside. I simply feel expanded and resource-filled in regard to the particular task I am undertaking. It is as if something else overshadows my usual consciousness and vastly expands its capacities and resources. In this augmented state of consciousness, I have full awareness of Simple Brugh's knowledge and informational systems, but I also have much, much more knowledge and information as well.

This expanded teacher aspect loves the adventure of spiritual development, yet tends to demean the simple and the ordinary. This part actually overvalues spirituality and expanded awareness. If he had his way, the whole world would be awakened by now.

Because I don't lose consciousness, tremble, or alter my breathing patterns when I change levels or invoke another self, and because I can effect a change in consciousness simply through gently lowering and then opening my eyes, most people are unaware of the dramatic inner shift that takes place, a shift that makes powerful resources available to me. I feel that this capacity to maintain consciousness while changing vehicles of awareness has come through the discipline of daily meditation and through the development of the Heart Center state of awareness over a seven-year period, a process I discussed thoroughly in *Joy's Way*.

A fascinating aspect of recognizing and appreciating the multiplicity of Being is in coming to understand that each part of one's Beingness has particular resources. Then what's important is to begin the process of Self-Realization through the discovery of the various selves, which may involve far more than just a few selves, and to master the access to each one in appropriate circumstances. Perhaps the basic cause for our societal anxiety is the lack of development of the mature selves through initiations, leaving most of us stuck with only a few monotonous infantile patternings with which to engage the mystery and the livingness of life. Even using just one of the mature selves for all situations encountered in life would force that self to struggle with stages and circumstances it was never intended to handle. No single sense of self has access to all resources. Perhaps our utilizing only a few of the potential resources in consciousness contributes to our heavy use of Valium and alcohol.

Having to rely on other parts of Self—autonomous parts—to come forward when circumstances dictate involves a tremendous vulnerability. This was dramatically emphasized to me several years after I began lecturing publicly. I was asked to give a talk at the Church of Religious Science in Walnut Creek, California. The audience was highly expectant and filled with members of the general public as well as physicians, nurses, and people who had attended my workshops, along with their friends and family members. They had come to hear this "heightened" Teacher of consciousness transformation and healing. I was feeling a particular need to perform to my utmost.

Everything was going on schedule. Simple Brugh was complaining that we shouldn't be there in the first place because he didn't have anything to say. My anxiety had reached a crisis level, which usually precipitates the appearance of the Teacher self. I could feel the beginning changes of consciousness as the minister began to introduce me.

Then, when I started toward the podium, Simple Brugh's worst fear came to pass. The expanded feeling drained out of me like water runs out of a bathtub when someone pulls the plug. I was left with Simple Brugh and a highly expectant audience. I could barely remember why I was giving this talk, let alone come up with anything that might inspire an audience. For fifteen or twenty minutes I stumbled through some simple anecdotes, literally praying for the more expanded level to come through. But nothing happened. After thirty minutes I could feel the audience becoming restless. I was feeling humiliated, betrayed, extremely vulnerable, and uncomfortably warm. Finally an original thought came to me. Why not just admit to the audience that nothing was happening?

I stopped telling the story I was using as a filler and made my incredible announcement, at which time the audience expressed its concurrence and responded with thunderous applause! I was even more humiliated. Obviously they knew what took me forty minutes to admit to myself ... that absolutely nothing was happening that could inspire or transform anyone.

When I am addressing an audience, I always feel some performance anxiety. There are also financial considerations and obligations to the sponsoring organization to consider, as well as my own future as a professional public speaker and the resources that are thereby generated. Needless to say, all of these things were concerning me. But whatever self comes in to teach didn't care about how I felt or what was happening to the audience. That self simply was not available.

When I suggested that it would be better for them to chant and sing rather than to be exposed to what I was presenting, the negative response from the audience began to subside. First of all, they did appreciate my honesty, whether they understood what I was experiencing or not. When I accepted the circumstance instead of denying it and masking my feelings, a transformation occurred in me. I suddenly didn't fear the rejection or the humiliation. My suggestion that we all take a break was met with even more thunderous applause, and I completed the evening in a quiet, simple storytelling mode, which some enjoyed but with which most were disappointed, as the postlecture feedback revealed. Interestingly, having actually experienced my worst lecturing fear ended lifelong, recurring dreams about forgetting my lines or walking down the street and discovering I am naked. Somehow, in that painful moment, I met and accepted a part of myself that does exist, is inept, and is closely kin to the Fool.

When I prepare to do healing work, whether using visualization during meditation or energy flow through my hands to work directly with someone, I enter an awareness that is different from that of the Teacher or of Simple Brugh. It is feminine. She is compassionate beyond anything I can possibly express in words. She is mature and has rich resources of natural understanding and wisdom. She has a profound appreciation for the miracle and mystery of Life and she instinctively knows how to touch and how to move energy into another person's body. She is, for me, the Healing Presence, Incarnate. She thinks in terms of ancient temples and healing altars. Her healing forces come through a Radiance of Unconditional Love and Compassion which I have learned to deeply appreciate over the past fifteen years. Through my experience of her, another renovating perspective has come to me. Only the feminine aspect of the human psyche can effect intrinsic healing. I have often thought that perhaps this is because of the intuitive understanding of the Feminine regarding relationships and wholeness. Certain masculine aspects can organize and set the staging for healing, whether through ritual, surgery, medicines, or a combination, but they cannot make the actual healing process take place. They rely on the wisdom of the body (which may be feminine, by the way) to effect the healing. The point is that some, but not all, feminine parts of the psyche can directly effect healing forces in the healer's body or in another person's body.

When I am preparing to do dream interpretation, the Teacher and the Healer have to step aside, as a most amazing resource of consciousness enters my awareness. It also feels feminine. She has a very highly developed intuitive sense and a psychic range far beyond my other senses of self. She loves to listen to dreams and to interpret them. If she is not in my awareness when a dream is being presented, whether it is one of my own or another person's, nothing will happen. The dream is just a dream, and mostly gibberish to my usual selves, including the Teacher. But when she is present in my awareness, dreams become magical displays of the fundamental patterning of the dreamer. Associations and insights, patterns and conflicts, become immediately apparent to me. I am often stunned as to how brilliantly she handles dreams, tying the images to meaningful material in the dreamer's life, often in areas that have not yet been broached in conversation.

The Unknown Driver

Having offered examples of a few of the different selves I explore and appreciate as parts of my own Beingness, I will now present examples of familiar situations that may reflect the principle of the multiplicity of selves in everyone.

The most commonly reported example in my Conference work is the experience of getting into an automobile to drive somewhere—perhaps to work, to church, or to a friend's house—then becoming lost in thought and suddenly arriving at the destination with no conscious recall of having driven the car. All sorts of complex decisions and actions have been dealt with by some aspect of the psyche capable of driving the car, yet they have not been handled by the part that is considered the conscious self. Something got the car where it needed to go, and that something is, I propose, another self . . . unconscious to the conscious mind. In this case, the conscious sense of self stayed with its own thoughts and lost contact with the self that was driving the car. And in my own life, before I began to think in terms of the multiplicity of Beingness, I experienced a number of occasions when, while dealing with an exciting, creative project, I would awaken the next morning and wonder who dreamed up what had been produced, since what lay before me was beyond what I knew or sensed I could do in my usual conscious level of awareness.

Ritual masks in primitive societies and the costumes worn during Mardi Gras and Halloween all reflect the multiplicity of the psyche in a single individual. People often report that when they put on costumes, they are released to be someone other than themselves. This is a very telling statement. Actors and actresses often are shy in their personal lives but quite capable of being dynamic and resource-filled when playing a character. There are cases of individuals who are practically helpless under the handicap of stuttering but who speak normally and powerfully when acting or singing. They will usually declare that the reason they can do it is that the person acting or singing is not themselves.

Those moments when we transcend ourselves are not under the direction of the ego or conscious self. They may occur while we are driving a car or working on a creative project, or they may spontaneously erupt in professional performances such as acting, celebrating religious rituals, speaking in public, healing the sick, or when we are handling a major crisis. Whatever heightened consciousness is, it is often more intelligent and certainly more resourceful than is the ordinary awareness. One does not have to postulate discarnate entities or intergalactic visitors to account for expanded ranges of human awareness, since we have so little understanding of what consciousness is in the first place. Much of what seems curious or alien becomes comprehensible when we begin to take a new perspective regarding human consciousness . . . one which holds that each individual has potentially at his or her disposal far more vast dimensions of awareness than just those of the outer conscious mind. Precisely because I regularly experience the contrast between my ordinary mind and the greater ranges of consciousness, I can make the statement that the ordinary conscious part of my Being is mostly comatose, has only a limited and superficial effect on my life, and is mostly a strongly biased and defensive witness to reality. I suspect the same is true for others.

The fact that some individuals go to Conferences where they are lifted into new potentials, feel great opportunity and possibility, then return home only to fall back into old patterns and old habits, does not diminish the significance of their encounter during the Conference with their own greater resources. It simply emphasizes that control over encounters with expanded or different selves is initially tenuous and easily interrupted. At least several months of constant attention to the newly encountered self or selves are usually required before a degree of stability is achieved. The majority of participants emerging from a gathering that inducts them into greater possibilities will follow the path of least resistance and fall back to the old ways of defense, control, and comfort. The path of Self-Realization, however, is one of courage, vulnerability, attention, commitment, and sacrifice. Neither getting on this path nor staying on it is easy.

Multiple Personality Disorder

Having a number of personalities in a single body is termed Multiple Personality Disorder by traditional medicine. The individual seeks treatment, or the family of the individual seeks treatment for him or her, because of the confusion and chaos surrounding having to deal with the various personalities, most of whom are unaware of the other personalities and what those personalities have been doing from day to day as the individual has lived his or her life. The problem is that there is no conscious continuous observer in the multiple-personality-disordered individual who can keep track of and integrate the various realities that are experienced. The usual approach to treatment in psychiatry and in psychology is to consider the existence of multiple personalities as abnormal and to strengthen but one single sense of self, the one that conforms to societal standards of value and behavior, or to the therapist's standards of value and behavior.

When I was in medical school, I heard during a psychiatric lecture that a diagnosis of Multiple Personality Disorder was considered to be so rare that only one hundred cases were recorded in the world's literature. These days, however, all of my friends know at least one person who is a "multiple," and many of them claim also to experience multiple senses of selves. Further, when I lecture to large audiences and query those gathered as to how many are aware of multiples or actually know a multiple, I am amazed that 30 to 40 percent of the hands go up. Of course, medicine is much more rigid in applying its criteria to possible cases of Multiple Personality Disorder than I am in my informal observations. Nonetheless, the multiplicity of Beingness experienced by large numbers of people points to a very different understanding of consciousness than traditional religious, scientific, legal, political, and medical perspectives hold, particularly in Western societies. The discovery of multiplicity in myself and in every individual I have worked with over the last fourteen years forms the basis, and accounts for a large part of the success, of my approach to helping people engage Self-Realization, fulfillment, and their inherent well-being. Indeed, having multiple personalities may be of extraordinary value to both the individual and the society.

There is excellent research material on health and disease in multiple personalities in the scientific literature. The National Institute of Mental Health, for instance, is researching how different personalities in the same body may affect health and disease. The best summary and bibliography I have run across on multiple personalities is published by the Institute of Noetic Sciences in Menlo Park, California.

For the reader who has never encountered the subject of Multiple Personality, I highly recommend one motion picture—*Sybil*. Two and one half hours of experiencing this film, and no one can forget what a multiple personality is. Classically, a multiple personality is someone who does not know he or she is multiple. The basic personality usually is unaware of the other personalities, yet the other personalities are often aware of one another as well as being aware of the basic personality. The different personalities may be of either gender and of any age. Some may have great artistic, musical, linguistic, or mathematical ability, while others may be relatively resourceless. They may or may not like one another. Each has a relative sense of self with a personal history that may overlap, to varying degrees, the personal histories of other parts. One or more of the personalities may have diametrically opposite viewpoints from other personalities on many subjects, including religion, sex, politics, and life in general. Some may give evidence of being dark and destructive, while others may be "good" persons. Some are like monks and nuns, and some are like prostitutes and street people. The chronological age of each self doesn't have to change with time as the basic personality does, and in fact usually does not.

When lecturing on the multiplicity of Beingness or related topics, I usually use some of the examples given by the Institute of Noetic Sciences, wherein they report cases in which allergies are detected when one personality is present and no allergies are detected when another personality is present. Doesn't that just boggle the mind? From the viewpoint of my scientific background, this information is simply a noncompute. We are supposedly allergic lifelong, not personality-long! Another example that upsets the physician within me is that of cases which have been reported where diabetes mellitus is present and detectable in one personality and not in another. (Remember this is the same body with a different self in charge of the consciousness.) Even eye color was reported to change in one case of multiple personality.

One of the most remarkable reports of multiple personality involves a woman who, when in one female self, has her usual menstrual period. If she happens to change to another female self just after her period, that self may be expecting her own normal period in a few days ... and she'll have it. When each of the female selves is questioned individually as to how many periods were experienced that particular month, each will answer, quite honestly, that only one was experienced and that it was on time. Her physician, in fact, documented that two periods would sometimes occur in her body during the same month.

An unexpected encounter with a multiple personality occurred while I was demonstrating the psychological aspects of disease in a very ill woman to a group of individuals who had come to study with me. This process involves my having the ill individual tell the group and me what illness is present and what has been done for treatment. I also ask the person to discuss what he or she thinks about the disease and what may have brought it about. As I have no prior knowledge of the patient, the problem and its dynamics unfold to me and to the group at the same time. I then commence a deep psychological dissection of the dynamics of the individual's disease process, guided by my intuition. I reveal how the disease and the psychological dynamics are reflections of each other. I find that recognizing this mind/body relationship is very significant in helping me to understand—regardless of what the individual's outer sense of self feels about the situation—whether he or she is going to get better, stay the same, or succumb to the disease and resolve the psychological and spiritual issues through death.

During this particular analytic process, the woman, who was in her late forties, revealed that she was dealing with widespread breast carcinoma and that she was depressed and wanted to die. As the session progressed, it became apparent that this part of her had never wanted to be in life in the first place, found little in life to inspire it, and felt basically unwanted and unloved. Then, suddenly, I thought to ask if she had any inner spiritual or psychological guides to whom she could attune, who might be able to help her.

A most amazing transformation began to take place. She looked curiously at me, then announced, "You know I channel, don't you?"

"No," I said, "but can you channel for us now?"

This woman, who, during the earlier part of the session, had looked as if she would die on the spot, perked up and, with a twinkle in her eye, sat erect and began to change levels of consciousness, until another personality—the "channel"—took over. The most remarkable aspect was the change in body posture and voice energetics as the channel discussed how pathetic this part of herself was—meaning the self who was usually in charge of her psyche—and proceeded to outline ways the sick part might live life more fully, as well as to discuss which of the suggestions I had given might be most beneficial and which the channel thought would be rejected or disregarded entirely by the sick self.

When the sick personality came back, she was unaware of what had been presented by this wonderful, wise, clear area of the woman's Beingness. The ashen skin color reappeared, as did her difficulty with breathing. If ever I wanted to demonstrate how changes in states of consciousness can influence the response of the body, this was it. One moment she had vitality and an aura of well-being. The next moment she had an aura of depression, illness, and rapidly approaching death. Fortunately, I tape-record all sessions when I am working, so this woman, for the first time in her life, could hear another part of her speaking, telling her how to get better and how to heal herself. It was truly a moving, mind-expanding session. Nor was it unprecedented in terms of scientific literature, for the material published by the Institute of Noetic Sciences notes that if the Multiple Personality can access the "helper," the part that can heal or knows about healing, any illness tends to heal more rapidly, and surgical procedures tend to be more successful and have far fewer complications!

The Muumuu and the Red Dress

Another rich example of selves contained in a single body is that of the grandmother of a truly great Hawaiian woman I am privileged to know, Hannah Veary. The grandmother was a pure Hawaiian woman who, in her ordinary sense of self, was a fanatical fundamentalist Christian who would allow no drinking, smoking, swearing, or impropriety of dress to occur within or near her home. She read the Bible daily and went to church several times a week. She worried over lost souls.

Because of the grandmother's fanaticism, few in the clan liked to visit her . . . unless the grandmother would start to get sick and run a fever, at which time a most amazing event would occur. When the fever reached a certain level, what was animating the body as "the grandmother" would disappear, and in would pop a Hawaiian Goddess, with an awesome range of psychic abilities, wisdom, and compassion. The "Goddess" would tear off her high-collar muumuu and call for her bright red dress, her pipe, and her whiskey, all of which would have been brought along by members of the family when they heard the grandmother was becoming ill. During the height of the fever, Grandmother, alias the Hawaiian Goddess, would prophesy, describe where the good fishing was to be that year, tell who should marry whom for the best interests of the family, provide Hawaiian names for the newborns of the family/clan, warn the family about difficult or dangerous times, and so on. It was a wonderful occasion for the entire gathering . . . until the illness would subside and suddenly in would pop "the grandmother," with all her prejudices and narrow-mindedness. The grandmother would be shocked, not only to see the people gathered in her home but also to see the color and kind of dress she would find herself wearing. She would kick all the heathen clan members out of her home, tear off the red dress and proceed to burn it, and completely cleanse her home of all demons and dark spirits. The clan would leave in a hurry, but not without appreciating the gifts the "Hawaiian Goddess" had showered on each of them.

Here we have a circumstance in which one self is so completely unable to handle the other aspects of Self that a state of trance-mediumship occurs, the usual outer ego-identity completely disappears, and an entirely different self enters. Edgar Cayce was such a medium. In his outer consciousness he was a Christian, with no abilities at psychic healing or psychic diagnosis. In his trance state, his perspective on life, spiritual matters, health, and illness was completely shifted into a remarkable range that was entirely incompatible with who he appeared to be in his ordinary state of awareness.

The preceding examples all demonstrate a form of channeling wherein the conscious mind is completely eclipsed by another aspect of the Self, one that has far more vast ranges of consciousness than does the outer awareness, the ego. I have come to believe that all forms of channeling—whether simply a heightened consciousness in which the outer awareness feels expanded yet is still aware of itself and its history . . . or the opposite pole, where the outer "normal" sense of self is completely overridden by another part and has no recall of what was said or what transpired—are examples of multiple personality. One does not have to postulate a discarnate entity or walk-ins or angels or possessions. The human consciousness is simply far more complex than the outer consciousness comprehends. From the perspective of the outer sense of self, all facets of this phenomenon of multiple personality must appear to be of foreign origin. Even more fascinating to me is the impression I have that a few of the unconscious selves in any individual may have access to collective ranges of knowledge and information beyond the individual's personal information system and may actually be a part of a more collectively shared human consciousness.

Seeing the Selves in Action

Becoming aware of the inherent multiplicity of our interior nature— most if not all of which is unconscious to our usual state of awareness—raises profound questions and stimulates realizations that impact all areas of our lives.

Might this not account for so many situations in which a person becomes almost the opposite of what he or she usually is, if only for a brief period of time? Or might it not account for people who seem two-faced, regularly professing one viewpoint and acting out another, often in secret? When such individuals are confronted about this behavior, their usual personality will deny that the other, less socially acceptable, aspect exists. This happens because, to their ordinary sense of self, the activity of that other part of self is *not* sensed as self, even if conscious recall about the other self is available.

From a perspective that acknowledges the multiplicity of Beingness, the situation is understandable. The ordinary sense of self is not lying. Rather it is speaking a relative truth about itself, which does not include an ability to see the counterpart and which is mostly, if not completely, unconscious of it anyway. The person just doesn't appreciate that there is more than a single self and that the usual sense of self maintains an unconscious defense system against the counterpart's being seen or being expressed.

Upon considering these things, I am amused by such issues as the reliability of questionnaires. Whenever I get one, I have to decide which part of me is going to answer the questions, since I can provide as many different answers as there are selves within me. Most people call this "answering from the mood they're in." If something changes the mood, then the answers change. Maybe changing moods is really much more profound than we realize.

Another aspect of the multiplicity of Beingness can be appreciated when a healer begins to work with a patient. Perhaps one important function of a healer, especially the kind of healer who does not focus on the disease itself, is to induct a healthy self, one that already exists in the patient, to take charge of the body at an unconscious level.

For instance, I used to be called in to work with patients undergoing chemotherapy. They would be apprehensive, weakened by the drugs, and complaining how terrible the chemotherapy made them feel. I would slice through this infantile response pattern, with its accompanying complaints, and suggest to them that perhaps, if they would see the chemotherapy as an ally and a great friend with a great capacity to eliminate the cancer from their body, the drug might not make them feel that way. I would ask them to hold the medication in their hands and, prior to taking it, bless it, being truly serious about what they were doing. This would empower the patients to feel much more in control and to be participants in a great struggle to survive, to gain back the right to live. Such a process, seen from the perspective of the multiplicity of Beingness, would involve breaking the hold of the child over the patient's psyche and helping to induct a more mature sense of self, one that had many more resources than did the child.

I was aware that patients who do not tolerate chemotherapy often have deep, unconscious, infantile resentments against authority figures, especially father figures such as doctors (of either gender). For this reason, their reaction to the medication is, in part, related to their projecting onto the medication all the negative and destructive aspects of their own psyche related to such feelings. By breaking the mind-set about chemotherapy, most of the patients began to experience far fewer side effects and greatly improved response to the treatment. In regard to the possibility that the mind plays a role, if not a dominant role, in matters such as these, a recent report in the newsletter of the Institute of Noetic Sciences noted that 30 percent of patients given nothing but water, though told they were receiving a chemotherapeutic drug, lost their hair!

In the case of spontaneous healings and dramatic changes in the outcome of a disease process, perhaps the patient shifts from one sense of self, wherein the pattern for disease is potentiated, to another sense of self, which somehow doesn't maintain the pattern of that particular disease . . . and the body recovers. At least this is a good initial working hypothesis.

Since, in my experience, the fundamental nature of the relationship of the mind to the body has been so thoroughly demonstrated, I still have difficulty remembering that most of the medical field ignores this critical relationship. I recall, for instance, that my sister-in-law told me her physicians laughed when she suggested that her crushing marital conflict might somehow have been associated with her bowel carcinoma. However, only after she had been involved in catastrophic psychological turmoil did the bowel cancer appear. There is no question in my mind that death through the cancer was her way of unconsciously resolving the guilt and pain centered in her marital relationship.

I realize that few conventional health practitioners are trained to probe the deeper, more unconscious aspects of a patient to draw out the emotional and mental factors regulating the disease process. It's the old story: When you don't know something exists, you don't perceive its influence. Further, a period of from forty-five to ninety minutes is required for a trained individual to display the unconscious dynamics of disease in a patient. This, understandably, is too much time for most health professionals with a busy practice to spend with patients. But without information in regard to the psychological aspects of a patient, the physician is working with only a portion of the important and useful clinical information and therefore creates limited treatment programs which usually do not take into consideration the patient's psychological makeup.

Perhaps we can train specialized personnel to ascertain the psychodynamic disposition of the patient. Such personnel would provide in-depth summary reports to the physician, who then could integrate the psychological evaluations with the physical evaluations before creating therapeutic approaches for patients. The key to my work with individuals is to encourage a courageous approach to the exposure of those elements of the psyche that seek death and disease for resolution of psychological conflicts, and then, if possible, to substitute other, more life-enhancing solutions. Traditional medical and psychological support and treatment can be conducted simultaneously and do not interfere with this technique.

Personal Values, Collective Values

Value systems and ethical and moral preferences are ordinarily regarded as consistent and relatively fixed in any individual, yet few people realize that diametrically opposite value systems can be held by different selves in the same individual.

One example I use is that of the medical triage officer. A medical triage officer is someone who, in time of war or catastrophe, makes decisions about who is to be treated and who is not to be treated, based on what medical supplies and medical teams are available. The triage officer assesses the condition of a patient. If the patient's injuries or wounds are sufficiently severe that enormous effort would be required to save that patient while others waiting for treatment died, the severely injured person will be sacrificed so the resources of the medical unit can be utilized for saving the greatest number of lives. This is evidence of a phenomenal instinct operating in the human psyche, and it demonstrates that a part of life seeks to salvage as many individuals as possible and will, when necessary, sacrifice individuals for the benefit of the whole.

Most of us could easily do such difficult work in times of emergency without hesitation, concern, or remorse. However, everything would change entirely if a member of our own family came through the door. Now a very different value system would be activated. We could no longer function as triage officers, for we would find ourselves determined to sacrifice the many for the sake of our loved one! We would have to release the position in which the collective event and its value system had placed us and take up the position of one who was personally concerned.

Personal value systems are tied into parts of Beinghood which—as with a mother who could kill someone threatening her child—fulfill personal and individual needs, those in which specialness, uniqueness, personal love, and care are appropriate. Collective value systems, however, like those of the medical triage officer, the physician, the politician, the military officer, the scientist, and the head of a large business or corporation, belong to very different parts of Self and function well only in the context of the impersonal and collective.

Without one's having the understanding that two entirely different value systems exist to take care of two entirely different aspects of life—the individual personal and the collective impersonal—some really dramatic errors in judgment can occur.

For example, war does not involve personal values. It calls for the implementation of impersonal, collective values. Personal value systems are sacrificed as a collective enacts larger-than-life war events. Actions deemed worthy of reward are those in which the individual sacrifices himself or herself for the benefit of the whole. The actions of an individual during wartime cannot be judged by the personal values of peacetime. That is why there is a military code of behavior and a court to uphold its values, and an entirely separate civil code of behavior with courts to uphold its values. Although there may be some overlap, one's rights in the military or during wartime are very different from what they are when one is a civilian in peacetime.

Disastrous consequences may often occur when a personal value system attempts to dominate an event that is organized under a collective value system, or when a collective value system attempts to superimpose itself on events that should be organized under a personal value system. An example of the former is the individual who attempts—with the feelings and values of the personal aspect of the psyche—to direct political forces, during peacetime or wartime, as if they were personal events. This is especially problematic if the person has little or no understanding of the deeper psychological needs that move large human collectives into and out of war and peace. Those needs—which can be met during times of chaos and change—include such things as access to heightened inner resources, initiation into manhood and womanhood, and gaining senses of redemption and meaning. An example of the collective superimposing its values on the individual would be that of a government with mechanistic, conceptualized values attempting to impose consensus and conformity onto its citizens, with no provisions for individual differences. There are other examples, some of which are revealing and even darkly amusing. For instance, well-meaning governmental agencies in San Francisco recently demonstrated their concern for the area's homeless by creating a program that provided free shelter, free meals, free transportation, and places where clothing and personal effects could be stored. But the program met with great resistance from many of the homeless, who rejected the city's solution, claiming that it imposed unwanted regimentation upon them. This bureaucratic approach failed to take into consideration the undisciplined life-style that was enjoyed by the complaining homeless.

I remember the polio epidemics of the 1950s and the people who, on several floors of Los Angeles County Hospital, were confined to iron lungs. I remember when we couldn't go to swimming pools or theaters during the summer because polio had been reported. Then, several years later, the Salk vaccine and other polio vaccines had virtually eradicated the disease. Experience has shown, however, that as a result of receiving the vaccine, certain people may experience severe side effects. But those incidents are so very few compared to the vast numbers who benefit that a physician has no problem recommending the vaccination. From the personal, parental viewpoint, the thought of just one baby being damaged by the vaccine might be enough to condemn its use and cause the parent to elect not to have his or her own child vaccinated. But such a choice, based on a personal value system, would not be appropriate to apply to circumstances involving the larger collective.

When personal value systems interfere with the control and/or eradication of a lethal disease such as AIDS, we are endangering our very species. We are essentially sacrificing the collective for the protection of a few.

Both values are contained within us. In the vast cycles of life and death, peace and wartime, adolescent rebellion and mature old age, we are destined to apply and to live with both of them, depending on the context and on the balance of personal needs in relation to collective needs. Each has survival value in the appropriate circumstances.

Thus, as we discover the selves that compose the Self, it is important for us to know which self has what values and which dimension of life is being served.

PART II

INDUCTION

CHAPTER FOUR

THE SAGE, THE SHRINE, AND THE SACRED OBJECT

In the previous chapter, I presented some initial material on the Multiplicity of Beingness, and included hints about how to access the resources contained in the separate selves. In this and the next two chapters, I will explore the theme of *induction*, how induction can be used to gain such access, and how it can be brought about through various persons and processes, including:

1. Spiritual Teachers, Religious Figures, and Elders
2. Sacred places
3. Images and objects
4. Imagery and meditation
5. Collective or group meditation
6. Ritual work, rites of passage, and initiations
7. Crisis

Each of these methods represents a powerful pathway into expanded consciousness, regardless of whether one experiences the results simply in terms of expanded consciousness itself or in terms of access to different selves.

When such an induction occurs, one is fundamentally altered and has access to profoundly different interior resources. The ordinary sense of self tends to dissolve—sometimes permanently, as in the case of rites of passage, and sometimes temporarily, as when sources of wisdom, clarity, healing, or general information are inducted.

I want to emphasize that permanently entering any expanded state of consciousness is not necessarily advantageous. Most of the people for whom I have respect who regularly deal with these states recognize the importance not only of the expanded levels of awareness but also of the ordinary levels. They recognize the worth of using expanded levels to gain counsel or access to resources for the needs of a particular moment, and they also understand the value of celebrating Life and its mystery on the level of the everyday and the mundane. They perceive the ideal, ongoing state as being *inclusive* and not *exclusive*. The outer mind, the ego, is not a mistake. It does have a role. It has a function in the larger community of selves that make up the Beingness of each person.

Centering

Another point I want to note emphatically in this context is the importance of *centering* . . . of being able to enter an expanded sense of self that is interiorly based, calm, clear, transparent to disruptive forces, and that relates one to transpersonal or transcendental resources. It should not be confused with the rigid, mentally based, nonemotional, invulnerable, defended outer-mind state which is often regarded as "centered." The best example I know of a centered state is the expanded awareness of an awakened Heart Center. The Heart Center is associated with the anterior lower chest area of the body and, in the East, is referred to as the fourth chakra, or Heart Chakra. The attributes associated with an awakened Heart Center are Unconditional Love, Innate Harmony, Healing Presence, and Compassion.

It doesn't matter whether one learns to achieve a centered state of consciousness through pathways of religious orthodoxy or through those of personal meditation and contemplation. It is only important that one be able to access some state of consciousness that has the capacity to take on the larger dimensions of Being without reactivity or imposing inappropriate value systems, and the Heart Chakra state of awareness is capable of just that. Meditative exercises that can stimulate and develop this quality of heightened awareness are fully described in *Joy's Way*.

What do I teach in my foundational workshops? I teach centering. What do I teach in my advanced workshops? I teach centering. What would I teach in my advanced, advanced, advanced workshops, if I had any? I would teach centering. I can't stress enough the importance of the capacity to center at a transpersonal level. Without this fundamental development in awareness—that is, if the ability to center at a Heart Chakra–like level is not established—most expanded resources are either unavailable or can be misused. Hitler and Jim Jones are good examples of individuals who had access to heightened states of consciousness and who were unable to handle the attendant powers. The modulating influences of the Feminine and of the Heart Center apparently were not available to them. The daily (and sometimes moment-by-moment) practice of centering is what marks the individual who is awakening into a balanced process of transpersonal development.

Until centering is mastered, little can be done to direct the rich resources of the deep psyche. And unfortunately, without some kind of training or discipline, most people, when stressed, will regress psychologically to an earlier developmental phase. This is especially evident if the frightened Child self gains control of the feelings and the awareness! The more mature, more expanded experiences in life are simply beyond the resources of the child and the outer mind.

Centering is also necessary when entering the deeper aspects of the Unconscious for purposes of Self-Realization. This entry is a journey into the soul and can be fraught with psychological dangers. To enter expanded awareness is not safe even with centering techniques, but the dangers are minimized when such techniques are used. Undertaking the interior journey is as difficult as entering one of the world's large cities and attempting to integrate all of its myriad aspects without making judgments, without making comparisons, and without needing to understand. There must be no tendency to deny or to assume responsibility for what is encountered. An ability to be open to the suchness and the deeper wisdoms of Life is required. Because the inner environment is so vast (and probably infinite) and because one can encounter what may appear to be alien forces—forces that hold very different appreciations of Life, Death, and the Mystery—the need for centering must be firmly understood, and the ability to do it established.

As far as I can ascertain, in all of the world's Mystery Schools—where students learn to enter and handle the larger dimensions of Beingness—a special image or symbol is memorized and contemplated as an aid in centering. The image may be that of the Buddha or of Christ or Mohammed. It may be a mandala, a dot in the center of a circle, a cross. With time and practice, the centering image becomes more and more capable of bringing about a centered state of awareness. What's important is that *something* be established and available for the individual to use for centering, no matter what is happening in either the outer or the inner level of Beingness. I usually suggest that beginners use one of the traditional images—probably that of a Spiritual Personage—and that they work with this image for five to ten minutes twice a day when their lives are relatively calm, and as often as necessary when they are not!

The Force of Induction

The power of the image or symbol to bring about a change in one's state of consciousness involves a phenomenon of great power and importance. It is an aspect of the phenomenon of induction. The word *induction* means "to introduce or to initiate, to lead." It also has another important meaning related to the phenomenon of electrodynamic induction in physics, in which a current is created in one electrical conductor when it is brought near another conductor in which current is flowing. This analogy can be applied to experiences we have with certain people and in certain places. Induction occurs with me, for example, when I sit in the presence of a great personage or a Spiritual Teacher. It is what happens to me when I enter sacred places, such as ancient temples or great Cathedrals. These people and these places are capable—through induction—of bringing me into the heightened dimension of consciousness that is somehow in and around them. It is as if they emanate a field of consciousness that has the power to stimulate an equivalent field in anybody or anything near or in them.

Induction by Spiritual Teachers, Religious Figures, Elders

When the deepest levels of consciousness are approached, an Example—such as a Christ or a Buddha—may be required. Such persons point the way, bringing one to a threshold of new possibilities that the outer mind, by itself, simply cannot imagine. They operate as Initiators into the grander, deeper possibilities of Life. The individual seeking spiritual development must feel for and directly experience the dimensions of awareness and Beingness *behind* the teacher's personality or ordinary self.

Often, these exalted figures are perceived as deified Parents—which may initially be helpful but cannot move the seeker beyond Mother/Father/Child patternings of the deep psyche. The situation in which seekers want a god or goddess to parent them, or where teachers need to parent others, eventually arrests spiritual development in most people. The problem with the parental images that dance us daily—images of father and mother, religious figures, political leaders, physicians, law-enforcement officers, etc.—is that each of us, in relation to those parenting images, unconsciously continues to play the child.

In ordinary day-to-day experiences, our relationship with our actual parents has a very powerful influence over us, even as adults. Just observing our own behavior when visiting one or both parents will bring this realization quickly to mind. At an unconscious level we take on, to varying degrees, the role of the Child in relation to the Parent. The parent or parents simply aren't going to be anything else but Mother and Father. They aren't going to act out the Lover or Teacher or Bank Loan Officer roles, which would induct us into other selves. They are going to act out Mother and Father, which means we will find ourselves relating to them very differently than we would to personal friends. There is usually too much secondary gain for us not to engage these individuals as parents. Unfortunately, therefore, they *stay* parents and we *stay* children . . . sometimes very rebellious and angry children.

The forces I am talking about are powerful and are contained in the deep unconscious aspects of our Being, so just gaining a cognitive insight into the dynamics of the process doesn't really amount to real maturation and development. To break the Parent-Child forces inevitably requires *the sacrifice of the child* ... and that is not easily accomplished, particularly if the dynamics are unconscious. However, in Chapter 6, with the material on rites of passage, I will offer some suggestions as to how this critical and difficult process may be handled.

In the early stages of spiritual awakening, no harm is incurred in playing out Parent-Child dynamics. To be dependent on the teacher in those stages, perhaps even completely dependent, may be appropriate, with the dependency diminishing as maturation occurs. In later stages, however, the deeper initiations cannot transpire and the fullness of Being is lost if the Parent-Child bonding is not broken. An inclusive path must include not only the Child, but also the Adolescent, the Mature Man and the Mature Woman, the Father and the Mother, the Elder, the Teacher, the Cosmic One, the Self/Source ... and many more selves as well. All these aspects are to be experienced in some degree in the fuller awakening of Being.

Therefore, select the Guru, Master, Teacher, or Religious Training as carefully and consciously as you are able. The appropriate teacher will open the doors and initiate you just through his or her Presence ... through the aura you sense around that individual. Often, the actual words spoken by the teacher are secondary or minimally important. Just "hanging out" with a heightened being is enough. Silence is enough!

Teachers may have times when the heightened Self is present and operating through them and times when less-heightened selves are present. Someone who maintains only the heightened sense of awareness may not be as fully developed as someone who engages the full range of Beingness, including the Simple Self. If you want the induction into heightened possibility from Teachers, then encounter them when they are heightened, but also appreciate the ranges they present when they are *not* heightened. In addition, recognize that some aspects of heightened awareness are antithetical to Life and to livingness, and that not all transpersonal aspects include an ability to appreciate the ordinary and the simple.

From an esoteric point of view, the twelve Apostles of Jesus can be regarded as representing twelve different aspects or qualities of consciousness making up the Being called Christ. The term *Christ* itself designates the transcendental aspect that organizes and harmonizes the various selves of Jesus. Thus, the psychological makeup, the Inner Beinghood, of Jesus is seen as consisting of twelve separate selves. Among the many implications of this is the fact that Judas is not separate from Jesus but actually represents one of the shadow aspects or disowned aspects of Jesus—one that doubts, betrays, and can destroy itself as well as those who are in association with it.

We can therefore appreciate that a Teacher, Guru, or Spiritual Guide is not independent of his or her parts. Personal Beingness—whether one's own or that of a Teacher—is made up of *all* of its parts and not just the good or preferred or acceptable parts. The inner community, a term I often use when referring to the interior selves, is part of who and what I am, and is not separate from or other than who and what I am.

Further, such is the Mystery that each of us, individually, already has all the selves we must have in order for the needs of our particular life to be met. This has nothing to do with our individual perceptions of fairness or equality. It has to do with uniqueness and with Life's deeper intentions.

Each of us has been given a unique combination of physical elements called a body. No ranting, raving, or jumping up and down and complaining will change this "given." Modifications can be made, but fundamentally we are dealt a body and that's that. The same is true for our psychological patterns. I feel that at the moment of conception, each of us is given a unique combination of both physical and psychological patterns that serve us for a lifetime. They are givens and cannot be anything other than what they are. How we play out "the hand dealt" determines the quality and fulfillment we are to experience in life.

To appreciate what we have and to bring from it the best we can is the only requirement in spiritual Unfoldment. Big problems arise when we ask ourselves to be what we are not or cannot be. It is Life that incarnates us. It needs us. We find peace when we take our place in the larger Mystery Play, appreciating that Life, in dancing us, has dealt to us the various combinations that will insure *its* continuity and *its* creativity, no matter what the outer, more self-centered sense of self has to say about the matter. Each aspect of Self is important to the Mystery Play, whether it be the Whore, the Saint, the Child, the Teacher, the Truck Driver, the President, the Lover, the Warrior, the Peacemaker, the Mother, the Father, the Black Sheep, the Betrayer, or any other from among the endless variety of immortal possibilities.

The great spiritual and political viewpoint of the West is that we are all equal and are all capable of developing into the same end product. Anybody who bothers to examine the facts can easily see that we are not equal. What we really are is not so much equal as *unique*. Not one of us is the same as anyone else. In this uniqueness is a profound Spiritual Realization: Life is infinitely creative and requires uniqueness for creativity. Nothing in our internal world or in our external world is the same as what is in anyone else's ... not one cell in our body or one organ in our body or one grain of sand or one blade of grass or one wildebeest. This understanding, this celebration of individuality, allows us to accept the unique aspects of our Beinghood. Once they are accepted, we can immediately proceed into the full living of life, within the context of the givens.

With this in mind, we can understand why holding a single image of God or Spirit can be a profound limitation when we seek to discover the richness of life. For example, my sudden appreciation for polytheism occurred when I realized that in order to catch a glimpse of the essence of God, I needed to be able to recognize the many faces of God. Likewise, for me to begin to know another person, I must experience many aspects of that person. For me to begin to know myself, I must appreciate many aspects of my own Beingness. In this regard, I am reminded of Eleanor Roosevelt's famous statement when she was asked about the purpose of life. "The purpose of life," she said, "is to live it!" And this may involve confronting aspects of ourselves of which we have been unaware, or with which we are not at all comfortable.

Owning the Warrior Self

In early 1986, at one of my Foundational Conferences, a young man about thirty, a truck driver named Steve, raised his hand and shared a powerful experience of inner imagery he had during a session of high-intensity music in which I had played Wagner's "The Ride of the Valkyries."

Steve hadn't expressed himself up to this point . . . several days into the twelve-day Conference. Now, describing his inner imagery, he said:

> I was coming in for a helicopter landing on some island . . . like in the film *Apocalypse Now*. My comrades and I were there to take the beach. I was killing men, women, and children with my machine gun. It felt terrific! Physically I was at my peak; mentally I was at my maximum; spiritually I felt totally fulfilled. This is what I had come to do and I was doing it!

There was an awesome silence in the seminar room when he finished, as if somebody had forgotten to tell Steve that nice people, particularly spiritual people, and even more particularly, sensitive New Age people, want nothing to do with war, killing, and violence, even if it is spiritually fulfilling. But because of the sincerity and innocence of his presentation, each person in the Conference room experienced—directly, and not through actors in a movie or characters in a book—the Warrior self.

In the few minutes Steve used to present his raw masculine consciousness, he inducted the men in the room into their own equivalents of the Warrior and he initiated the women into the part of the Feminine that is attracted to a powerful Masculine. In that moment, Steve was strong, virile, uncomplicated, and completely inspired. He celebrated his Warrior self and shared it innocently and openly with us.

I later told this story to a group at an Easter retreat. One of the men, who had been in the Vietnam War and suffered deep depression afterward, got the message. He became immensely excited as he told us he had experienced his own Warrior during that conflict, though he had no way of dealing with the fact without also feeling tremendous guilt and shame over his peak experience of killing during the height of battle. But upon realizing that he could appreciate his Warrior self for what it was, his depression suddenly lifted and he felt redeemed.

War is a destructive force that serves Life. Human nature, in this, its most chaotic eruption, insures change, the death of that which is to fall away, and the propagation of new life . . . through the Warrior. In moments of battle, ordinary values dissolve and attitudes and beliefs to which the Warrior orients become primary. Pain, suffering, destruction, life, death, and sexuality all take on different meaning and importance to the Warrior. The major function of the Warrior, the *only* function in time of war, is to fight on a battlefield. Dying in battle is as much a spiritual fulfillment as being victorious.

Millions of years transpired during which the Warrior meant the difference between the survival of a society or its collapse. Now, along comes the twentieth century, in which our society suddenly demeans a fundamental aspect of itself, the Warrior, by disowning it. The important point is that we called hundreds of thousands of Warriors forward during the Vietnam War, then failed to give them the status and honor each deserved. The Warrior remains unfulfilled in both our collective consciousness and collective unconscious, and will continue to seek expression until it is released appropriately by the collective. We must appreciate the Warrior or it can turn on both the individuals who carry its forces and the society that invokes its powers. In fact, doesn't the Warrior self remind us of immune cells, which defend and destroy invaders when called forth but also can and do turn against the body?

The Warrior patterning that becomes ours at conception is activated the moment someone who is actually living the Warrior pattern begins to influence us. Boys don't learn to become Warriors through military training. They may learn military techniques and survival methods, but they don't learn the Warrior state of consciousness. They are inducted into it by inner and outer teachers, inducted to the degree that the Warrior self/selves are already present within them. The Warrior is innate. It is immortal. It has always been and it will always be, and the degree to which the Warrior itself will manifest in an individual depends on the degree to which the Warrior pattern is present in that individual.

The biological gender of an individual is not what determines the gender of a psychological self or selves which may be activated. Thus, the Warrior self may also be inducted in a woman, though when that occurs, it is not a feminine self. It is a masculine self, experienced in a woman's body and psyche. Women who are particularly attracted to the Warrior self often had periods of time during childhood and adolescence when they experienced themselves as "tomboys," with strong male feelings and attitudes. Sometimes this was an attempt to be a son to the father rather than a daughter, due to feelings that the father preferred sons over daughters. Regardless, the induction of the Warrior in a woman is, in my opinion, an example of the activation of a countergender self. Athena may be a woman biologically, but her prowess at times is definitely masculine. After all, she was struck from the head of Zeus! And the Amazons may be female warriors, but they don't think twice about cutting off their right breasts to accommodate the strings of their bows. Indeed, I strongly suspect all Warrior women represent the masculine Warrior in a woman's body.

Induction through Saints

The same induction process occurs when an individual who carries a strong Saint pattern inducts a devotee into the state of consciousness the Saint represents. The devotee doesn't *learn* to be a Saint. He or she is initiated into the state of consciousness that represents the Saint, and to a degree that is a function of how much of the Saint pattern he or she contains. This may be less than or greater than the degree to which it was present in the Initiator, and it is not determined by the individual. It is determined by Life and Life's needs. Whatever your combination may be . . . that is your lot.

For the induction to take place, the pattern of the initiating Spiritual Teacher, Religious Figure, or Elder must be close enough to one's own interior pattern of spiritual teacher, religious figure, or elder. The deep psyche reads only the *pattern* of the forces in the Initiator. If there is approximation, the induction occurs.

It is also important to understand that relatively few individuals are destined to walk the traditional spiritual path or to be inducted by a Spiritual Teacher, just as most people who are to follow a traditional spiritual path will never walk the path of the Police Officer, the Book Publisher, the Drug Czar, the Senator, the Astronaut, or the CEO. Each of us must fulfill the destiny of our own soul, and the soul finds peace when it accepts its part in the Mystery Play. This, however, is not to suggest that we have only one part to manifest in our life. The Mystery Play is very dynamic, constantly changing, calling forth many possibilities from a single individual. We limit ourselves if we fixate on but one possibility, no matter how empowering that possibility may be . . . even if it is Sainthood.

Religious Figures are well known for having the power to induct certain states of consciousness or to stimulate unconscious resources through what they symbolize to the student or devotee. It doesn't matter whether the Figure is in the form of a statue, a picture on a wax candle, or an actual person. It doesn't even matter whether the picture or statue actually portrays the Religious Figure of whose resources one desires to partake. What is being *symbolized* is important, not the object being used as the carrier of the symbolized resource.

A quaint but powerful example of this is a simple prayer to St. Anthony that can be used when a lost object is sought:

> Dear St. Anthony, please come around.
> Something is lost and needs to be found.

One enters a sincere, reverential state of consciousness and recites the prayer three times, substituting the name of the lost object for the word "something." Each time the prayer is recited, a deeper state of consciousness is attained, and with the final repetition, one has the feeling of having reached a sacred state and of requesting the help of a sacred resource. The trick is to recognize that the forces invoked by the prayer—not one's personal resources—are responsible for finding the object and then to wait expectantly for the object to turn up or for its location to be revealed. My experience with this inner ritual is that the object *always* returns to me, sometimes within a few minutes, sometimes within several days.

In using this simple prayer, I induct within myself what I call the Finder. St. Anthony represents the pattern of "knowing how and where to find lost things," that part of one's Beingness which knows where everything is in time and space, and functions to reconnect the lost object to the person. The inner equivalent of what St. Anthony symbolizes is activated in the Unconscious of the person with the need, time and space are influenced, and a reunion is effected.

Two of my friends, Carolyn Conger and Michael Hughes, are gifted with inner Finders that seem to be able to see the location of any object in time and space, regardless of whether either of them has actually seen the object or knows anything about the person requesting the information. All that is required for their inner sense to be set in motion is that a need be present or that someone has requested that something be found. They are not 100 percent accurate, *but when they are accurate* in this particular demonstration of extended awareness, they are really remarkable.

The induction phenomenon is also evident, for when Carolyn or Michael activate their paranormal resources, their state of consciousness tends to evoke similar resources in individuals who are in close physical proximity to them. This is why I continue to suggest that people simply hang out with those individuals who manifest ranges of resources they wish to discover within themselves.

Sacred Places

When I travel in the world, I go to those places which move or quicken something inside of me. Each of us has particular combinations of patterns in the deep psyche that cause us to feel a special affinity for certain cultures, certain historical periods, certain locations, certain civilizations, and certain temples or sacred places, and to be completely uninterested in others. This intuitive attraction can transcend family, ethnic, social, or cultural conditioning. Sometimes it can feel as if one belongs to another and very different ethnic or social grouping than the one in which one was born. I refer to this intuitive attraction to a completely different yet vitally familiar culture or civilization as unconscious "vibrational banding." It is as if these bandings, or patterns, are innate in the deep, universal human psyche—like signatures or motifs.

Each civilization and each ethnic grouping, past, present, and future, manifests these innate patternings. Though, in my opinion, they are not contained in time and space nor in the genetic code of biological inheritance, they are capable of incarnating in generation after generation without regard for social or cultural limitations. Thus, individual reincarnation need not be postulated to account for a sense of familiarity. Something is familiar because a person has inherited one of the great human collective patterns, not because he or she actually lived in a certain civilization or in a certain era. Though we may not be immortal, the patterns are.

Of course, traveling to the actual place where you sense a powerful vibrational banding is the option of choice if you seek, through induction, to access the resources it contains. If you do so, you may find the following suggestions valuable.

Most important, don't read about the location or ask guides about its significance. Follow your intuition and let it tell you what the location means to you in the deep layers of your Beingness. This is how you can access the self or selves that are part of the pattern to which this outer location is equivalent or nearly enough equivalent to stimulate the deeper inner resources. So-called facts and information about the sacred site or place may not really be why you are attracted to the location in the first place.

When people travel with me to the great energy vortices of the world—Machu Picchu, Greece, Egypt, Jerusalem, Lhasa, Glostonbury, Stonehenge, Kyoto, Kauai, Kathmandu, Cambodia, India, Chartres—I ask them to experience the trip functionally rather than factually. Their intention should be to experience the possible induction into profound and rich arenas of their unique, individual Being, not to verify facts about a place or the people. The same, I may add, is true in regard to the experience of a Spiritual Teacher. You are not there to verify facts about the Teacher. You are there to experience some aspect of your Self.

Remarkably, however, photographs can accomplish almost the

same inductive purpose, especially video and film. This is true because your deep psyche experiences audiovisual material as if you were actually present at the site. The deep psyche reads *only the patterns presented* and doesn't quibble as to whether the pattern is "real" or not. A good book of photographs or a *National Geographic* article on the place that quickens you will do just fine. A video or movie is even better, as time and space are presented more naturally. But the best option is actual travel to the area so you can enter the three-dimensional hologram and be guided intuitively to places, feelings, thoughts, and aspects that are not necessarily present in a video, movie, or photograph. Nevertheless, pictures are an excellent way to begin the induction, especially if you can't afford world travel at the moment.

I begin the journey to a sacred site several weeks before I actually depart, calling forth an image of it in my mind's eye just before falling asleep each evening. I allow myself to be inundated by feelings and impressions of it. Sometimes a dream appears that helps guide my attention to what significance the sacred site has for me individually. All sorts of interior movement are initiated through this technique.

When I actually arrive at the site, I sit quietly at a place to which I have been intuitively led and, in a meditation/prayer, state my purpose for being there and request permission to enter and to access the resources of realization the site can bring to me. My purpose is the same at all the great sacred sites of the world: to fulfill my soul's destiny. I will often present a gift or an offering . . . something I have brought specially to the site, such as flowers or a crystal I intend to bury there. Sometimes it is just a wonderful sense of appreciation for the site. Don't ask me why I personify the sacred site by asking its permission. All I know is that when I do, a deeper relationship to the location is somehow established in my mind.

When I sense intuitively that permission has been given, I begin to meander and let whatever is going to happen, happen. I have no expectations. I simply open myself to experiencing the location as fully as I am able, through as many dimensions of my Being as I am aware. The most amazing experiences occur when I do this, as I am not forcing anything, but merely being open and *allowing*.

Obviously, engaging a sacred site in this fashion takes longer than a standard tourist's visit, so I always customize my trips. I allocate ample time . . . perhaps five or six days at a major site or at one that is particularly sacred to me. When I am ready to awaken deep inner resources, I don't want to take the usual commercial "quickie" tours that involve hearing a twenty-minute talk, taking some pictures, and getting back on the bus. I arrange for overnight stays if possible. I usually spend the night, even if doing so isn't officially sanctioned, since sleeping in a sacred site is an awesome experience if it really *is* one's sacred site.

I meditate, meander, muse, touch, sing, dance, chant, pray, cry, laugh . . . letting myself really get into what wants to happen. If one is too "cool" about being in a sacred place, one may only experience being cool. I let my selves be inducted as fully as possible by the forces of the sacred place in order to reach my own Sacred Place inside. That, after all, is why I came. When the experiences are nearing completion, an intuitive knowingness tells me so. I thank the site and all those forces and beings that attend it on all levels. I share the Gift of a Radiance of Love with the site, an offering of my Heart Center, then I request permission to leave.

Wondrous possibilities may emerge at the great sacred sites of the world when you are not encumbered by information and details . . . or by convention or regulation. *Live your life!*

Objects and Images as Inductors

In some of my seminars I ask all attendees to bring photographs of a beloved Teacher, a loved one, a person who is ill, or someone who has caused them harm or hurt, and a cartoon. My intent is to demonstrate how an image of something is experienced by the deep psyche very differently than it is experienced by the outer awareness.

The deep psyche is that part of the individual's unconscious which transcends the personal and blends with the universal collective. My working hypothesis is that images are patterns of interrelating forces, and that the deep psyche is in contact, to varying degrees in each individual, with a vast *collective* hologram (as distinct from personal holograms of memory), containing every pattern that is, ever has been, or ever shall be manifested in what we call outer reality. Patterns in the deep collective psyche's hologram are not confined by time and space.

In order to access the deep psyche's equivalent of a certain image, either a "live" image we are actually seeing at a certain moment or a photograph or drawing seems to be equally effective. The pattern of forces is what is important, not whether the outer mind sees something "real" or a photograph or drawing. Then, through accessing expanded, more transcendent levels of conscious awareness, we can tune in to the deep psyche's hologram and access its information about the image we are looking at—information that vastly transcends what is in our outer memory or what we might gather through reasoning. Such information, because it is accessed from the deep psyche's connection to the universal collective hologram, is not confined to time, as is the outer awareness and its informational systems. The deep psyche may therefore reveal information from the past, the present, and the future concerning the image being contemplated.

What is more astonishing is that when one has accessed or "tuned in" to the deep psyche's equivalent of a certain image, the individual or object being tuned in to can be influenced by the person who is tuning in. And, not surprisingly, the object or individual being tuned in to can also influence the individual who is tuning in. This is the theoretical basis of many well-known but often apparently mysterious phenomena, such as distant healing (the ability to favorably influence the outcome of an illness in an individual when the healer is not anywhere near the ill person); so-called voodoo curses (where individuals are made ill or are caused to die by an individual working with transcendent forces at a distance); remote viewing (the ability to see objects or events at distances beyond the range of ordinary sight); and telepathy. These are only a few of the awesome possibilities that are explored by individuals who learn to access the resources of the Unconscious. The outer mind thinks it is just looking at an image or a photograph in a certain moment, but the deep psyche is working with patterns that operate both in time and space and out of time and space.

The process of accessing and using transcendental states has many names. It can be called a "reading" or "channeling." The process may be referred to as psychic, intuitive, "knowing," getting information from "higher sources," or "receiving transmissions," and its mode of presentation to the person in the heightened state can be in the form of (to mention the most common modes) voices, images (moving and/or static), visions, direct realizations, dreamlike pictures with sound, automatic writing, and physical body manifestations (such as pain occurring in the heart area of the reader when the person who has been tuned in to is having a heart attack). Sometimes the mode of presentation may have overlays, in which one is looking at an image and then another image is superimposed over the original. Both images are seen simultaneously. This can also be accompanied by further information in the form of voice commentary or direct realization. All combinations are possible.

What I am presenting here, incidentally, is merely a contemporary version of what has been explored in Mystery Trainings throughout the world for thousands of years. It is hardly new! What *is* new, however, is for the techniques to be made available to individuals who do not have the slightest idea what Mystery Training is about and probably couldn't care less. My intention is to inspire individuals who operate mostly at ordinary levels of consciousness to seek and to explore the vastness of what it means to have existence and consciousness.

The Patterns Behind Telepathy

The ability to obtain information from interior sources other than the ordinary senses of self is an extraordinary development. In the area of telepathic rapport, Carolyn Conger, with whom I have lived and creatively explored a number of ranges of awareness, has, in my presence, most consistently demonstrated her abilities in all of these areas under all sorts of circumstances through the years.

As a result of some remarkable experiences with Carolyn, I first began to suspect there was more to language communication than just the linguistic components. For example, she can be with Hopi people or with Eskimos and still be in clear telepathic rapport, though she knows no Hopi nor any of the languages of the Eskimo peoples.

The persons speaking may not know English, but Carolyn receives the impressions in English! This suggests to me that there is a universal pattern level of communication beneath the word-level of languages.

Language, in addition to being word patterns, is also energy patterns in the form of sound that carry the force of the intended expression. In fact, linguists have maintained that communication with just words, inflections, and tone changes is impossible. They maintain that something must be going on in addition to what we encounter at the auditory level. We have the feeling that we are speaking spontaneously, yet the infrastructure of our consciousness, before it delivers up even a simple sentence, has combined and associated the material in ways and to degrees that are beyond our wildest imagination. Truly, we are but extremely limited witnesses to profound mysteries.

Most people, upon first coming into contact with the notion of telepathy, think only in terms of the mental areas . . . someone else's thoughts. There are, however, many other arenas of telepathic rapport, and some individuals are telepathic in more than one mode of consciousness. For instance, Carolyn is able to be in telepathic rapport at mental, emotional, and physical levels with an individual. This is true whether she is near the individual or at a distance, and it is not a function of whether or not she knows the person.

One can be telepathic at the emotional levels and immediately have "hits" and "impressions" about someone else that reflect emotional disturbances in that individual. Through this kind of telepathic rapport, one can "read" the deeper aspects of the individual, so even if he or she is feeling happy in a particular moment, one can be picking up patterns or selves of that person that are not happy and in fact may be enraged, but are not expressing through the body at that time. Unless we have a sense that we are, both in the moment and through time, multiple and mostly unconscious of many of our parts, we can't possibly understand what is happening when a sensitive picks up unhappiness, anger, or other emotional pain that is being expressed on different levels, though the conscious mind is not aware of it.

One can be telepathic in regard to sexuality. Individuals who are telepathic sexually have usually run an "availability check" on every person who is attractive to them. They know when others are sexually attracted to them even if they are being ignored or rejected at the outer levels. One can also be telepathic at the physical or body level and know the physical status of any individual ... even to the point of being able to diagnose problems or of knowing where pain or disease are located or what injuries have taken place.

An image (photograph, object, or person) we engage with our conscious mind acts as a "witness," an esoteric term describing something that is related to a "target"—an individual or thing about which we seek expanded understanding. The witness helps to direct and focus access to the deep psyche's equivalent of the target individual or thing. The witness could be an object worn by the target, hair from that individual ... or anything else associated with that person or thing.

Pictures of a Guru or Beloved Teacher can be used to maintain a deep connection to the forces these individuals symbolize when that physical person is either at a distance or no longer incarnated. Regular meditation on or contemplation of statuary, an image, drawing, or personal article of the Beloved Teacher has the power to induct. Anything the Teacher owns or has worn or touched will do. Listening to the voice of the Teacher is another remarkable way to tap the forces of the revered individual. Hearing the unique voice qualities of the Teacher when he or she is in a heightened state inducts one as powerfully as if the Teacher were present and speaking directly. Remember, it is not the words or the thought content that are important. Nor is the image important. It is *the forces behind the sound or the image* that are important. Thus, photographs can be appreciated as far more than just photographs. Images can be appreciated as far more than just images. Objects can be appreciated as far more than just objects.

People who collect autographs or memorabilia are involved with these principles. So is the Church when it maintains bone fragments of saints, the Muslim religion with its preservation of a sandal of Mohammed, the Tibetan Buddhists when they encase the seated body of a truly great Lama in gold, and the American Indians when they maintain a feather or the skin of an animal as a totem. Just carrying pictures in our wallets of those we love involves the same principles.

Placebos and Sacrifices

The powerful unconscious interplay between the object and the observer is not merely intellectual and is the reason there is such a thing as a placebo effect. There is a dimension of awareness in each of us that can actually *tap the forces behind an object*, bringing to us certain resources that are unavailable through only the outer mind.

Placebos are powerful because the deep psyche reads their *patterns*, whether the patterns are those of the physical form or those of accompanying information (i.e., a suggestion that pure water is actually a chemotherapeutic agent). And here is the real mystery: The Unconscious, if it believes the placebo is what it is represented to be, will respond to the placebo as though it contains the forces that are in whatever it represents. In other words, the placebo is a surrogate, a close enough approximation of the actual object or function that the forces behind external manifestation respond *as if the placebo were the actual object or function*. The shroud of Turin is a good example. This cloth with the Christlike image, which has been venerated by the faithful for centuries, is close enough in patterning for the Unconscious to respond as if it were the actual burial shroud of Christ, whether it really is or not. The deep psyche only reads patterns and is not concerned about the "genuineness" of the object. This accounts for the power of the whole spectrum of substitution responses, including the phenomenal forces and experiences behind *substitution sacrifices*.

The stage is set for a substitution sacrifice when a situation calls for death. This can happen when a person is dealing with a life-threatening illness or is preparing to walk on a particularly dangerous high-mountain pass. It is seen in eye-for-an-eye situations when the death of a leader, whether through illness, accident, or actual killing by an enemy, requires the death of another person to balance the forces of the pattern. It is seen in the Christian patterning where, for redemption to transpire, a death is called for. It is seen in the Judaic patterning at Passover, where the death of the firstborn son has been called for. It is experienced where two deaths have already occurred and a third death is necessary to complete the pattern. Among the early peoples of the Pacific Northwest there are stories in which a perfect stranger, just happening along, would become the substitution sacrifice to balance the forces surrounding the death of an important person in the tribe or clan.

In the Christian mystery, the Son is sacrificed for the sins of the collective. In the Passover ceremony, the lamb is slaughtered in place of the firstborn son so, when the angel of death passes by, it will know a death has occurred when it sees the blood of the lamb over the portal. In the traditions of folk wisdom, a chicken or goat may be sacrificed in place of the person who is very ill and about to die. *Death is called for*, though not the death of a particular person. The deeper forces that lie behind manifest reality are impersonal and respond to the balancing of patterns. Substitution sacrifice is one of the most powerful ways humanity assuages the "gods," which, from my viewpoint, are simply impersonal patterns of energy, in a suchness of Being. All of what appear to us to be "events" are organized by unconscious patterns dancing in time and space, and we can satisfy or fulfill a pattern by creating an event that completes it.

This brings us to the rich arena of television, movies, and theatrical drama.

Television, Films, and the Dark Side

In the late 1970s, I spent several weeks in Los Angeles at the home of my intuitive and gifted friend, Michael Hughes. I was feeling the need to open certain psychic areas, and Michael displayed the range of consciousness to which I wanted to find equivalents in myself. I knew that just hanging out with people who carry the desired aspect, and being very open and receptive when the individual is expressing it, are all that is required.

Early one morning, as we were completing our time of meditation together, Michael suddenly announced that the "big California earthquake" was going to happen that day. He described huge forces beneath California pushing and straining, and the terrible collapse of buildings and bridges. I had been around Michael enough to know that his accuracy in such matters was not good. What disturbed me, however, was that I also had the impression of an earthquake, though I had dismissed it. But when Michael started talking about the quake, I felt different. Intuitively I sensed that an earthquake was going to occur. It felt close.

Following the meditation, I quietly slipped into his office and called my insurance agent to get earthquake coverage on some personal property that I could little afford to have crumble into a big heap. I then went on about the day's activities. Not that I ignored the warning, as I did stay out of tall buildings and I kept in mind that the "big one" might occur, but I didn't feel fear or panic.

Later in the evening, midway through a board meeting I was attending, I abruptly announced that I had to leave. I had remembered that the film *Superman* opened in Los Angeles that very day, and seeing the film felt as though it would be far more enriching than what was going on in the board meeting. I excitedly rushed off to Mann's Chinese Theater in Hollywood.

As I was entering the theater with a mob of others, I saw Michael in the crowd leaving the theater. He did not see me.

I hadn't known exactly what the film was about, and to my great surprise, there was a whole sequence in which the long-anticipated California earthquake was precipitated by a nuclear bomb released by the bad guys. There was a really massive earthquake, with huge landmass movements. The Golden Gate Bridge collapsed; well-known buildings crumbled. I suddenly began laughing. *Here was the California earthquake Michael and I had sensed in our meditations.*

I repeat: The deep psyche reads only the patterns and not whether they are outer or inner events, not whether they are "real" or not. Thus, this film presents a most fascinating situation, in that the eyes and ears experience a movie event as real. To all who are watching the film, the earthquake is happening. In my meditation, the deep psyche had been reading a future event that was transpiring only in the awareness of the film's audience and not actually taking place in outer reality. God only knows what the Japanese monster films of the 1950s and 1960s and the latest batch of world wipeouts by American film companies are doing and what they did to the consciousness of someone such as Nostradamus!

When an event can be viewed by literally billions of people either simultaneously (as with films on television) or on occasions that are relatively near to one another in time (as in the theatrical release of a film), what must be happening in the deep psyche?

I have often wondered if the film *Earthquake*, which is specifically about the California earthquake striking Los Angeles, didn't in some unsuspected way act as a substitution sacrifice by which the earth-forces that had been building for years might somehow have been influenced so an earthquake did not need to manifest. Of course, this would mean there is an extraordinary and unrecognized connection between mind and matter, a connection far more radical than what is currently being explored merely in terms of mind-body relationships.

It may therefore be that films which show awesome destruction and chaos somehow satisfy the dark side of the Mystery. I find it important to note, for instance, that the United States produces a greater number of horror, violence, and sex films than any other nation in the world—sometimes with all three elements combined in a single film. However, at the outer level, the level of the mask, our society doesn't even let Little Red Riding Hood get eaten by the wolf (which happens in the original European version), we profess antiwar sentiments, and sex is a sacred act only to be experienced in the context of marriage. I wonder: Are the films of horror, violence, and sex stimulating the expression of such behavior in people (as is commonly believed) or is the deep psyche seeing them as a substitution sacrifice and thereby being satisfied and brought into a more harmonious balance as masses of people are exposed to the disowned aspects being depicted? These are profound questions, which emerge when one begins to appreciate a different perspective of human reality and the power the deep human psyche may have over events.

When we take this kind of overview, we can clearly see the schizophrenic behavior of our society in its collective form. We are willing to pay money to experience vicariously what we are not willing to allow in our day-to-day reality. Further, from the perspective I have been presenting, the person who exemplifies only the positive pole of duality and denies its opposite is involved with *creating* that opposite polarity and its eruption into physical reality, whether the eruption occurs in that individual's home or as violence and chaos in another part of the world.

We must not forget that we are all in this together and that duality and its consequences are aspects of Life's Wholeness.

CHAPTER FIVE

INDUCTION:
FROM INNER IMAGERY
TO GROUP MEDITATION

Through induction, we may be brought closer to a heightened awareness . . . a sacred state of consciousness, a transcendental state of awareness, a more vast aspect of Self—one that has little to do with the personal sense of self. This heightened awareness can access and experience a dimension of the Unconscious that has unimaginable resources and possibilities. I refer to this dimension as the "universal collective hologram," to imply that when one accesses a small part of it, its totality is potentially available and experienceable. This collective hologram—in the form of patterns that I suspect are external to time and space—contains equivalents of everything that has been, is now, and ever will be.

All of this may sound bizarre, yet it is a way to appreciate phenomena that are otherwise impossible to comprehend, such as psi abilities and the Akashic records of Eastern esoteric religious practice. The labels are unimportant, however, as they are only pointers. *The experience* is what is important. "How" and "why" are secondary questions, germane only to the needs of the intellect.

A mental or conceptual model can be valuable, though. Even if it is incorrect, it does help to stabilize the intellect while phenomena beyond the scope of the intellect are embraced. There is ample psychological evidence that the human psyche tends not to experience a reality when there is no model or framework with which to engage it. For example, when there is no conceptual model for seeing auras, most people simply never see auras. However, when they are presented with an understanding of how to begin seeing the energy emanating from their hands and their bodies, they soon begin to see it and are invariably stunned, awed that they were unable to see the auras prior to the training session. Likewise, the function of any Spiritual Pathway is to give us a model, a pattern, that helps us handle experiences and realizations beyond our ordinary senses of reality.

Learning to generate and work with images and sounds from one's own imagination and thereby to stimulate induction into expanded states of consciousness is not difficult. After all, the very existence of dreams informs us that we can generate alternate realities spontaneously and effortlessly, without conscious awareness. When we study the content of dreams, we further discover that the dream self/selves are thoroughly capable of participating in images and conversations quite different from what we are familiar with in our daily activities. The images and conversations can be amalgamations of outer experiences, but they also can be completely new experiences.

The key to working with inner images and conversations is to recognize that *beneath them* are patterns of forces, communicating and interrelating with one another! The outer awareness conceives of reality in terms of people, places, and objects . . . all of which represent conceptualized abstractions of something deeper and more fundamental. With dreams, we are still experiencing in terms of concepts and forms and are not yet to "ground reality," as the Buddhists refer to it. Creating images and dialogues, as is done in guided imagery, also occurs at the conceptual and form level. But beneath all these phenomena is an innate pattern of dancing forces that allows us to experience reality.

There are meditative dimensions in which images spontaneously appear that have not been retrieved from memory. Especially when they take geometric form, I believe we are seeing more nearly the basis of reality . . . the level of pattern interacting with pattern. Eunice Hurt, the Spiritual Teacher I wrote about in *Joy's Way*, maintained that geometric images are the highest form of mental imagery. She also stated that experiencing the forces behind the images was far more important developmentally than just seeing the images.

Until one does come into contact with images that are spontaneously delivered from the Unconscious, using images from ordinary memory—ones that can be held while the eyes are closed—is a good substitute when imagery is being used to access heightened states of consciousness. Though many people cannot image with their eyes closed, even as many people cannot remember their dreams, in most cases they only need to practice visualization for good imaging capabilities to become available. If good inner images are unavailable, one can still work with hazy forms, impressions that are more feelings than images, or sounds, smells, and inner textures.

When one uses memory to re-create an image and its associated feelings, the deep psyche responds as if the actual object or person is once again present in the outer levels. This is really important to understand, as many people dismiss interior images as being false or not valid because they are entirely self-created, or "imaginary," not realizing that doing so may be a psychological defense against vast interior dimensions the ego-awareness is not prepared to handle. Of course, the question of which self is in charge when the deeper forces and powers are being accessed is very important. Infants have the resources of infants, and children have the resources of children, and mature adults and elders have the resources of mature adults and elders. That is why centering and accessing more transcendent aspects of Self are fundamental in preparing to enter the most resource-filled of the inner levels of Being.

The approach I suggested for use when accessing an external sacred place is based on many observations and experiences I have had while visiting with people living in cultures very different from my own. Each of these cultures used a ritual to enter the sacred space, whether it was one of purification, sacrifice and prayer, meditation, or gifting. I began to realize that a pattern is always followed, one which leads to changes in consciousness that permit a much fuller access to deeper resources, not only those of exterior sacred spaces but also, and much more important, those of the interior sacred spaces to which the external ones point.

With this in mind, I developed a meditation called "The Sacred Temple by the Sea," which uses inner imagery to induct changes in consciousness through which one can reach these Sacred Spaces. By the time one has arrived in this inner Sacred Temple, one has entered a centered and heightened dimension, a dimension very different from that of the sense of self which was present before the meditation began.

What follows is an overview or map of the meditation ritual to reach the Sacred Temple. On pages 123–24, the steps are summarized for the convenience of those who wish to practice this pathway with a minimum of distraction. Or the reader may wish to tape record the following material so no distractions at all are introduced and a deeper awareness of the actual changes in consciousness can be appreciated. I have also prepared a professionally recorded audio cassette tape of the entire Sacred Temple by the Sea meditation for those who desire a direct experience of the state of consciousness I enter for teaching purposes. That recording is only a convenience, however, and not essential to actual practice of the meditation.

Entering the Sacred Temple by the Sea

The key to approaching the Sacred is to find a way to access very different selves from the ones with which you usually engage the world. In this case, you are going to use images, feelings, and impressions generated by sequences of inner experience I will present.

Taking advantage of the virtually universal experience of renewal and well-being that people feel when they go to the seashore, you begin your change in consciousness by making yourself very comfortable and imagining you are going to your own special seashore area, where you can be alone to renew, to refresh, and to touch back into your deeper spiritual values and sense of well-being. This can be a spontaneously created seashore or it can be one drawn from memory. The important point is that it be a secluded place, one where you can have the feeling of being away from the usual impingements of life.

As you go deeper and deeper into relaxation, you want this special seashore to begin to appear clearly in your mind. It is always early dawn when you arrive at the beach. This represents the time when the augmenting forces of life begin to gather. (Many cultures, including some of the Native Americans and Hawaiians, use this powerful, serene period between early morning and sunrise exclusively to effect healing and to perform initiation ceremonies.) You want to feel unburdened of worries, concerns, illnesses, and conflicts, and released from all the responsibilities you carry.

Take in a few deep breaths of the wonderful ocean air and feel the gentle breeze caress your face and gently move through your hair or ruffle your clothing. Your intention is to make this experience as real as you possibly can ... feeling the sand beneath your feet, seeing the vegetation, experiencing the waves moving toward the shoreline, hearing the sea gulls, activating inner images of the sights, smells, sounds, and tastes. The degree to which you make this experience real is the degree to which you have access to the resources of the forces behind the images!

Now ... open to the Mystery, to the miracle of Being and the gift of Life. Find the deep sense of appreciation you have for the privilege of existence ... a profound realization that transcends all other concerns, no matter what the circumstances of your life may appear to be, no matter what challenges may beset you.

Sit or stand quietly and feel the balance and harmony of the elemental forces as they renew, strengthen, heal, and harmonize those aspects over which each has psychological and physiological dominion:

> Open to Water ... the ocean. Feel its forces renew, heal, and harmonize. Recall the mystery of the Unconscious and the deep Feminine as you gaze on the ocean and open to its prana. Breathe in the wondrous healing power of the sea.
>
> Open to Earth ... the Earth Mother. Recall its gifts of regeneration and creativity. Let the energies of the earth penetrate your body to heal, harmonize, and heighten those aspects over which it has influence.
>
> Open to Air ... Spirit. Feel its forces renew, heal, and harmonize. Recall the gifts of the wind and of the breath of life.
>
> Open to Fire ... the Awakened Mind. Feel its forces renew, heal, and harmonize. Recall the gifts of light, purification, and clarity.

At this point you have the choice of returning to ordinary consciousness by simply gifting the sacred seashore area with the Radiance of your Love and Appreciation or proceeding into deeper levels of consciousness in order to enter the Sacred Temple. You may have engaged the first part of the meditation only to renew and refresh yourself. Or . . . you may have entered the meditation to deepen your inner experience of sacred states of consciousness, and therefore you proceed.

Continuing to prepare for the evocation of and entry into the Sacred Temple by the Sea, you deepen your feelings of well-being and inspiration. Then, without the slightest sense of self-consciousness, you ritually undress, in your mind's eye, until you are completely naked at your special seashore area. The feeling you seek to touch upon here is that of unmasking the self—feeling your naturalness in relationship to this healing and harmonious environment—as you prepare to enter the most sacred arenas of awareness you can engage.

The Purification Bath

A ritual of purification prior to evoking the Sacred Temple by the Sea is your next step in inducting deeper and more expansive vehicles of awareness. The entry to all Sacred Temples everywhere, whether inner or outer, requires some sort of conscious clearing of chaos or conflict, as well as a heightened state of consciousness. This can be accomplished by a ritual bathing or by entering some kind of field of energy that has the power to purify. The important point is to become involved with an experience that has the potential to induct a feeling of purification and of heightening consciousness.

Here are three possibilities from which you might choose: First, a sacred seashore pool of ocean water, protected from the waves . . . warm, clear, and pure. Second, a sphere of light and energy into which you can step. Third, a clear pool by a waterfall, a pool that then flows on into the sea. These are only suggestions. When the time comes to enter the purification experience, one of these—or perhaps another not mentioned here—will appear in your mind's eye.

Now, as you are naked and free, feeling a deep sense of communion with nature and the elements, image in your mind whichever purification process wishes to manifest in your awareness. Just before moving into it, remind yourself that you are entering this experience to change *levels of consciousness, to move from the ordinary and inspired to the extraordinary and inspired, then move into the purification forces. As you do move in, completely surrender to the forces of purification.* Let the forces do you! *Completely immerse yourself in the heightened forces and remain there until you can actually feel the changes taking place in your body at the deepest level possible, perhaps even at the molecular or the atomic level. Feel the purification! Don't just think about it or wonder about it.* Be *the force that is doing you.* Ask *the purification forces to* clear and cleanse *you, bringing you into fresh possibility and new beginnings; to* balance and attune *you, bringing you to a fulcrum point of your Beingness; to* harmonize and heighten *you, bringing you into an inductive, heightened energy.*

As you prepare to exit the purification ritual, be aware of how light you feel. Stepping out of the purification force, experience, as best you can, the first rays of the sun that are now breaking in the east. Feel the light pass through *you. Feel the gentle breeze, not striking your skin, but passing* through *you. Let the sound of the seashore pass* through *you. You are now reaching into the vehicle of awareness that suggests the etheric . . . that has a sense of transparency and of extreme refinement. Make this as real as you possibly can.*

And now . . . light, refined, and inspired as the sunrise occurs, stand to face the ocean with your arms uplifted. By right of your inheritance as an awakening Being and by right of your having purified yourself and entered a heightened state of consciousness, you call forth your Sacred Temple by the Sea.

Evoking the Sacred Temple

At this point, a few comments are necessary. Some people have found that when they evoke the Sacred Temple, it appears in the ocean or somewhere else other than the seashore. That is entirely all right. Go with whatever the Unconscious delivers to you. Don't get picky or misjudge what the Unconscious is doing when images appear during meditation. During the first few such meditations, the Temple may be in different places, it may look different, or it may even change during the same meditation. Let this happen. Even if the Temple is dark and disheveled . . . allow it. Some people have Temples that appear in full form, while others experience the Temple as manifesting gradually. It may be only a circle of rocks or a mud building. Allow it. Trust your deeper Beingness to bring to you the Sacred Temple that is most appropriate for you at this stage of your development. Do not try to make the Temple be what you want it to be or try to change anything that appears. If no Temple appears, perhaps the whole seashore area is your Temple. Perhaps your Temple has nothing to do with buildings or structures.

As you evoke the Temple, you may feel a temple garment swirl around your body. Most people find that a garment spontaneously appears on their body or is otherwise made available for them to put on. Others feel no need of a garment in their Sacred Temple by the Sea. The garment, if one does appear, symbolizes the new state of consciousness, just as a costume in a Mystery Play symbolizes a certain aspect of Being.

The next step is to inwardly request permission to enter the Sacred Temple and to state your purpose for seeking entrance. This is done with all the sincerity and humility you can possibly generate. (Some people find that as soon as they invoke the Temple, they are already in it. Permission to enter should be requested anyway.) If you approach the Sacred in a demanding way or with a "taking for granted" attitude, the Sacred will play with you for a while, then dismiss you. However, if you approach with humility and with a profound appreciation, the deep psyche will shower you with all its resources.

Some people find that the Temple won't give them permission to enter. Should that happen, wait and continue your purification and the deepening of well-being outside the Temple. Then, if permission continues to be denied, dissolve the Temple, put on your clothes, return to the outer levels of awareness, and approach another time with the freshness of a beginner's mind. Remember that the right to enter the Temple is granted by the deep psyche. The self that evokes the Sacred Temple does not have the right to enter without permission.

Entering the Sacred Temple

When you have stated your purpose and permission has been granted, step into the Sacred Temple by the Sea. Feel as if you are stepping into one of the great Cathedrals/Temples of the world. Allow yourself to be further inducted by wonderment and reverence for the Sacred. Feel the Temple. Smell the Temple. See the Temple. Hear the Temple. As you do so, realize that you are again changing vehicles of consciousness, as the Priest/Priestess/Healer awareness embraces you. Then, move to the Sacred Altar or to the most sacred portion of the Temple, the Holy of Holies.

All temples, regardless of where they may be in the world or of which culture—whether they be a cave or a crystal temple on a cliff overlooking the vast ocean and a night-fading sky—have a place considered the most sacred in the Temple, the closest to Essence. It is usually, though not necessarily, where the Altar is.

Find this Holy of Holies and approach it with a sense of reverence and awe. As you step across the threshold into the Holy of Holies completely surrender yourself to the experience. Don't try to direct or to anticipate what will happen. Make yourself vulnerable and fully open. Just as a bird entrusts itself to space, so do you entrust yourself to Source. This is the moment of deepest communion with Essence ... Source ... God ... Spirit, or however you may conceive of the Most Transcendent. Let yourself be embraced by the Essence of your Temple. Open to alignment, to infusion, to redemption, to forgiveness, to Love, and to the Peace that transcends all.

Leaving the Sacred Temple

When the time comes for you to prepare to leave the Holy of Holies, you will know it. You will feel it. As you do feel ready to leave, give back something of yourself to the Altar. Share with it from your sense of harmony and well-being. Unveil your sacred inner Light, which is concealed deep within you, and fill the Temple with this Radiance of Love in appreciation. Then re-veil the sacred Light.

Now, walk through your Sacred Temple by the Sea. Observe the ocean if you can, and experience the morning light filling your Temple. Smell the sea air and hear the seashore sounds. As you do so, recall that you are going to leave the Temple and again take up each of the vehicles of consciousness through which you originally came. Welcome into your awareness what it means to be inclining toward incarnation into the physical ... the miracle it represents. Seek the ordinary, outer levels of consciousness with the same spirit and devotion as you feel when seeking the Transcendent. Then request permission to leave the Sacred Temple by the Sea, realizing that you can always return for renewal and suste-

nance. The Sacred Temple always grants permission to leave. Requesting permission to leave is a way to honor the forces of the Temple and is not related to rights and to privileges, as is the request for permission to enter the Sacred Temple.

As you leave the Temple, feel the light of the morning sun pass through your body and hear the sounds pass through you. Once again, feel the etheric vehicle as you face the ocean with your arms uplifted. Now ... dissolve the image of the Sacred Temple by the Sea. Feel it return to nontime and to nonspace. Feel the temple garment, if any, dissolve, and feel your denser physical form return. Appreciate it! Welcome it! You are naked, renewed, and deeply attuned to the seashore area, where just to be is a wonderment in itself.

Feel the light strike your body, and feel its warmth. Feel the air caress your hair and skin. Hear the sounds of the seashore. Make this as real as you are able. Change vehicles.

Now find your clothes and ritually put them on, realizing that they represent but one mask—one aspect or one self—the one that feels comfortable wearing clothes. When you are finished dressing, grace your sacred seashore area with a sense of deep appreciation and well-being. Let your inner Light shine in a Radiance of Love, then turn and walk away from the seashore and enter into this time and this place, the time and place from which you began your journey.

Celebrate your return with Joy and Inspiration. The sense of excitement about returning to the outer levels is as important as the sense of excitement about going to and entering the Sacred Temple by the Sea. Thus, you honor each aspect of your Self you encounter—in particular, the Simple Self, which carries the primary responsibility for most moments in the outer levels. It has a tough job. Give it the recognition it deserves.

At this point, most people feel that although they are back in their usual sense of self, something has been added. A deep calm is present, a greater sense of resourcefulness.

The world is different, and so are the possibilities and resources that are now available to engage Life.

Here, then, for quick reference, are the steps in the Sacred Temple by the Sea meditation:

1. *Relaxation and preparation to go to the sacred seashore*
2. *Approaching the seashore and experiencing the elements*
3. *Undressing and preparation for the purification forces*
4. *The purification experience*
5. *The experience of the etheric body and of transparency*
6. *Calling forth the Sacred Temple by the Sea*
7. *Requesting permission to enter and stating a purpose*
8. *Entering the Temple and letting it induct you*
9. *Approaching the Holy of Holies*
10. *Fusion with the Essence*
11. *Leaving the Holy of Holies and exploring the Temple*
12. *Requesting permission to leave and looking forward to the return to the outer levels of awareness*
13. *Leaving the Temple and being at the seashore area in the transparent body*
14. *Dissolving the Temple and releasing the Temple garment, and the simultaneous entry into the denser physical body*
15. *Naked, natural, and renewed, locating your clothes and ritually dressing*
16. *Final appreciation for the sacred seashore area*
17. *Return to the place and time from which you started*

The Sacred Temple by the Sea meditation uses sacred images supplied by the deep psyche for induction. It is composed of sequences that encourage changed states of consciousness and, thereby, access to the deeper ranges of one's Being. It is a powerful meditation and should be used in moderation. To overuse the meditation will, as with any overuse, dilute the experience. I suggest that it be reserved for weekly use, for a special one day in seven, a day you can look forward to, when the deepest communion with Spirit is desired.

The Sacred Temple by the Sea meditation also reflects a complete cycle of going out and then of returning with added resources that augment Life. In this regard, the meditation has the same intrinsic pattern as does the Zen story depicted by the ten woodcut drawings of "The Search for the Ox" as presented by D. T. Suzuki. This is an ancient Chinese story, later modified in the Zen tradition, communicated in ten simple pictures, with ten equally simple accompanying commentaries. There are several versions of the drawings, so you may want to find the set that most moves you.

The Ox represents the Mystery of Being, and the search for the Ox represents the search for spiritual enlightenment. The first of the ten pictures depicts an individual in a marketplace, realizing there is more to life but not knowing exactly how to find the deeper meanings and fulfillments. The one hope in the first woodcut is the footprints of an animal leading out of the marketplace. We sense the person's excitement, for at least there are tracks to show the way. In the succeeding pictures, the individual sees the Ox at a distance, catches the Ox, tames the Ox, then the Ox tames the individual, the Ox and the individual become one, the individual forgets the Ox (forgets the *search* for enlightenment), and then finally, at the eighth picture, forgets both Self *and* the Ox. Both the Ox and the individual have disappeared into a state of fully awakened enlightenment.

This is where most spiritual paths leave us. The individual has fused with Essence, and the journey to Realization is complete. But the wisdom of the later Zen masters produced the two final pictures in the sequence.

The ninth picture depicts the formless Void of final enlightenment emerging into form again, though without losing its formlessness—a demonstration of perfect Wholeness or unity. Now there is no Ox differentiated from the individual. The person stands alone.

The tenth picture shows the individual back in the marketplace ... laughing! At last, the spiritual cycle has completed, celebrating Life and Spirit, contributing to Life from the deepest resources that are available through the inner spiritual journey.

Inductions through Collective or Group Meditations

Whenever and wherever people gather, a special factor is present which must be considered in regard to induction—the collective force field. It can be experienced at many different kinds of mass gatherings, such as rock concerts, Christian revivals, political rallies, and public benefits that focus on charismatic individuals. The phenomenon is experiential and transcends just the presence of the Initiator(s). It requires the collective! This phenomenon can be easily understood by comparing one's experience of watching a rock concert (or other mass participation event) on video or film to actually being in the crowd experiencing the event. Watching an event alone in the privacy of one's home or with just a few people is simply not the same as watching that same event with a large group.

I first became conscious of the collective force field when I was visiting the ashram of Sri Satya Sai Baba, outside of Bangalore, India. Thousands of people had gathered to catch a glimpse of this remarkable man. It was never announced when he would come out of the small house to make his appearance, so people just sat and waited. They sang, socialized, ate, and meditated. The days were hot, but the evenings and early mornings were cool, and therefore the most pleasant times for waiting. Water for the large crowd was supplied by men who came by with large-spouted containers and, one by one, poured streams of water into the mouths of the thousands gathered there. Everyone but me seemed to be able to swallow the water. I simply got a drenching, since I couldn't master the art of swallowing at the same time the stream of water was pouring into my gullet.

The people were extremely friendly, sharing food and stories of the wonders performed by Sai Baba. Just being in the collective field at this level of induction was healing and harmonious.

Then, as though a distant powerful wind were approaching across a vast plain, the mood and energetics shifted. The crowd went from pleasantries and camaraderie to mass hysteria, in which the rational and intelligent dissolved and a primitive mass mind began to manifest. Sai Baba was making his appearance.

I was about seventy-five yards from Sai Baba. It took every last effort of rational consciousness I had not to be swept up in the mass mind, which had only one intent . . . to touch or to be seen by him. I managed to pull to the periphery (about a hundred yards from him), where I could feel and observe what was happening, but not lose consciousness. I realized that Sai Baba was a master of crowd control, for with the slightest movement of his fingers, he had people moving back, sitting down, or otherwise doing as he wished. It was as if the crowd were an entity, belonging to Sai Baba, which he could mold and sculpt as he chose.

All public speakers, actors and actresses, ministers, rabbis, rebbes, priests, and priestesses know this state of Beingness, in which one isn't dealing with individuals in a group but with the group entity itself. The group entity, in fact, is what I am most attuned to when I am doing my Conference work. With the twelve to forty people who gather at the various kinds of residential workshops I offer, there is always a group induction effect. The key task for me is to keep this field balanced and heightened. If I pay attention to this group entity and not to each individual contribution to the force field, all goes well. Some members of the group will be "down," exploring the pits, so to speak. Some will always be flying high at the same time. However, it is the group oversoul, as the individuals coalesce into a collective induction force, that determines the success or the failure of the Conference for the group as a whole.

When a few individuals go up or down, the collective Conference force field will automatically balance itself. The danger comes when the collective force field is swept to one or to the other extreme by someone who seizes control of it. This is rarely a conscious act on the part of that individual. He or she is not conscious of how vulnerable the collective is to strong inducting forces in either direction. My task in such a circumstance is to diffuse those who are attempting to gain control of the collective field and bring the group entity back into balance and harmony. This is part of what I teach to individuals who are studying with me in preparation for teaching and working with large groups of people. What is important is to be able to read the collective force field and not be distracted by what is happening at either end of the bell-shaped curve. As long as the collective force field is heightened and balanced, all will go well.

There is always the danger of collective collapse, hysteria, or other kinds of problematic inductions in large gatherings. But when the leader has confidence and integrity, and has experience in handling large groups of people, nothing can induct a heightened state of consciousness faster and more intensely, for any purpose—whether for healing, inspiration, creative thinking, meditation, performance (as in theater or dance), religious conversion, or moving people to any action, including war.

The Collective Force Field

Collective forces influence us whether we are aware of them or not, and there is no way to deny or to run from those collective forces of which each of us is a part. Nor would we want to when we realize the contribution those collective forces make to the quality and possibilities of life for all people.

Just after I turned forty, I had a sudden realization about the collective force field, or, as it sometimes is called, the "vibes" of a group. I am sure many others have come to a similar understanding, but I was having this particular insight for the very first time. I realized simply that the collective force field of any grouping—whether family, committee, town, city, religious/denominational, or political—can itself be out of balance or "ill" in any and all the ways an individual's field or presence can be out of harmony—physically, sexually, mentally, emotionally, psychically, socially, environmentally, or spiritually. There may be perfectly normal individuals within the collective vortex, but the overall group pattern can be diseased. Just because a few might claim personal balance doesn't mean the collective of which they are a part is balanced. We, as a collective, generate this powerful field or entity, and only when a large enough grouping within the collective reharmonizes and reattunes to the natural healing and balancing forces can the greater collective energy be shifted, rebalanced, and integrated at the collective level. Thus we can understand the potential importance of periodic collective attunements through which such integrating experiences can be entered into.

With the advent of television and satellites, the real possibility of our entire society being simultaneously brought into an integrated accord is now at hand. Yet the danger of a single perspective or a single morality being imposed on the human collective is also a distinct danger. Before we contemplate realigning the force of a collective, even in peace, we must first understand how chaos or an apparent imbalance may be serving aspects of the collective in ways outside of our conscious awareness. This requires that we have a real depth of understanding of the disowned forces in our own personal and local collective unconscious.

For example, it is absurd and infantile to conceive in terms of only peace and harmony for a collective when much larger and more important forces may be moving it, and therefore the individuals in it, to new potential. For that reason, I decline to enter into prayers or marches for world peace. I realize only too well that such action, when divorced from its counterpart—chaos—sterilizes and fixates, and, in the end, constellates the very actions that the prayers and marches intended to abolish.

Human life and interaction are based in unconscious patternings that have as their basis the laws of rhythm, change, and creativity ... the Alpha and the Omega ... and war erupts whenever there is fixation of creative evolution. The unconscious motive for desiring permanent peace is the need to control, but Life in its profoundest sense is not controllable. This must not be taken as a statement that I am for eternal war or for eternal chaos. I am not! I am for the natural unfolding of Life, and I accept its cycles. There is a time for all things ... and there is a place for peace ... but not peace *forever*.

The human psyche during this century has been and remains in a period of great flux. The chaotic forces have not completed their service to the future of humankind. Thus, in regard to balancing the collective field, we need to be deeply circumspect before we allow the value system of the outer mind to dictate what the collective state should be. I trust the Unconscious to such a degree that I am willing to surrender my personal desire so the greater forces of the Unconscious can dance, renew, heal, break up, and re-form the collective in *its* timing, which may be over centuries—and certainly is beyond my personal lifetime.

Oh, the impatience of the personal self when it is confronted with rhythms and cycles far more vast than those of a single lifetime. Yet we are the inheritors of rhythms and cycles set into motion thousands of years ago ... and people thousands of years in the future will be the beneficiaries of our contemporary contribution. Human life and, indeed, all of life may not be in the final form of its evolution. We may actually be in very early stages of Unfoldment, stages that require exactly the toxic and chaotic forces engaging us today to elicit the full potential for the future. Certainly there is ample evidence from the geological and biological past to indicate that this may be the case.

I am reminded of the recent devastation that occurred in Tibet. What most Westerners don't appreciate about such an event is the long history of collectives that interact with one another, sometimes over thousands of years. In the case of Tibet, sometimes the Chinese win . . . sometimes the Tibetans win . . . sometimes the Mongols win. Nor have we seen the end of the story, and we cannot even contemplate it if we fixate only on the moments of chaotic change. Whenever the demon of destruction appears, the energies contained in the demolished forms and structures of the past are freed up for new possibilities. Witness what has happened in Japan and Germany in just fifty years. This doesn't diminish the sense of loss or pain I can experience about any of these events at a personal level. But deeper forces than the personal are operating. Harmony and balance can sometimes only be seen through extended periods of time and not in the little slice of time we are viewing. We are better off trying to sense what is happening from a standpoint that reveals and enlightens rather than from one that denies and compounds.

Therefore, just as I do when I am working with an individual, when I begin to work with the collective field, I want first to appreciate as much as I can of the dynamics that are operating, to be sure that by shifting the forces, I am not actually doing a disservice. "When in doubt, do nothing!" was one of the wisest teachings I learned during my medical training.

Still, there is something we can do in all circumstances. We can attune to Wisdom, celebrate our Beinghood, and attune to other collective forces with a deep intent to appreciate Life and Spirit. We don't have to wallow in problems that are either created by or exacerbated by our own unconscious projections of disowned and unconscious material onto the larger world. We can reown these images and begin to mature as Beings. The world and the life to which it has given birth can begin to unveil their deeper wisdoms and intentions. We can begin to live the Mystery instead of only living to control the Mystery. We can finally begin to incarnate fully into Life.

CHAPTER SIX

INDUCTION THROUGH RITUAL, RITES OF PASSAGE, AND CRISIS

Rituals and the rites that make them up have been used since antiquity to change states of consciousness. Or, in the language I prefer, they have been used to induct from the interior community those selves that have specific resources and possibilities that the ordinary self does not. Rituals that involve entering either an external or internal Sacred Site or Temple are good examples. So is the ritual of the Mass or the rituals around marriage, birth, and death.

A ritual is not something invented by the outer mind for entertainment or as a show or display. Ritual, when carried out with conscious intention and reverence, is a sequence of experiences that can evoke and then give direction to changed consciousness. These states have resources that can augment any action or process, whether it be healing, affecting the weather, or communing with Source. Certain rituals—those surrounding rites of passage—are also pathways by which the death of one stage of life and the incarnation of the next stage of life can occur.

In ritual, one goes through sequences of changes in consciousness to reach into parts of Self that are not usually perceived as self. The specific pathway is innate, already established within the Unconscious. Each part of the pathway must be followed, and in sequence.

In baking a cake, a specific pathway—a recipe—must be followed if the result is to be a cake. One cannot put all the ingredients except water into a pan, place that combination in the oven, cook it, then add water. One will get a result, but not the intended result. The same is true with ritual.

When the priest transubstantiates bread and wine in the Catholic ritual of Mass—meaning that the priest has reached a state of consciousness where the bread and wine *actually are*, at the psycho-spiritual level, the body and the blood of Christ (which, in turn, symbolize a Mystery beyond the body and blood of Christ)—the self who usually is that priest is not present. Through the ritual, the priest changes vehicles and enters the aspect of the inner Self that can perform the act of transubstantiation. The priest's ordinary sense of self does not, cannot learn how to, and never will be able to transubstantiate. It does not have the resources. Through the ritual, however, the ordinary self seems to withdraw, as the consciousness is absorbed into a more transcendent state. The ordinary self learns to "die" to another part of Self that now knows, always has known, and always will know how to transubstantiate.

Transubstantiation involves changing one substance into another, and the principle of transubstantiation is active whether one is changing bread and wine or changing a vehicle of consciousness. The self that can transubstantiate is first inducted in the novitiate by a priest who is already able to transubstantiate both himself and the bread and the wine. The ritual itself is merely a scaffolding to direct the awareness toward the sublime, while the state of consciousness infusing the ritual is what has the real power to induct the corporate Church into the transcendental. Therein lies the power of the ritual for the collective. Unfortunately, only rarely does one experience a priest who can achieve the transcendent state that the celebration of the Mass is intended to bring about.

The way I approach ritual is to observe many rituals that deal with the same theme, synthesize what I have observed, then do one myself. Finally, I teach one. This learning sequence—called "see one, do one, teach one"—is probably a universal training technique, although I initially encountered it in medical school. It is effective and necessary because seeing is not the same as doing, and doing is not the same as teaching. All three are required for a person to gain the full empowerment offered through any ritual.

First, a person goes on a "coattail trip" and is inducted into the ritual states of consciousness by being with someone who knows how to enter those states and has the power to engage the ritual forces. This is equivalent to the "see one" stage. Though the effect of the forces on the inductee is strong, it is relatively minor compared to what is experienced by the inductor when he or she is in the state of consciousness that actually empowers the ritual. (This is why any spiritual priesthood guards the enactment of its sacred rituals, since actually practicing the art of entering heightened states of consciousness to perform the rituals showers the individual with all of the associated resources.) Thus, the inductee must next demonstrate his or her capacity to enter the heightened state of consciousness without an inductor present. This insures that the capacity to enter heightened awareness has been completely transferred to a new individual. And finally the newly empowered person inducts someone else into the state of consciousness, which allows that additional individual to perform the ritual for others, thus completing the three-stage experience for oneself and insuring continuity through time.

Who Heals?

My realization that seeing is not the same as doing, and doing is not the same as teaching, was very important, and it came about as a result of the following experience.

From time to time, in order to maintain my medical license, I am required to review my skills at cardiopulmonary resuscitation. During the presentation of the latest findings and changes in the techniques of cardiopulmonary resuscitation, most if not all of the physicians in attendance are drumming their fingers with boredom or are doodling. The material, except for the new information, is quite familiar to them.

Then a most embarrassing situation occurs. It happens when the time arrives for what is called "the practical." The physician must change from being a passive listener who intellectually knows the information to being a person who can actually perform the new techniques. This transition is not smooth for most of them, as the chaos in the training room usually demonstrates. Whereas a physician may have virtually total recall when listening to the information, the same physician may not have that information available when action is required. The problem is not just one of performance anxiety, but is also one of state-bound consciousness. The fact is that one's awareness is complex and constantly fluctuating from one resource to another, with the result that the self that was listening knows the material, including the new material, but the self that must perform—the doer (which is a very different and much more complex self)—may have access to only part of the information or perhaps none of it. Thus, one can talk and talk and talk and think and think and think about induction processes, but have little knowledge during the experience itself and be able to produce only limited results, and maybe none at all. Conceptual realization is not the same as experience.

In all of my Conferences, we explore induction through ritual, and in Foundational Conferences I watch the confusion on people's faces when I say the part of them that is listening to what I am saying is not the part that will be able (for example) to do healing work. That part will never be able to heal. Its job is to listen, to think, and to be ordinary. Another self *already is in* the healing state of consciousness. One's task is to let go of the ordinary and enter the extraordinary.

Rituals that deal with individual and collective healing can do just that, reconnecting us to the resource that actually does the work. We, at the outer level, don't do it, just as Simple Brugh doesn't do it.

One of the most powerful experiences I have had in observing ritually induced healing states of consciousness occurred while I was still practicing traditional medicine in Los Angeles. I was invited to witness the charismatic Christian Kathryn Kuhlman calling in the Holy Spirit for the healing of members of her audience. Before the service started, I—along with various curious physicians, rabbis, priests, nuns, psychologists, nurses, and other health care professionals—was invited to come onstage and be seated in a section that would permit direct access to those who were affected by the healing service if I wished to examine them.

Ms. Kuhlman began simply, with an opening prayer, soft music, and song. Slowly she built the forces in her audience until, after an hour—during which the lighting, music, prayer, and preaching all combined with increasing intensity—I could feel that the whole auditorium was in an unstable field of energy. As Ms. Kuhlman entered her most inspired state, she called for members of the audience to come to the stage. By now people were falling down, crying, screaming, praising, and praying. It was formidable! I felt as if my own body might collapse if I attempted to move about in the vortex she was inducting.

Many of the individuals sitting in my section—those who had been invited to act as conservative and objective witnesses, including the doubters, the reporters, and the doctors—were swept up in the forces and awakened to find themselves on the floor after having passed out when Ms. Kuhlman touched their bodies during the service. I was really moved by what I saw and felt. It definitely was not something out of a medical lecture. It was powerful, emotional, and electric.

Investigation of her work by other traditional physicians had demonstrated that a full spectrum of possible results came about—from healings that seemed miraculous to no response at all. But physical healing as a goal seemed less important to her than entry into some kind of heightened state of consciousness that invoked mental and emotional catharsis, followed by inspiration and high-level well-being. I have since observed the same phenomenon—and the same results—when charismatic healers of any faith or no faith at all work with heightened states of consciousness, so Christians don't hold a monopoly. But the forces she invoked continue to amaze me even today, fifteen years after the event.

Importantly, the ritual with which Ms. Kuhlman would call forth the healing energy was the same each time, and Kathryn Kuhlman, the woman who initially came onstage, was not the same Kathryn

Kuhlman who was there at a critical stage when the laying-on-of-hands phenomenon began to occur. She would pass through a ritualistic series of changes until she reached the state that "took her," so to speak. Whether one is healing or conducting a Mass, a change from the ordinary consciousness into the extraordinary is required.

As members of an audience, we are empowered through the heightened state of consciousness of the inductor, but our actually entering the inducting state—doing so directly—is usually precluded. (The same is true if we are patients in the hands of the physician, for if we are only passive, we will benefit to some degree but miss the augmented healing interaction that can be ours when we take an active role in our own healing.)

To deal with this matter of the observer's passivity, I sought a way that all the participants in any healing interaction might directly enter into and partake of the sacred, inducting states of consciousness.

The Rosette Ritual—A Circle of Healing

The process I evolved is the essence of simplicity. It can be used with any number of people, though gatherings of several hundred or more people are preferable, since the effects both of the induction into heightened states and of activating the healing potentials of the group are greater as the number of participants increases. The only thing required is sufficient space for the entire group to be able to divide into small groups of six to seven people.

Before proceeding with the introduction of this induction process, we need one additional understanding. We need to understand about physical touching.

Touch is primary. It is probably the most ancient of our sensory systems. Even the eyes and ears are nothing but specialized touch organs, responding to photons and to sound vibrations. I have had two powerful realizations about the experience of physical touch. The first, an extension of my recognition that the self who learns is not the self who "does," was that the self who touches is not the same as the self who feels and appreciates the touch. The second was that the deep psyche doesn't know who or what is doing the touching. It reads the patterns. It simply knows it has been touched and recognizes the quality of that touch, while only the intellect pays attention to such superficial details as who or what did the touching. Therefore, when you touch yourself with the same caring and compassion as you would touch a sick friend, an injured animal, or someone who requested your most caring and healing attention, your deep psyche only knows you have been touched by a compassionate, heightened healing energy and is not concerned at all with who did it.

By integrating these two realizations, we can vastly augment the experience of the collective healing ritual. We can explore the amazing difference between touching ourselves or another person while in an ordinary state of consciousness and touching ourselves or another while in a heightened state of consciousness. We can also sense the difference between the "doer" self and the "receiver" self at both the ordinary and transordinary levels.

Preparation

Just prior to the commencement of the ritual, an individual who will not participate is selected from the large group to act as group leader to guide the entire experience. Alternatively, a tape recording of the instructions can be made in advance and played to orchestrate the actual ritual, so everyone gathered can be fully involved. For the convenience of those who prefer a prerecorded tape or who desire to experience how I actually bring this ritual through for groups, I have prepared a professionally recorded audio tape cassette of the entire ritual sequence.

The group leader now asks the large group to break up into small groups of six or seven persons apiece, then asks those in the small groups to number off sequentially, starting with one, until each person has a number. The size of the small groups is important, since working with fewer than six people can be less satisfying energetically and technically, and working with more than seven people simply takes too long. Breaking into smaller groups might seem to diminish the effect of the process, but it does not, for the ritual itself is being conducted in the context of the larger group. Thus, a synergistic effect comes about as the small-group members work with one another and simultaneously work as parts of the overall group field.

At this point the leader announces that heightened energy can cause some individuals to lose consciousness. If any person does begin to lose *consciousness or feel faint any time during the experience, he or she should just sit or lie on the floor and wait for the feeling to pass, rejoining the group when doing so seems appropriate and comfortable. The group leader points out that the experience passes quickly and does not harm the individual, but since most people are unaware that such a phenomenon can occur at all, they could be frightened if they were not warned ahead of time. If an individual does elect to sit or lie on the floor, the group simply fills in and continues the ritual without that person. Most group rituals proceed smoothly without anyone having to take these measures, however.*

With these logistical considerations out of the way, the ritual itself can commence.

The Ritual

The group leader asks the members of each small group to form a circle without holding hands and to attune inwardly to the Sacred for a minute or two with their hands on their hearts. During this time, each person is quietly aligning with an inner harmony and well-being. Images that are sacred to the individual are called to mind. These can be images of a Sacred Being, a Spiritual Teacher, or inspiring phenomena in nature. A line of poetry or an uplifting melody might also be used for this inner attunement. Each individual is reminded to touch his or her heart area with the same sensitivity and compassion he or she would have for someone in need.

Next, the group leader asks the members of each group to close their eyes, hold hands, and attune to the energy of the small group for a minute or two. Then, as the group members hold hands with their eyes closed, the group leader asks each person to visualize having stepped into one of the great Cathedrals or Temples of the world. Each person is asked to visualize a wondrously radiant energy bathing the Cathedral/ Temple, protecting, harmonizing, and heightening all who are within it. Thus the room is energetically sealed and protected. Instead of a great Cathedral or a great Temple, some individuals visualize ancient temples, sacred ritual centers (such as a circle of massive stones), or a beautiful natural setting. The important point is for them to use images and impressions that are individually sacred and that have the capacity to cause a change in their state of consciousness.

Deepening into the Heart

The group leader now asks the individuals who are designated as number one to enter the center of their circle and, with their hands on their heart area, to prepare to receive an influx of heightened energy. The people in the center of the small group circles are now referred to as the center partners. Those forming the circle are referred to as the circle partners.

The circle partners are asked by the group leader to reattune to their own sacred images and to one another. The group leader asks the circle partners to turn the right side of their bodies toward the center of their small-group circle and move closer to the center partners, so their own right sides are gently nestling the person in the center. The circle partners' left hands are placed on the shoulders or backs of the partners in front. Their right hand is placed on their own lower anterior chest area (the Heart Center).

The circle partners are asked to connect to an Infinite Source of Energy which manifests outward at their Heart Center like an artesian well. They are further asked to explore the attributes of the Heart Center . . . feelings of Compassion, Innate Harmony, the Healing Presence, and the experience of Unconditional Love . . . first one attribute and then the next, one by one, slowly and experientially, with sufficient pause between each to permit an unhurried experience. The group leader suggests that the circle partners feel as though they are connected to all those individuals who have ever experienced the embrace of Compassion . . . and let that feeling pervade their own sense of beingness, also feeling as if the Compassionate embrace is reaching through their sense of self to embrace others in the circle and in the room. The group leader asks that the circle partners each feel as if Compassion itself is embracing them, rather than their simply feeling compassionate and sharing this feeling with the others. It is important for them not only to feel the embrace but also to feel the embrace reaching through themselves to others.

Each of the additional attributes of the Heart Center—the Healing Presence, Innate Harmony, and Unconditional Love—is handled in exactly the same way, guided by the group leader.

This initial induction introduces the ritual participants to the concept of levels of consciousness beyond the ordinary sense of time and space. The rational mind has a real struggle when I ask each person to connect to all those individuals who have ever lived who have felt the embrace of Compassion. Yet through the mystery of the inner imagination, such an experience is psychologically possible. The moment I suggest that the group members are in touch with a larger Beingness in time and space, both the individual energy and the group energy take a big leap in intensity and possibility.

Transmitting Healing Energy

The circle partners are then directed by the group leader to image their hands being like radiant balls of light ... like radiant suns ... and to begin to share this energy flow, this state of consciousness, with the partner in front through their left hands and with themselves through their right hands, which are still being held against the lower anterior chest, the Heart Center. This is called the experience of Sacred Touch.

The circle partners are then asked to imagine themselves collectively becoming a vortex of Light and Energy, surrounding and enveloping the partner in the center of the circle. This is done by having the circle partners surrender their sense of individuality and separateness in order to blend and fuse with one another, to form a collective sense of Self ... a vehicle of consciousness capable of transmitting a Sacred Healing Energy. The circle partners do this by receiving the energy flow from the partner behind and simultaneously transmitting an augmented energy flow to the partner in front, and by continuing to imagine the collective vortex of energy that is forming. I refer to this part of the ritual as the act of Sacred Communion.

As the energy builds—and you can't miss it—the circle partners are instructed to turn inward to the center partner, in this case partner number one, and to enact the experience of Sacred Touch with him or her by placing both hands on the center partner ... lightly and sensitively. The circle partners should intuitively determine for themselves where to place their hands. We now have a rosette of heightened collective energy focused on the individual in the center.

The circle partners are reminded to continue to imagine they are in the center of a great hallowed place and that they are being held in the Heart Radiance of this sacred place. They are then asked to experience themselves as the spokes of a wheel, radiating energy to a central hub ... directing to the center partner the energies and forces they are accessing. The circle partners are asked to feel their hands being like radiant suns and to sense the energy flow penetrating the individual in the center. They are asked to fill the center partner with light and energy ... to illuminate the body tissue beneath their hands ... to nourish and to heal at Soul level. The center partners are asked to open themselves fully to the inpouring of the heightening, healing, harmonizing energy, and to become open to receive as they have never been open before. The center partners are asked by the group leader to imagine themselves bathed in a healing, heightening, harmonious sphere of light and energy.

The leader should allow about ninety seconds to pass (which is a long time in these states of consciousness) before asking the circle partners to return their hands to their own Heart Centers, to place their left hands on the back or shoulder of the circle partner in front, and again to enter Sacred Communion with one another. The circle partners' right sides are still turned in to the center, gently supporting and nestling the center person.

The circle partners are now asked to reconnect again to their individual sacred images and again to feel the Heart embrace of the sacred place in their imaginations. The circle partners are sensing energy as being simultaneously given and received, allowing this collectively and personally nourishing experience to deepen and to heighten. The center partner is asked to enter a deep, calm, clear pool of Beingness.

The circle partners are then asked to join hands while partner number two changes places with partner number one, who returns to the circle. The whole sequence is then repeated for partner number two except that the left sides of the circle partners are turned in to the center to gently support the center partner, their left hands are placed on their own chests, and their right hands are placed on the shoulder or back of the partner in front. This reversal accomplishes two things. It keeps the arms from fatiguing by alternating the hands, and it develops a facility in both hands for delivering heightened energetics. Thereafter, each time the sequence is repeated, alternate sides are turned toward the center.

Near the end of the ritual, those in the circles that had only six persons, and who finish before the seven-person circles do, should stand, *arms around waists, and enter a simple communion with one another while the final individuals in the circles of seven complete.*

When sharing with the last individual in the small groups is complete, the group members form a complete circle with no one in the center. With their arms around the waists of the partners on either side, everyone in the circle enters into an appreciation of each member ... a simple, nonverbal communion with one another.

All participants are then asked to sit or lie down on the floor or to return to their seats and, after a silent meditation which focuses on deepening the energy experience that has just occurred, to leave the ritual area in silence, each in accordance with his or her own sense of appropriate timing. Often silent, warm embraces are shared as the ritual comes to completion.

The Importance of Collective Rituals

There is a great need in our culture for collective healing and nourishment rituals. The touching itself is beneficial enough, but when the forces are ignited into Transcendence, the experience is *awesome*. A once-weekly gathering of any group of individuals—friends, temple goers, church members, committee members, members of the police force or of street gangs ... office workers, physicians and nurses—for touching, healing, heightening, and entering the Sacred together might just transform our society and the world we live in.

I hope groups will use this format for collective and personal healing. Most rituals in traditional religions still maintain the power in the priest/priestess or the minister by having only that particular person enter a heightened state of consciousness and share it with those in attendance. In this ritual, however, everyone is asked to enter a heightened state of consciousness and to share the energetic experience with the others. Everyone in attendance is therefore empowered. It also allows people of all faiths and all backgrounds to work together, beyond dogmas and differences, to touch one another and to touch the Essence together while still honoring the images that are sacred to each of them.

Rites of Passage

My intent thus far has been to present rituals that allow one to experience induction into other arenas of awareness yet still return to the Simple Self at the end. The Simple Self is, after all, the aspect of us that experiences most of what we call our life. Now, however, I want to focus on the rituals involved in *rites of passage*, initiations that induct a new, long-term vehicle appropriate to a new biological staging . . . initiations from which we do not return to being the same persons we were before.

Rites of passage separate one developmental staging from another and initiate the next vehicle of consciousness, the one that has resources appropriate to the new stage. The early initiations—from fetus to infant, from infant to child, and from child to adolescent—are, for the most part, unconscious. As we pass through such stages, we are not aware of the actual initiations. Yet, in many cultures, there are rites and rituals around conception, pregnancy, birth, and various stages of childhood, performed by family members, the religious community, and/or Elders. Each stage grants to the individual greater responsibility and authority. But the major conscious initiations, wherein the individual is challenged to his or her maximum, begin with puberty, when the most powerful aspect of Life—the procreative—becomes actualized.

An exceptional film called *The Emerald Forest*, written by Rospo Pallenberg and directed by John Boorman, features some of the male initiation rites of puberty and the subsequent rite of passage into marriage.

I will briefly summarize the story. A Caucasian boy about seven is abducted by native Brazilian forest people while he is on a family outing near a dam on which his father, an engineer, is working. The father spends the next ten years trying to locate his son, but without success. Meanwhile, the son is being raised by the chief of the forest people and has developed into a resourceful though still youthful boy of about seventeen. We see him at that age playing in the river with a male friend. They are teasing the young girls of the tribe. The boy dives underwater to sneak up on a girl to whom he is attracted. As his head emerges from the water, we see his tribal father and tribal mother standing nearby on a large, flat boulder, tall and serious, close to the water's edge.

The forest father says the time has come for the boy to die. We see apprehension on the face of the boy and yet excitement, too, as he realizes his boyhood has come to an end. His forest mother tells him she is lamenting because she will never see her little boy again.

The next images explosively present the ritual of the rites of passage, in which the boy can no longer afford to be a boy. His initiation requires all the strength and courage of a young man if he is to pass through it without humiliation or physical death. What then transpires is the death of the boy and the birth of a young man who has the resources to engage and to support his society as well as to initiate the resources for handling marriage and procreation. This is a very different self from the Boy self.

Since the induction into the next stage will be long-term, the passage back into boyhood must be permanently closed. My working hypothesis is that through the extreme crisis of the initiation, as well as through the forces of tribal social sanctions, the psyche is forced to withdraw its animating forces from the Boy self and to infuse the Young Man self. The young man is empowered and celebrated while the boy is ritually released and sacrificed. There is no going back. It is as final as the physical initiation from the fetus to the infant.

When the original father finally finds his son, the boy has already been initiated into young manhood. The biological father asks his son if he won't return for his mother's sake. But, as the young man's wife says, "He has no further need of a mother." The father is himself initiated and realizes that his "boy" no longer exists.

The End of Childhood

For the majority of males in our culture, war is the only experience that even comes close to a circumstance that can generate sufficient energy for the rite of passage into young manhood. In wartime, the boy is ripped from the breast of the mother and from protective family and social conditions. He is exposed to forces that the child or boy cannot handle or resolve, and in the face of which the initiation into manhood can potentially transpire. The next developmental vehicle of consciousness, which has far greater resources and capabilities, is birthed.

The deep psyche is not concerned that a devastating event is transpiring to initiate the male. It is only insuring that the resources contained in the next staging are engaged and manifested. The young man has a new power base, and the society is benefited by his energetics and resources. Obviously the same also holds for the female, provided that her initiation is equally as deep and as powerful. In fact, the task for women is even more awesome, as the women must integrate the vast Feminine principle and break from the power of the father.

Unfortunately, the significance of initiation has been lost on our society. We maintain the child/parent relationship far too long, significantly arresting the deeper Unfoldment required for full empowerment of the individual. The Child self is hardly ever completed and is also ridiculously overvalued. The psychological Young Man and Young Woman are never quite birthed. In addition, the sensitive masculine and the masculinized feminine are extremely popular in today's American culture, while the Eldership stages are demeaned. The gods and goddesses of Youth reign supreme. Immature stages are not properly sacrificed, and the later stages are ill-defined.

Even when there are rituals of confirmation, as in Catholicism, or rites of passage, such as those in most bar mitzvah and bat mitzvah ceremonies, a strong tendency has arisen to diminish the severity of, or to minimize, the trial through which the child must pass, thus to insure that all children do actually pass. In other words, the sensitivities of the child are protected and the actual force of the initiation is diluted to such an extent that the initiation is, in fact, a sham and does not actually take place. The whole purpose of the initiation is thereby lost, as the person remains in the psychological vicinity of the earlier staging, or has easy access to that staging. The probability of a psychological arrestment is high. (One should recognize, however, that not all initiations have been diluted in this fashion. Indeed, some carry the threat of permanent physical and/or psychological injury or even death. These possibilities are present in many Eastern spiritual rites of passage, the rites of passage for the aboriginal adolescent in Australia, the initiations of street people and ghetto people in our own American cities, and, of course, the initiations of war.)

I can't begin to count the number of individuals in my Conferences who are surprised to find that they are arrested at the infantile and sometimes even the fetal psychological levels. The outer awareness thinks it is an adult, doing adult things, until the deeper nature is unmasked through projections, dreams, or, under stress, regression. In fact, much of my initial Conference work involves helping individuals prepare for birthing into (1) life, (2) the body, or (3) the next appropriate stage of psychological patterning.

Regardless of what our prior difficulties may have been, an initiation can commence and staging can proceed once we are aware that an arrestment has taken place and how the forces that are operating to maintain the arrestment can be handled. Even if we don't consciously initiate these stages of development, Life from time to time will create the circumstances that offer rites of passage. Mature stagings are too important to Life for Life not to have found ways to force the initiations from generation to generation. In such cases, not all individuals in a group will have the opportunity to be initiated, but there will always be a few who are initiated into more resource-filled vehicles of consciousness.

The Mystical Marriage

I was particularly struck by comments regarding the rites of passage into marriage that were made by Joseph Campbell and Bill Moyers in their PBS television series, "The Power of Myth." Campbell noted that in a mature stage of marriage, neither partner surrenders to the other. The true process involves both partners' surrendering into the unity represented by the marriage itself! In my terms, both enter new vehicles of consciousness which are based in the mystery of blended forces. The senses of self present prior to the rites of passage into this new, more mystical relationship must "die" and give way to the deeper, more resourceful, more empowered selves which can fully engage the challenges and requirements of marriage.

The first general staging of marriage satisfies procreative and survival needs. The second general staging brings the couple into mystical union, in which their separate selves dissolve. But where are the marriages that have achieved this mystical relationship, this circumstance that demonstrates the selflessness inherent in the mystery of that second major stage? It's no wonder the divorce rate is so high, not only because most individuals entering marriage have failed to appreciate how powerful the unconscious infant, child, and adolescent are, but also because rites of passage no longer exist that might put them to rest.

The rites of passage into marriage bring us into a crucible of development that is beyond anything we imagined in the premarital stages. We certainly aren't prepared to understand that there are many selves in each partner and that no marriage can possible contain and fulfill all the aspects of each partner. There are selves that the partner cannot satisfy or fulfill even if his or her life depended on it. As this is understood in the mature relationship, one partner will help the other partner to fulfill those aspects through other people . . . outside the marriage. This prepares both partners for the selfless aspects of the mystical marriage that, potentially, can occur later on.

I also do not want to imply that heterosexual rites of passage into marriage relationships represent the only possible, or for some, even the most desirable, pathways into the mystical marriage. Outer mores and standards are mostly ignored by the deep psyche anyway. Life has created many paths and many possibilities to engage the mystical marriage.

Induction through Crisis: Trauma as Life Teacher

We come now to the most popular and most successful method for generating the energy to change vehicles of awareness: creating a crisis. Enormous energy is required to initiate the unawakened person into heightened ranges of human consciousness. For instance, war not only initiates individuals, but it also initiates an entire society into resources not ordinarily available nor ordinarily experienceable. Author Doris Lessing, who was born in Turkey, lived in Africa and then England during World War II, and now resides in Canada, has written a book called *Prisons We Choose to Live Inside*, wherein she makes note of people who are psychologically fixated to the times of the great wars. These people continually live and relive the excitement and the drama of their war years. They talk as if the war was the peak experience of their lives. And, of course, it was! The moment-by-moment threat of devastation, the existence of great causes, the moments of laughter and humor in the face of horrific events and challenges, and the feeling of aliveness are all reported and remembered by these people. The crises of the moment contributed to a heightening of the experience of life by opening them to greater psychological resources than were available during peacetime.

Long periods of peace are often soporific in character and lead to stagnation. Lawrence Blair and his brother Lorne, two adventurers into Life, recently filmed a documentary on the Indonesian people who live on the sides of active volcanoes. The Blairs' observation was that the constant threat of eruption and chaos contributed to a heightened sense of daily life and moment-by-moment experience for these people. They did not take their lives and homes for granted.

How many of us have lived through natural disasters or major calamities and found we were strengthened and awakened through such events?

One of the most powerful thoughts I ever had about medicine was a previously taboo concept which, when it occurred to me, renovated my entire understanding of health and disease. I asked myself how a particular disease, injury, or emotional trauma might be serving the deeper aspects of a person. It was as if the gates of awareness parted. Most people experiencing cancer or other life-threatening illness will tell you they came alive under the crisis of the diagnosis. Priorities were suddenly revalued. The petty and infantile were discarded for the meaningful and fulfilling. Relationships that had been taken for granted were heightened. Other relationships, long dead, were discarded.

Crises in the form of disease, injury, and emotional pain are forces for change. However, if the underlying patterns of change can be discerned and if the *willingness* to make the required changes is substituted for the illness, injury, or emotional pain that is *forcing* changes, a miraculous potential to dissolve disease and injury patterns can be discovered. Yet there is so much unconscious secondary gain in disease and injury that most individuals will not want either to see a need for, or to effect, the required changes. But when the individual is ready for a difficult initiation, the deep Self showers its resources and gifts on that part of self undergoing the change.

Crises and stress themselves are not evil or wrong! What makes the difference between our being aborted psychological cripples and mature, natural, and ever-expanding beings is how we deal with crisis and stress. Stanislav Grof, Ph.D., in his book *The Adventure of Self-Discovery*, presents some interesting views on the relationship of the birth crisis to life patterns of one's later experience. He notes that during the birth trauma, the fetus is brought to a critical stage with all alarms on—instinctual, physical, emotional, sexual. This can cause a transcendental experience in the fetus/infant, a peak experience. We also know that massive amounts of endorphins are circulating in its body, introducing a narcotic component to the crisis.

The fetus/baby is experiencing the end of the aquatic phase, all it has known to that point of life. The future is unknown, and the trauma of contractions and movement through a very narrow passage, along with bursting into light and air, represent *the* most dramatic physical and consciousness changes it will ever experience, except possibly the changes in consciousness at death. From my perspective, these difficult events are necessary for the next stage to fully initiate. This fetal peak experience also sets the stage for the individual to attempt later to return to that same experience *unconsciously*, utilizing the same energetics that are present during the birth crisis, including the pain.

During the initiation of birth, the trauma is important in activating many physiological and psychological systems. Just as the effort put forth by the chick to peck its way out of the egg is necessary for the chick to gain strength for physical survival, the crises surrounding birth are fundamentally necessary. If the chick is helped by someone who good-heartedly opens the egg . . . the chick usually dies.

When I am assisting people with their personal growth, I usually urge them not to redo the birth trauma and not to redo childhood crises. The fact is simply that the infant vehicle of awareness had to enter, appearing through the struggle of initiation, because the fetus could not handle the new circumstance. Likewise, each subsequent vehicle of consciousness must also enter through the struggle of initiation, or major problems occur in later life. This has become even more clear to me as I have worked with large numbers of people, for I have discovered that they are often trying to use infantile psychological patterns to deal with adult crises, while the vehicles of consciousness that could easily handle the crises or the changes are prevented from entering their awareness.

Crisis has the potential to activate rich and mature states of awareness, with capabilities that are not stimulated in unstressed and overly protected infants, children, adolescents, and young adults. In fact, many of the world's most remarkable individuals—whether they have worked for the great Good or the great Evil—have come from very disruptive or abusive early environments. Difficult circumstances are the basis of great maturational potential if the psyche has been initiated in a way that permits the individual to embrace the necessary sacrifices.

CHAPTER SEVEN

THE IMMORTAL PATTERNS
BEHIND REALITY

Throughout this book I have been presenting information about patterns and the importance of being able to read the pattern level of reality, whether such patterns are experienced in the inner reality of the psyche or in the outer reality of the manifest world.

What are patterns? Dreams are patterns of interrelating, intrapsychic forces. Visual images are patterns of electromagnetic energies. Patterns are the basis of scientific, mathematical, and psychic regularity and predictability. The various personality aspects of the conscious senses of self are patterns. The transcendental senses of Self are patterns. The basic themes of our lives reflect patterns of the Unconscious.

Patterns, though perceived as either single events or as series of events in time and space, are, from my current perspective, independent of time and space. Whether we are aware of them or not, patterns, the relationships of patterns, and sequences of patterned Unfoldment are what give each of us the experience of reality. Patterns of forces are what give objects, events, and ourselves reality and meaning. These patterns and the realities that are generated through them are essential and intrinsic ... the givens that underlie manifestation ... having nothing to do with right or wrong, good or bad, preferred or not preferred.

We can begin to approach this profound arena of understanding by thinking of Life as reflecting a great Mystery Play ... a Play ingeniously well orchestrated, determined by the very nature of matter itself, and flawlessly enacted by characters generated out of matter's mysterious yearning to come into being.

Most writers of such art forms as plays, novels, short stories, operas, and ballets know there are only a few basic plots and that all of their creative endeavors will reflect one or the other or a combination of these relatively few basic patterns or themes. Great works of fiction as well as great individuals will often have many or all of these plots interwoven into one great expression of Life. The fundamental dynamics of Life reflect this same fact ... that there are only a few basic patterns around which life, as we know it, infinitely dances. Current theories regarding matter and chaos suggest, in fact, that there are approximately one hundred fundamental patterns into which chaos can move and become coherent. Through the interaction of these approximately one hundred possible patterns come what appear to be infinite variations of expression. I am likewise intrigued by the fact that, at the time this is written, only 109 chemical elements are known to exist. Everything we encounter in the physical world, whether organic or inorganic, is comprised of patterns of one or more of these basic chemicals. Then, when one reviews the subatomic composition of each of the chemical elements, one is appreciating the unique pattern of each chemical element itself, in space and time. The patterned way that elements, compounds, and mixtures get along at the physical level is very similar to how human beings get along at the psychological level and is the basis of my working hypothesis for understanding the relationship between mind and matter.

A good example of how basic patterns appear over and over again can be discovered in examining the basic theme of Shakespeare's play *Romeo and Juliet* and of Leonard Bernstein's musical *West Side Story*. A brief perusal of both reveals the classic theme of Ill-Fated Lovers. The basic similarity of theme or pattern is concealed by the differences in culture, geography, historical period, backgrounds of the characters, and manner of presentation. Nonetheless, love entangles two "innocents" in a circumstance that precludes their being able to have a relationship. Tragic death resolves the conflict in both stories.

We don't grow tired of seeing this pattern depicted in any number of apparently different stories. I believe the reason we don't grow tired of this recurring pattern is that it is fundamental to our very nature, and somehow essential to our Beingness. It is fundamental to the nature of matter! We can have an infinite number of different men and women play the parts of Romeo and Juliet and have them engrossed in an infinite number of conflicting family circumstances, but the pattern remains the same and always resolves through the death or through the substitution sacrifice of one, the other, or both of the Ill-Fated Lovers. From the transpersonal viewpoint, the pattern is immortal, dancing in certain people of each generation in every culture of the world.

A psychically sensitive person, meeting the young lovers before death ensues and reading the pattern correctly, would know the Ill-Fated Lovers pattern is active and that resolution through death is called for. This need for death can be satisfied through the ending of the lovers' relationship. Or the need for death can be satisfied through a ritual substitution sacrifice, in which the psychological senses of self of one or both lovers are sacrificed in place of the physical bodies. The need for death can be satisfied through the ritual substitution of one life for another, as with human or animal sacrifices in the Jewish, Christian, and Islamic religions of the West and the Near East. Or the need for death in the Ill-Fated Lovers patterns can be satisfied through the death of one or both Lovers. Activating any of these options will satisfy the pattern, and death will cease to stalk . . . until, of course, one of the lovers who carries the pattern reconstellates that pattern in the next encounter with Love.

Patterns are carried for life but may remain latent, and a specific pattern may not be activated in one's lifetime. We must remember, however, that the purpose of Life is not to escape from or avoid patterns, but to recognize that they are what give our lives meaning and, therefore, represent our pathway to fulfillment. Thus, for example, from the transpersonal viewpoint, individuals swept up in the

Ill-Fated Lovers pattern, rather than trying to escape from the lethal configuration to fulfill their lives, actually fulfill their lives, and therefore Life, *through* the pattern. The sacrifice of life for love is not uncommon in our society. It simply means that the personal and mortal are sacrificed into the Transpersonal and Immortal. The outer mystery is sacrificed to the inner Mystery.

We are basically, then, but witnesses to the myriad physical and psychological patterns living through each of us. The patterns are immortal, and our unique relationship to them is, I believe, struck at the time of conception. In terms of the usual ways of expressing human existence, Life lives us. We do not live Life! Only through Self-Realization is there even a remote chance of our living a life with option over which patterns are activated and which patterns remain latent . . . and even then we are restricted to those patterns which are intrinsic to our individual makeup.

Unconscious Patterns in Relationships

An example of the pervasiveness of patterns and of patterned phenomena can be seen by examining two powerful, closely related unconscious patterns that are at the basis of attraction into the marriage relationship. The first deals with unconscious bondings to the countergender parent during infancy and in early childhood. The second, which is related to the first in a most remarkable manner, involves the fact that what one sees and becomes involved with in the outer world has a preexistent and coexistent counterpart within the interior Self.

We can only relate to the outer aspects of Life through the inner correspondences. The outer is only a reflection of the inner patterns. The attraction to another person is actually the attraction to a self contained in one's own Self. We literally fall in love with parts of our Self—not with conscious parts of our Self but with unconscious parts of our Self, which have been projected onto whatever in the exterior world most closely resembles them.

When those of us who have been through or are presently in a first marriage realize that we have married the pattern that represents our countergender parent and that, unless we become conscious of what is happening, we are destined to form sexually based primary relationships only with persons who carry the basic patterning of that countergender parent, we begin to realize the personal importance of awakening into Self-Realization. There is no hope of escaping these dynamics if we remain unconscious of them. No matter how many marriages we enter into, the Unconscious will dance and control the relationships. Of course, the Unconscious controls *all* relationships, but the primary spousal relationship contains the most powerful unconscious material, as it is based in parent/child pattern dynamics. This has biological and psychological survival value in that the attractive sexual forces of parent/child are transferred into dynamics that attract us to a spouse and lead therefore to continuity of the unconscious physical and psychological patterns that are being transmitted through the family or clan. Yet, we scarcely recognize the profound incestual components to the marriage, nor do we recognize how unfulfilled other aspects of the Self are when the primary dynamics being fulfilled in the marriage are those of the parent/child. If we want to appreciate these dynamics, the first marriage will tell us everything we need to know ... if we can only recognize that a pattern is present, that it has to do with powerful and unconscious relationships with the parents, and that when this pattern is made conscious, new potential in the relationship as well as within the experiences of life is more readily available.

A particularly astute reader of unconscious patterning can observe a child for a short time and discern all the patterns, or at least the major patterns, the child will enact in adult life. An intuitive person can hold a baby at birth, sense the patterns, and predict the general life-themes of that particular infant. A highly intuitive person can hold that same baby and predict with astonishing accuracy not just the general patterning but also actual, specific events that will coalesce around those basic patternings.

When well-developed intuitives (sometimes also referred to as *sensitives* or *psychics*) give a "reading," they are reflecting patterns in the deep psyche. In my experience, such intuitives are 90 to 95 percent accurate at the general pattern level and, at best, 60 to 70 percent accurate at the specific level. In fact, all sensitives are more accurate in reading general patterns. Of course, these percentages are not precise, and they cannot be applied to any specific individual. But they do point to a trend, and it is this trend about which I wish to comment.

My own particular gift involves being able to read the general pattern levels of the deep psyche ... to recognize the fundamental forces that are operating. I am only moderately accurate in reading specific levels. Some people are gifted in regard to the specific levels but may have no understanding of the general patterns, so they can miss the relationships between the general and the specific. Carolyn Conger is an example of someone who is gifted in both areas.

One person I often recommend, who was also the first person to do a formal reading on me, is Bella Karish, whom I mentioned briefly in Chapter 2. I was overwhelmed by what Bella presented to me. In three hours she took me apart on every level you can imagine and put me back together with deep intuitive insight and compassion. Had I known someone could read me that deeply, I might not have gone. No matter how integrated and balanced you usually feel, anxiety and vulnerability quickly erupt when somebody sees you more deeply and more intimately than you usually see yourself. This experience of anxiety and vulnerability in the presence of someone who knows things about you that you wouldn't want anyone to know can be really disturbing, at least until a more mature self develops which can handle such candidness. I know this well from being around such people as Bella and Carolyn Conger—especially Carolyn, as I lived with her for a number of years and was exposed to her intuitive awareness of me on a daily basis.

I have also experienced the other side of this situation at my own Conferences, where participants become anxious when sitting next to me in the dining area or in the seminar room because they assume I am reading or "seeing" their thoughts. Quite to the contrary, though, my intuitive awareness is usually only active in the context of sessions in the seminar environment, when I am specifically working with an individual. At the dining room table, I am only interested in eating and being simple. And even when I am aware of material that may be uncomfortable to an individual, it doesn't mean the material has the same meaning to me as it does to that person. Most of the time it is only a "suchness" to me, just a bit of information, without a value system attached. Sometimes—although this possibility doesn't usually occur to the participants—I am just as concerned that they will pick up my thoughts or feelings. Most of the time, however, when I am not working, I am simply not interested in information coming in from heightened states of consciousness or from intuitive realms. This can shock the beginning students, who tend to overvalue the expanded ranges of awareness.

When I have listened to recorded sessions of Bella Karish's individual readings, I have been impressed by the phenomenally detailed revelations of deep unconscious patterns associated with the individual being read. Each reading covers sweeps of time and dimensions of consciousness far beyond the usual ranges addressed by sensitive readers. Bella reads on many levels, using metaphysical themes and drawing heavily on reincarnational structures to tie her material together. Wayne, her partner, works with her during the reading but stays in the background, using his highly developed intuitive capacities to pose questions and to direct the overall reading from level to level. The result of such a reading is, in terms of Bella's model, a myriad of "past lives." In my model, each "past life" is a pattern that is present in the Unconscious and potentially active in the individual's life.

Past Lives/Present Patterns: An Alternate View of Reincarnation

Although I expressed a belief in the reincarnational viewpoint in my first book, I am now exploring another possibility, one that can be used to understand the same material from an alternate perspective. My current view is that the key to understanding and appreciating what Bella and other past-life readers are presenting is to reinterpret "past life" anecdotes in terms of their being active, current patterns in the multiple selves of the Unconscious, rather than events in the past. There is, in fact, nothing in a past-life reading—no character, plot, or theme—that cannot be understood as a force presently acting in the Unconscious. When this is recognized, one can ferret out the key unconscious patterns that are operating in one's life without getting stuck in literal or denotative interpretations of psychic readings.

This shift in attitude about past lives occurred because I discovered that when I went to different sensitives, each would read the supposed past lives differently, yet the same basic themes or patterns would be embedded in these ostensible scenarios from the past. The names, places, and most of the superficial details of the "past lives" would be very different—just as *West Side Story* and *Romeo and Juliet* are different—though the patterns of these stories were basically the same.

Through these experiences with many different readers, I suddenly became aware of the Pattern Level of Reality. I saw the eternal dance of but a limited number of themes and plots, combining and recombining, dancing us generation after generation and having nothing to do with the personal self, that self which is but an illusion of consciousness and has only limited resources and options in relation to the forces that are actually manifesting us. Instead of seeing karma as personal and individual, I suddenly saw it as collective, impersonal, and immortal.

All the patterns being read by the reader are those of impersonal forces manifesting through us. Each individual has a unique combination of the immortal patterns, determined by the energetics at conception. Life incarnates us and needs us. These patterns renew themselves in each generation and are present now, not somewhere in the past! We are only the latest vehicles acting out the forces in the great Mystery Play called Life. Our only spiritual responsibility is, to the best of our ability, to fully live out those patterns that relate us to the wholeness of Life.

My fourth year of medical training brought me into obstetrics and gynecology. During the many deliveries I personally managed, not only was I awed by the process of birth, but I was also awed by what I sensed about some of the newborns. A few seemed predominantly to carry the Angelic patterning of goodness and wholesomeness, a few others seemed to carry the Artistic patterning of struggle and crisis, some carried the Athletic patterning, some carried the Abandoned Child pattern of self-rejection or of being not good enough. And a few, much to my amazement, carried a sense of the Dark and Destructive.

As I have lived more and more of my life, I have begun to realize that some individuals are destined to live out, almost exclusively, the good and "acceptable" side for the collective, some individuals are destined to live out, almost exclusively, the dark and disowned side for the collective, and most of us will be somewhere in between.

Not only is an individual danced by these immortal patterns, but so also are groups of individuals in their collectivity. By reading the collective group pattern and not the individual patterns making up a group at one of my Conferences, I can usually predict the overall outcome of the Conference at the group level. As I noted in Chapter 5, at any moment during the Conference, there will always be a few people who are miserable and unhappy with the Conference and their relationship to the material being presented. There will also be a few people who are ecstatic and intoxicated by the Conference and their relationship to the material being presented. Most of the participants, though, will be engaged by and grounded in the material. I cannot predict which individuals will be the high fliers of the collective and which will polarize around the shadow content. But it is possible to predict that a high flier will revert to the pits, and the individual who is in the pits will move into the high-flying experience. Both may oscillate for a while before they finally take up a position in the experience of the main group, but when they do, generally two or more other individuals will enter the energetics of the polar opposite. This is a fascinating observation, similar to what occurs in quantum mechanics, in which the behavior of huge quantities of light particles can be predicted, but a prediction regarding which particular photon will go where cannot be made.

The phenomenon of mass predictability is evident in many areas, a well-known one of which involves the ability of insurance companies to make a profit despite the unpredictability of individual policyholders. It is also evident, of course, in the field of medicine, where group behavior in regard to any particular disease can be statistically displayed and is therefore predictable, yet no one can accurately predict how any one individual in that group is going to respond to the disease or to its treatment. Actually, the whole field of medicine is based on predictable collective responses, within the boundaries of which is a remarkable range of possibilities for each individual. However, for the collective pattern to be fulfilled, only a certain proportion of individuals can satisfy each aspect of the range.

Here, between predictable group behavior and unpredictable individual behavior in the group, we confront a profound mystery. Is there a general pattern that superimposes itself over a collection of people and influences their overall behavior, while individual behavior can, to varying degrees, be independent? And if one individual's behavior is consciously directed into a certain area of action, is another individual's behavior unconsciously forced into a balancing reaction in order that an unchanged overall group response might be maintained? In regard to healing, is it possible for certain individuals in a group process to consciously latch on to the "remarkable cures" category of response and thereby force others into the "nonresponsive" category? Psychologically, when one group of people polarizes in the direction of the Great Good, is another group moved thereby into polarizing with balancing forces in the direction of the Great Evil? Of course, from a rational and intellectual perspective, such dynamics can easily be shown not to be valid, but from the nonrational and intuitive standpoints, they seem to be operating as fundamental principles in the Unconscious.

How we perceive events and think they have transpired, and how these same events in fact *do* transpire represent two different orders of reality. We bump up against the psychological perspective versus the factual perspective in the field of religion, as, for example, in Christ's Virgin Birth and in the Buddha's having been born from his mother's side. In the field of law, psychological versus factual orders of truth display themselves daily in the courtroom. There are many examples to support the assertion that there is a psychological/subjective reality *and* a factual, intellectual reality, and thus I am further encouraged to pursue the realizations around group dynamics and the patterns that seem to be operating in terms of both the rational/intellectual and the nonrational/intuitive perspectives.

Some interesting considerations along these lines became evident to me when I started to look into sibling dynamics within families.

I was struck by how often the brothers and sisters seem to divide up the pie of the possible kinds of sibling behavior, as in the case of the sibling who becomes the black sheep of the family and the sibling who becomes religious, the sibling who becomes intellectual while another sibling becomes predominantly athletic. An unconscious tendency seems to exist for distribution into these and other basic sibling patterns. Even when an entire brood takes on "black sheep" characteristics, perhaps another family grouping somewhere will act as a counterbalance by having children who are *all* saintlike and angelic.

I was disturbed when I realized how individuals in my medical school class, in just twenty years, had been distributed into a classic bell-shaped-curve pattern of life circumstances, from those involving drug addiction and alcoholism to others involving accolades and high achievement, as well as practically everything else in between. We had become yet one more predictable grouping of physicians satisfying some unconscious and powerful pattern.

In seeking to recognize and understand patterns more clearly, I have come to believe that large cities may be a perfect reflection of the basic composition of the human Unconscious. They appear to exhibit the same intrinsic patterns the world over, patterns that seem not to have changed in thousand of years. All of the immortal characters, from the most dark and malignant to the most beatific and celebrated, seem to incarnate each generation in every great city of the world. Is there a fundamental pattern of energy, innate to the human psyche, that guides or controls such development, so all great cities of any culture in any era—past, present, or future—will always display such a similarity? And just as all the divergent elements in the vast complexity of a large city are able to coexist . . . is the same also true in regard to the human Unconscious? Does this great city-pattern force the individual elements to dance its dance or do the individual elements create the dance of the city? I am strongly leaning toward the former view, and from that perspective I am awed by certain insights.

All possibilities of existence are maintained and nurtured in the matrix of the city. All human potential is incarnate and renewed generation after generation. No aspect of any city is either "right" or "wrong." All aspects reflect only the full creative suchness of human life. All individuals of a city are interrelated and need one another for the entity of the city to survive and to procreate. When someone interferes with the balances, by such actions as attempting to do away with the ghetto or to provide homes for the homeless, the entity called the city will reconstitute itself through time, initiate others into the ranks of its depleted, and restore the balance between the haves and the have-nots. As disturbing as this perspective sounds, there is much evidence to support its validity, as anyone knows only too well who has attempted to change the balance of life-styles in a city. The poor will always be there, as will the sick, the indigent . . . the prostitutes, the corrupt . . . the exploiters of humanity and the humanity that seeks exploitation . . . the good side of town and the bad side of town. Such aspects are natural and intrinsic to our deeper nature, and *Life is served by the maintenance of these balances*. The individuals who make up these aspects may change, but the aspects themselves do not change, as they are innate.

When I am traveling in the world, I often have difficulty realizing which city I am in. The same squalor, poverty, criminal elements, respectable restaurants, architecturally magnificent monuments, first-class hotels and flophouses, and bureaucracies and black markets all exist together! Saints are saving sinners, and sinners are unsterilizing the saints. The wealthy are do-gooding and exploiting the poor, while the poor continue to be initiated into rites of survival and passage, enabling them to be able to pass through calamitous circumstances without batting an eye, while the more sophisticated and well-off often crumble under the impact of chaos.

Want to reach full Self-Realization? Go live in and be reflected by the spectrum of the city. Be careful, though. You can't apply value systems appropriate to the family or to rural living when engaging the full force of a city. All aspects of life are represented there, and all of those aspects—even the most apparently unsavory—are necessary and appropriate from the psychological perspective. The situation is no different from that of cells in the human body. In the body, some organizing force takes potential cells and directs their development into specialized parts that allow the overall survival and well-being of the whole body. Some cells are directed to live as anal cells, while other cells are destined to live as sole-of-the-feet cells, and still other cells are destined to live as Betz cells in the central nervous system. This isn't a matter of right or wrong, or of good or bad. It is the suchness of things, and cities likewise reflect the suchness of our psychological being in a vast, complex, and vibrant manner.

Tools for Perception: Pattern Projections

Numerology and its relative, astrology, are two additional reflections of the fundamental psychological patterns contained in the human Unconscious. While a rational, intellectual perspective tends usually to view numbers in terms of arithmetic and counting, an intuitive perspective can also see them in terms of psychological symbolism. To a psychologically awakened individual, the numeral one, for example, not only represents "a single thing," but it also represents unity, oneness, totality, indivisibility, and that which is initial, the most important, or of the first order, to mention but a few of the most obvious aspects.

Again, if systems such as numerology or astrology are approached only from the intellectual and factual viewpoint, they seem not to have a rational basis. Yet when they are regarded from the psychological and symbolic viewpoints, they can be of immense help in understanding the principal dynamics of life and the human Unconscious. Mystics and intuitives have no problem living with both the psychological and the intellectual realities of life, though the priesthood of Rational Science can become enraged by such thinking.

Carl Jung, the great twentieth-century explorer of patterns of the Unconscious, commented that the most amazing thing about numbers is that they communicate the same symbolism no matter whether they appear in the outer consciousness, in dream states, or in states of meditation. Numbers are consistent between dimensions of the human psyche.

Signs of the zodiac are also basically patterns of the deep psyche projected out onto configurations of stars. Mind and matter ... the deep psyche and manifest reality ... are as one at the level of the Mystery. The reason complex relationships among planets and zodiac signs can be used to predict the future or to reveal the basic life-forces carried by an individual is that the deep psyche is behind the projected patterning. Crystal ball reading, an enigma to the uninitiated, is merely a way to focus the awareness while unconscious patterns display themselves as impressions and projections into the crystal ball. These same general processes are used in palmistry, phrenology, iridology, reflexology, Tarot card reading, divination with the *I Ching*, dream interpretation, and psychic readings in general. All are based on projection of the innate, unconscious patterns of the human psyche.

When discussing how images and visions can be projected onto outer reality, I am reminded of a powerful exercise I mentioned in *Joy's Way*, called the trespasso. As one gazes steadily and unblinkingly at any object (usually, with the trespasso, at the face of a partner or at oneself in a mirror), images begin to manifest in outside reality in a most dramatic manner. This same phenomenon is sometimes used by sensitives when they are doing readings. The person for whom the reading is being given can tend to dissolve in the mind of the sensitive and other images will begin to appear, images that may contain information about the person being read. If the sensitive reports seeing an Indian or a little boy or an angel, he or she is not talking about outer, material reality. Indeed, the images appear to be "out there," but the source of the image is the deep psyche of the sensitive, which is somehow in relationship with the individual being read. The Unconscious is projecting its impression onto outer reality, whether that reality be a crystal ball, the face of an individual, celestial configurations, or tea leaves. The really startling aspect of this process is that the genuine reader is not projecting something imaginary or concocted in his or her own mind (although that's always a possibility), but is somehow picking up information directly from the individual who is being read.

A very powerful way to work with pattern-level phenomena is to do cloud readings, as some Hawaiian Kahunas do. When one enters a heightened, intuitive aspect of Self, the deep psyche (which is not bound by time and space) can project onto the clouds a pattern that is germane to a question that has been posed. Or one's attention may suddenly be seized by a particular cloud pattern that alerts the outer mind to an event that is to take place in the future or even at a distance in another part of the world.

Predictive patterns manifesting as events can be seen in many other ways as well. For example, I was sitting on the front porch of a house on the beach on the island of Kauai talking to a young woman who, because of a carcinoma of the breast, had recently had a mastectomy. The biopsies of her auxiliary lymph nodes were negative, and all studies pointed to her having a complete recovery.

She had been expressing to me her appreciation for angels and the angelic dimension. As she continued to center the conversation around her love of angels, I began to experience her seemingly innocent talk as her Unconscious contemplating and orienting toward death. Then as she was speaking, a single sea gull flew by, swooped a few times, then flew almost straight up in the air and disappeared. I knew she would soon die of her disease. An omen had been delivered through the very unusual flight pattern of the sea gull. I cannot describe the extent to which this process is disturbing to my intellect or how the process actually works, other than to report that the intuitive knowing about her impending death was inescapable to me. I did not have the courage to tell her what I "knew," and I supported her sense of recovery and well-being. She died a year later.

Clearly not every external event will be predictive, and an observer must discriminate between fantasy and actual psychic information. What is most likely to have psychic import is an unexpected event that breaks into or interrupts normal consciousness and has the feeling associated with intuitive knowing, a certain "zing" that distinguishes actually *knowing* the meaning of the event from merely being aware of possibilities and probabilities about the meaning of an event.

A sequence of events that constitutes an omen for me, one that makes my hair stand up on end whenever it occurs, always begins late at night when I become aware of the sound of a bird's wings beating against the window and the sound of a bird's beak pecking against the glass. As I approach the window, I see a bird frantically trying to enter through the closed window. Even when I turn on the light and go to the window to scare the bird away, it persists in the extraordinary behavior for ten to twenty minutes before it stops, then it just sits on the sill outside. Later it disappears in the night. Invariably, and I do mean invariably, someone close to me dies within two days of such an episode. The bird is different each time, but the pattern is always the same. These events, incidentally, are actual events and not dreams.

I have two conscious associations with birds and death. One is that my mother used to be afraid a bird might fly into our house, as she believed it would mean a death was about to occur. The other is a very sad experience I had at about age ten, when I was given a BB gun. I shot at and, to my surprise, hit a bird that was sitting atop a telephone pole. It fell to earth, wounded but not dead, and in my panic and guilt, I buried it alive. I have never quite forgiven myself for such an unthinking act, even though through that act, a compassion for other life forms was birthed in me.

My psyche reads an omen of death in birds that act bizarrely at night. From the viewpoint of my rational mind, I have no idea how such events could happen. I only know they do. And of particular interest to me is the fact that the sequence, the pattern, is not reflected by events that might ordinarily be present in my outer reality. This unnatural behavior by birds seems somehow intended to catch my attention. Is it caused by my Unconscious, which already knows the death will transpire and activates the omen pattern, even causing a bird that happens to be around to act in a bizarre fashion, to stimulate communication between the unconscious and the conscious parts of myself? The relationship between mind and matter often stuns me.

Sacred Creative Patterns

In the area of what would generally be regarded as aesthetics, *sacred creative patterns* can provide moving ways to experience the phenomenon of patterning, whether in the form of sacred geometry, sacred proportions in architecture, sacred combinations of sounds in music, sacred combinations of light and color in painting, sacred (or classical) proportions in masterworks of sculpture, or sacred (heightened) expression in literature, such as poetry and drama (the Shakespearean plays of the West or the No plays of Japan).

What distinguishes the sacred from the nonsacred is the object's resonance with or its closeness to a fundamental pattern. What a human collective calls beautiful, masterful, or aesthetic is related to correspondences between one of these inner patterns and an outer object or person. The more nearly the outer object or person corresponds to the unconscious original pattern, the more greatly it inspires and lifts us.

There are, for example, ways to divide a line into proportions that create a pleasurable resonance in the human psyche. One, the so-called "Golden Section" or "Divine Proportion," is produced when a line is divided into two unequal segments such that the ratio of the whole line to the larger segment is equal to the ratio of the larger segment to the smaller segment. A rectangle whose length and width correspond to this ratio is called a "Golden Rectangle" and somehow evokes a pleasant and uplifting response, inspiring us to recognize the innate harmony of Life. We feel a sense of peace and at-one-ment . . . a resting place, so to speak.

We can look at all sorts of architecture, but that which has been created by master architects employs sacred proportions in various ways, sometimes obvious and sometimes concealed, to achieve an effect on the observer, whether the intent was conscious or unconscious. There is a profound mystery that relates these sacred patterns, forms, and matter to human consciousness. There is sometimes chaos in form and matter, and there is sometimes harmony in form and matter. What allows us to distinguish between the two—to "know" when we experience harmony and to "know" when we experience chaos—are the sacred patterns in the Unconscious.

The ear can experience aesthetic sound and chaotic sound. The great masters of composition discovered the sacred relationships between sound frequencies and produced timeless classics. Composers have often said that the next note falls into place because of the notes that preceded it, so there is no choice when composing what turns out to be a classic piece of music. The composer is merely discovering the pattern that already exists. The music had already been struck at the pattern level.

Pattern is not only experienced in the melody but also in the intensities and in the relationships of sound to no sound. All these aspects can be appreciated in a classical piece of music. One distinctive quality of a classic is that it cannot be improved on. It seems to be a perfect reflection of the ideal pattern that underlies the composition. Not one note or its timing can be changed if it is a true classic. If something can be changed, the piece of music is good, or perhaps a near classic, but not yet a masterwork.

I observed this phenomenon while viewing the *Venus de Milo* in the Louvre Museum in Paris. No matter from what angle I looked at the statue, it captured me completely. Less masterful sculptures may thrill the eye in certain views yet assault the eye from other views. However, people can take pictures of *Venus de Milo* from the back, the sides, and the front, and a masterwork is still evident. Michelangelo's *David*, in Florence, Italy, can also be viewed from any angle without one's losing the sense of viewing a masterwork. All classics have this attribute. Every part reflects the perfection of the underlying pattern on which the work is based. You can try this with any statue. Note that for the vast majority of statues, there will be "dead" angles or views where the sense of the masterful collapses.

The same holds true in the case of lesser musical compositions. Some parts work and others don't. The composer was not able to attune completely to the Master Pattern and went astray in places.

Obviously the same can be stated about any kind of art . . . painting and poetry, for instance. Sometimes the artist or poet can birth a painting or poem effortlessly, one that is fully developed, in which nothing needs to be changed. Here the Master Pattern has been reflected perfectly and directly. Most of the time, though, the artist needs to struggle and wrestle with the material until the Master Pattern is finally revealed. I have often thought that the artists of words, light, sound, and matter create the many crises in their lives in order to maintain connection to the heightened states of consciousness that can directly access the primary pattern level of reality.

A distinctive artist who has tapped one of the master forms can commit a whole lifetime to exploring a particular combination of energy, no matter what type it may be. Thus, perhaps the music unique to such greats as Bach, Mozart, Beethoven, and Wagner are actually intrinsic patterns of sound that each of these men *discovered*. The compositional modes and styles of Wagner or Bach or Beethoven or Mozart were not created by them, nor is the music unique to them, but rather each of them tapped a unique, classic sound pattern that always was, is now, and forever shall be. The name of the composer gets attached to the master form or pattern he or she discovers, but the composer does not actually create the pattern! The same would hold true for all distinct signatures in art, no matter what the medium.

A well-known controversy raises the issue of whether Shakespeare actually wrote the masterful plays that carry his name. Could it be that William Shakespeare, relatively inept in his ordinary consciousness, may have tapped a master form of play writing and poetry that transcended his outer awareness? His name gets attached to the form, but he may only have tumbled into the dimensions of awareness wherein the Master Patterning of "Shakespearean" plays exists. This is clearly similar in principle to the phenomenon of Simple Brugh and Teacher Brugh, two very different aspects of my Self with very different resources which are contained in the same body.

Such a possibility may also account for people who, as they compose, claim to "channel" the music of Delius or Debussy or of other composers. Perhaps they are in contact with the Master Patterning that Delius or Debussy channeled.

Incidentally, the great problem with tapping a Master Pattern is that, as an individual, you can be absorbed into it and, psychologically speaking, "die" an early death. The pattern seizes you, and you are no longer free to express other patterns available to you. You become a stereotypic android.

Many artists struggle with this problem. When they find one Master Pattern, its intensity is so great that they have difficulty breaking free from it to discover others. Not only might an individual become trapped in the expression of certain artistic patterns, but he or she might also become caught up exclusively in expressing the Artist pattern itself, and thereby sacrifice other important patterns in his or her Unconscious. Either of these alternatives means the death of individuation on the path of Self-Realization. That is why I noted in an earlier chapter that the Saint may be but one aspect of the whole. To be absorbed into only one aspect is not Self-Realization. It is a sacrifice of multifaceted, individuated life to a single, eternally dancing form.

The Dance of Patterns

Each of the master forms or patterns also has power and stature associated with it. Whether a person is conscious or not conscious of what is happening determines whether that person gets seduced by one of these forms or learns how to draw from its wisdom and resources while continuing to deepen the awakening into Selfhood.

The outer mask—the dominant, preferred sense of self—is never a full reflection of the forces that make up an individual. It is usually only a compensatory aspect, and to maintain it at the expense of the other aspects of Self costs the individual dearly. Until a vehicle of consciousness is birthed into the awareness that can handle the unconscious forces driving the psyche to wear the compensatory mask, no true awakening occurs. Furthermore, in the outer levels of awareness, the ego structure of most people can usually only sustain positive, ego-enhancing images of Selfhood. Images that evoke universal, loving responses are particularly attractive to an individual whose underlying unconscious dynamics are those of unworthiness and self-rejection. What births the Saint is the inner Sinner. The person who is attracted to the Warrior image is not attracted only because of strong, warriorlike inclinations but also because unconscious feelings of inadequacy and inferiority are active and present, driving the outer self into expressing the Warrior.

The larger population rewards and honors many of these compensatory masks—which are needed for collective completion, pleasure, or satisfaction—and the individual thus is tempted to become a sacrifice to the patterns of the collective for such rewards and honors. But the individual can become dronelike, with no freedom of soul expression. If you can't give up the power that is yours through identification with the deity that is dancing you—whether it be the Warrior, Saint, Healer, the Mother, the Father, or anything else, pleasant or unpleasant—you are seduced and in danger of losing your soul . . . the unique combination of selves that forms your individual Beingness—which includes, but is not contained by, the outer sense of self.

These themes are, in fact, what underlie stories about selling one's soul to the Devil. What is not discussed, however, is that one can also sell one's soul to the Saint or to the Good Daughter or Good Son or to the Warrior or to the Monk and be in just as much trouble as Faust got into. At least Faust realized his dilemma and managed to regain his soul, which rarely happens to the Saint or to the Good Son or Daughter. Psychologically, they are unaware of what they have sacrificed, as the secondary gains are too wondrous to give up.

How is the power of such Master Patternings broken? By surrendering the attachment to the power the Master Patterning provides! This may mean humiliation, powerlessness, chaos, and collapse of sacred value systems, but it also may mean the fulfillment of one's soul. As our culture sees it, being a failed Sinner is not humiliating, but being a failed Saint is. However, such prejudice is what seduces the immature. Being able to give up attachment to "good" power is just as important as being able to give up attachment to "bad" power. It is the addiction to any power that enslaves the individual to a Master Pattern.

There is a degree of absorption into a Master Pattern beyond which the individual psyche cannot balance itself, leaving the individual completely enmeshed in the Master Pattern for the rest of his or her life. The unconsciously held counterpart to the Master Pattern— that is, the Sinner in relation to the Saint, the Female to the Male, the Male to the Female, the Whore to the Virgin—will constantly try to establish balance, and if the absorption hasn't gone too far, the eruption of the counterpart will establish psychic balance and harmony. Unfortunately, the individual's outer awareness, enslaved to any Master Pattern, will read this eruption as a test of faith or a test of loyalty and continue to generate even greater sacrifices to maintain the desired conscious polarity. However, the awakened path is to realize that the unseen, unconscious aspects of self are real and form part of the Whole. A Saint is not Holy without the Sinner. A Male cannot be whole without the Female. A Female is not complete without the Male. The Virgin is not complete without the Whore.

Through having been danced by patterns of the Sun God, the Divine Child–Divine Mother, the Puer, the Christ/Healer/Saint, the Monk, the Prostitute, the Sinner, the Artist, the Magician, the Orchestrator, the Spiritual Teacher, and the Fool, I have some conscious realizations to share about such patterns. I know they are ever-present in my Unconscious ... changing from time to time from latent to active and back to latency again. They, and others of which I am as yet unaware, form an orchestra and play my symphony. The only difference between my life in the past and currently is that a deeper, more mature aspect of me is becoming conscious of each of them and appreciates each one unconditionally. What I know about my inner community of selves is this: They are in harmony with the Unfoldment of my life. There may be parts that do not like other parts, but in consideration of the deeper purpose of my life ... all aspects support its expression.

Dying to Death: A Repatterning

In 1984 I was ending the Puer/Christ/Healer/Saint patterning. The change was overdue. I was forty-five, and many who carry this particular pattern die before they reach forty. It is, in fact, an esoteric axiom: Healers die young. Death may come through illness, accident, or suicide, and there is no right or wrong involved. It simply is part of the patterning.

In October 1983 I had the following dream:

> I am given the opportunity to see the Book of Death ... a large black book filled with the names of those who are already dead and those who will soon die. As I look through the pages of handwritten names of those who have died and who are going to die, I unexpectedly run across my full name. In the date column is written, "Easter, April 1984." In the cause-of-death column is written "Heart Attack."

I couldn't tell if the dream indicated a psychological death or actual physical death. The problem for me was that as I examined my life, I sensed that all the great patterns to which I felt attuned were concluding. I felt as though death at that point would be appropriate.

I began consciously to prepare for death, setting all my affairs in order and organizing each moment of time around an appreciation of Life and of the soul-stirring experiences I had had the good fortune to encounter. I saw Death as a natural part of my patterning.

I entered a month of complete surrender to the idea of cessation of Beingness. Parts of me grieved and cried. Other parts were simply fascinated by the idea. Still other parts would panic and feel terror. And other parts were experiencing heightened awareness as Easter approached. Three days before the Easter weekend, I had the following dream:

> I am sitting in a pastoral setting, watching a strange event take place. A white, triangular tent, covered at both ends so I can't see inside, is in an open area. I hear a small boy's laughter coming from inside the tent. Long, multicolored sashes, tied together and forming a multicolored snakelike pattern, are being pulled into the tent through a sphincter-like hole at one end. Suddenly, seated next to me, appears an East Indian Sage, about forty to fifty years old, with a radiant face. He, too, is laughing. He is dressed in orange saffron robes, which he wears comfortably and causally. He has a graying beard. The Sage informs me that I need a teacher to help guide me into my next initiation. He suggests that I go to the bookstore and see what strikes me as interesting.
>
> He then tells me to lie down on my stomach. He places one hand on the back of my head and the other on the lower end of my spine. I suddenly feel a current of energy, as though I were plugged into an electrical outlet. I begin to cry tears of appreciation. The Sage tells me he is healing my body . . . and I awaken.

But the most remarkable event was occurring. Though I had awakened from the dream, the current persisted! I was in bed, on my stomach, still experiencing the sensation of his hands, one on my root chakra and one on the back of my head. The incredible current of energy coursing through my spine lasted some thirty to forty minutes before subsiding.

I interpreted this dream as follows: The pastoral setting signals the healing power of nature and of the natural elemental forces. The multicolored snakelike sashes penetrating the sphincterlike orifice of the pure white tent represent the fundamental mystery of creation, with the masculine energy fertilizing the womb and creating a new conceptus, which, in this situation, is the laughing child not yet born. This is the new incarnation that will replace the form that is to die, as was announced in the pre-Easter dream.

The boy-child is basically happy, and humor is natural to him. The womb is symbolized as a white, triangular tent, reflecting the stability of the basic trinity ... Mother, Father, Child ... and the virginal qualities of the womb that carries the new creation. The tent is on the ground, symbolizing the "earthing" of the new self. There is a single child in the tent, meaning that the twin energetics, which I have carried with my actual twin brother, have been integrated into a single individual. The long, multicolored sashes, tied end to end, making up the masculine contribution to the union, suggest that many colorful personalities or selves will comprise this new manifestation and that the child is actively engaged in pulling these parts of Self into itself.

The sphincterlike orifice was like an anus ... an entrance into a mystery, just as with the mouth or with the vagina. Because the first, or root, chakra is in this area, there is an implication of the awakening of the root or physical and instinctual state of consciousness, with access to the kundalini energy. It may also reflect the anal compulsiveness of the Child.

The boy-child is still within the protection of the womb and has not birthed into outer life. He is still gestating in my Unconscious. As the Child and the Sage are frequent pairs in the Unconscious, the Healer/Sage, as represented by the East Indian Guru, acts as the mature healing agent to prepare my actual physical body and my mind for the new incarnation. The East Indian's good humor again reflects the connection to the boy-child in the womb and to the humor of the family into which I was born in 1939. It also reflects the power of healing through humor and laughter, pointing to the notion that one can break the pattern of disease through the unexpected and disarming aspects of humor, which slices through deadly seriousness and cracks open doors to new possibilities.

The suggestion that I go to a bookstore for direction was a gift that I took to be both symbolic and literal. Thus, I went to the Rainbow Book Store, the only bookstore on the island of Kauai that carried material which interested me. There, I discovered *The Portable Jung*, edited by Joseph Campbell. I had avoided Jung's work from the moment I heard about it. I knew if I ever began to study him, I would need years to come out from under his influence and discover my own creative center again. To my delight, however, some of his work simply validated what I had already discovered for myself, so it became a wonderful confirmation as well as a profound opening into deeper and more difficult arenas I might explore.

The healing experience in the dream was formidable. There is simply no question in my mind that my physical body had been reorganized into a healthy patterning that was capable of sustaining a new incarnation. My concern about dying died in the experience of the dream.

Although I realized that the new entity which would carry my life force was already conceived and was gestating, I still did not have any image of the vehicle that was to dance the next season of my life. I felt like the nineteen-year-old girl who had no role model for her own next staging. Then, six months later, I had the following short dream:

> I am facing a deep, dark pool of water. Slowly, from its depths, rises the body of a man. At first, he is floating face-down and seems to be dead. He then becomes animated and I see that he is actually a healthy older man in his seventies or eighties. He stands on the water's surface, smiles, and embraces me as I smile and embrace him.

My interpretation is as follows: The pattern of the Elder was activated and birthed into my awareness from the depths of my Beingness. This Elder is related to the Christ, which is apparent by his standing on the water. This indicates also that the Elder is supported by the Unconscious and rests on the Unconscious. There has been a maturation from the young, mother-complected, puer energetics that Jesus represents, into the mature Elder. The embrace of the Elder by my dream-ego symbolizes the acceptance, at an unconscious level, of the stage that is to embody the new incarnation.

I was ecstatic when I began to fully fathom the implication of the short dream. Not only did I have an outer direction to unfold into ... from maturity to Elderhood ... but also the culminating stage of the Human Cycle was going to be mine to experience in the outer reality. I had somehow survived the withdrawal of earlier patterns that often end in youthful death and had been picked up by the Eldership pattern.

I recognized that a long cycle of preparation, apprenticeship, and full empowerment of the Elder was now awaiting!

CHAPTER EIGHT

EXPERIENCING THE UNCONSCIOUS: DREAMS AND PROJECTIONS ONTO THE SCREEN OF REALITY

Upon the most famous and powerful oracular temple of ancient Greece were inscribed the words "Know thyself." At a simple level, this timeless admonition invites one to seek basic self-knowledge within the ordinary ranges of consciousness. At more profound levels, it encourages an exploration of the whole Self and the multitudinous unconscious aspects of Being, an exploration made all the more difficult because *the outer mind doesn't know the unconscious aspects exist.* Further, the outer mind, with its egoistic defenses, must protect itself from unconscious material that is not acceptable to it. Not that the Unconscious and its content are wrong, evil, or bad. Rather—and this is the important point—unconscious material is often of an order of intensity and power that can easily overwhelm and even break up the tenuously constructed ordinary consciousness each of us usually senses as being awareness itself.

One of the most powerful initiations we experience in the early stages of psychological awakening is the realization that there *is* an Unconscious and that it is vast. This means that the outer mind—the aspect of Self upon which we usually base our entire understanding and definition of who we are—isn't even an important aspect of consciousness when viewed from the perspective of the whole scope of Beingness. The Unconscious, by contrast, is so enormous that the more deeply one explores it, the more closely it resembles what is traditionally called "God."

The formal entry into the unconscious aspects of Beingness has long been conducted in religious orders and esoteric schools through a process I referred to previously, which is generally called the Mystery Training. This training is necessary to prepare the individual for such inner experiences as dealing with the collapse of the sense of self, engaging time and space relationships foreign to the outer awareness, handling unusual powers that may spontaneously become available (referred to in the East as "siddhas"), confronting fears of mortality, and dealing with tendencies toward intoxication with power elements. The trainings are rigorous and dangerous. The capacity to handle the unveiling of the unconscious aspects varies from student to student, and only a few individuals in each school are ordinarily capable of engaging the deepest material. Remarkably, however, most of this esoteric material, at least in the form of intellectual insight, is already available to the public through the wide selection of books in any good metaphysical bookstore! Still, even when the great wisdoms and techniques are laid out, if one doesn't approach them with a vehicle of consciousness that can make use of the information and the resources they offer, those resources cannot be accessed. To most people, in fact, the material will seem paradoxical or even senseless, because, as in a dream, the realities and languages of the Unconscious are very different from those of the outer level. Thus, there is little danger that the powers and forces will be misused or mishandled by an undeveloped individual. Furthermore, initiation or induction by a teacher (outer or inner) into the required vehicle of consciousness is usually needed before the resources can be fully activated and fully appreciated.

Many labels are applied to the processes by which the Unconscious is elucidated. Psychiatry and psychology are two contemporary Western approaches to the relationship between the conscious and the unconscious parts of the Self, though both of these approaches tend to view the Unconscious through intellectual, rational filters. While I do not have formal training in the thinking of either Freud or Jung, what I know of their work causes me to regard the psychology of Jung as the most enlightened and far-reaching. Except

for some of the behavioral sciences, the field of psychosomatic medicine, and certain aspects of psychoimmunology, most of Western
science, medicine, religion, law, and politics ignores or denies the
existence of the Unconscious.

Thus, we recognize the two major, alternative perspectives from
which we may regard the experience of the Transcendent. One is the
view in which the spiritual dimensions are understood to be beyond
ourselves and therefore exteriorly based. The other is one in which
the Transcendent is seen as part of a vaster dimension of Self and
based interiorly. The view one takes depends largely on whether or
not one recognizes the existence and significance of the Unconscious.
Either view is therefore relatively correct, though I regard the interiorly based view as more appropriate and useful to a genuinely expanding sense of Self.

We tend to experience only what we can conceive, or worse yet,
only what we are told is possible to experience. Unfortunately, the
religious models that are presented to most peoples of the world are
simply too controlling and too limited to be used exclusively as models to guide development, except perhaps in the very earliest stages
of Unfoldment. Thus, whichever approach one takes to expanded
states of consciousness and to an exploration of the unconscious aspects of Self—whether the transcendent is regarded as being within
the individual or outside the individual—one should recognize the
importance of having a working model or hypothesis that is inclusive
and expansive enough to be able to handle the experiences encountered in the expanded states.

Because the Unconscious *is* unconscious, it can be observed in
only a few ways, and nearly all of them are indirect, like watching a
shadow play in Bali. The most common ways of seeing its influence
and power from the *ordinary mind* are through attention to such
phenomena as dreams, projections onto the screen of reality, repeated
life experiences, doing the opposite of what we think we ought to be
doing, slips of the tongue, delayed responses to word-association tests,
and (primarily with children) sandbox play and drawings.

The most common ways of viewing the Unconscious from the
nonordinary mind are through attention to such phenomena as peak
or transcendental experiences that occur during extreme crisis, mor-

tification of the flesh, illness delirium, and drug experiences, as well as through the induction of heightened states of consciousness by an Initiator.

This chapter will concentrate on approaching the Unconscious through the first two major pathways available to the ordinary mind . . . dreams and projection.

Dreams

Many excellent books on the Unconscious and dreams are available, and I particularly recommend those written by Jung himself, as well as those by other Jungians that are recommended by branches of the Jungian Institute throughout the United States and Europe. At the same time, I want to emphasize that the approach to the Unconscious I am presenting does not conform to the Jungian viewpoint. I approach life and dreams eclectically. Further, since the subject has been so broadly covered, my intention here is not to take a technical approach to dreams but rather to make a few fundamental comments on how I view dreams and how I personally engage them for myself and for others. To begin, and to help the reader break up mind-sets about images and therefore about dreams, I will present a brief introduction to the basic and relevant physiology.

Around thirteen billion cells in the occipital cortex fire off with every image we experience, whether or not the image reaches consciousness and whether or not the image is of endogenous or exogenous origin. The fact that something has caused at least thirteen billion cells to fire off in the brain must be appreciated as wondrous. Thus, even before we enter an exploration of the meaning and intention of dreams, we recognize that just from the most elementary physiologic viewpoint, they are miraculous and complex manifestations of interacting forces.

We can also remind ourselves that the phenomenon of seeing is based in a physical/chemical reality that is quite different from the reality we experience subjectively. The biochemical reactions involved in the process of seeing are too complex to even begin analyzing here, but we can at least note that they are *very* complex.

Actually, just perceiving an image of something "outside" ourselves confronts us with quite a mystery. For example, in tracing the neuro-pathways of sight, we find that when a biochemical image arrives at the occipital area of the brain—the part at the back of the head—it is upside down. How the image gets to be right side up again and perceived as "out there" is not known. Let me stress this point. *No one knows how the image gets back outside the head again.*

We can well imagine the many possible ways the original image might be influenced interiorly before the conscious part of us ever gets to view it. Which unknown parts of Self are viewing it before our ordinary consciousness does? What is the influence of intrinsic, inherited patterns within us? What is the significance of the relationship between the experiences in our life and the events or objects we are viewing? By the time the biochemical image reaches consciousness, it has been manipulated and altered in ways we scarcely conceive of, much less understand. And there are scientific data showing that often we are, in fact, not watching outer stimuli at all ... that we are actually watching simulations of reality—"movies"—wherein our mind fills in the details and only updates an image when important shifts in the original stimuli occur.

The blind spot, a very large area where the optic nerve exits each eyeball, cannot register light stimuli, though we don't experience a large hole in our vision. But such a hole does exist in our visual field, and its existence can be demonstrated through special testing devices used by opthalmologists, oculists, optometrists, and neurologists. When that is done, objects—amazingly—simply "disappear" when they are in the area of the blind spot. But the mind somehow uses the surrounding peripheral images and fills in this blank spot, with the result that what we see is not what is actually out there.

In addition, most people are not aware that they usually see mostly through one eye, their dominant eye, with the nondominant eye being supportive, though not the primary visual pathway. This can be verified by pointing the index finger of either hand at an object twenty or more feet away, then alternately covering the left eye and the right eye with the free hand. The finger will appear to jump back and forth, pointing directly at the object when the dominant eye is looking and pointing off to the side when the nondominant eye is looking.

These simple techniques and exercises demonstrate the larger principle: What we see is a function of external stimuli *and also* of the apparatus with which we see (which translates the stimuli into biochemical forces that represent the stimuli); plus, at some point, the Unconscious aspects of Self; and, finally, the state of the outer consciousness at the time of seeing. From this we can appreciate that what we see and experience is not a report of a single, unvarying, objective, external reality but a mosaic of interacting forces from both the exterior and the interior. And the contribution from the interior is important. In fact, it may be the most important factor. This is also true of hearing, as the following account indicates.

After a particularly long period of giving Conferences, I had taken some time off and found a bed-and-breakfast manor house in Wales, where I began to unwind. It took six weeks for me to find the simple place of Beinghood, one that wasn't swept up in my being a Teacher, a Healer, a Saint, a Guru, a Friend, a Brother, a Physician, a Boss, an Organizer. It was Simple Brugh, and I was delighted to reacquaint myself with him. Life was reduced to a simplicity of interaction with nature and people at very basic levels.

One day, when I had just left the manor house to take a walk along one of the ancient canals that run through many parts of Britain, I suddenly heard my shoes crunching on the gravel walkway in an extraordinary fashion. When I put the experience into words, it loses something, but what happened was that *I was hearing that I heard the sound.* I was experiencing sound from a completely different place in my awareness, and it was fresh and exciting. The sound of the shoe interacting with the gravel was simply beyond words. I was shocked into a dimension of ecstasy. I had known from personal experience that there were states of consciousness in which sound, light, and touch are perceived very differently, but this was my first spontaneous experience of such a phenomenon involving sound, and without induction through a teacher, drugs, or meditation.

This experience was comparable to hearing in super, super, holophonic high fidelity! By comparison, my normal hearing seemed like listening to a tin can tied to the end of a string. The event was followed within several minutes by a similar phenomenon with my sense of sight, and I was now engaging reality with my two most dominant senses in a spectrum beyond my wildest hopes for expanded experience. It was a gift from Life that I had not expected nor even sought. It simply happened, and I am very appreciative it did.

I wrote my friend Carolyn Conger and told her I now knew what a dimension of Zen Lightning was. A sequence in the film *The Emerald Forest* depicts something of what I experienced. The father and a newspaper reporter are deep in the Amazon jungle searching for the father's son. It is a stormy night and the men are using fireworks to attract the natives. Suddenly they become aware that when the lightning flashes or the fireworks ignite, they can see natives who have gathered and are standing in the darkness at the edge of the encampment. The natives are abruptly visible, then abruptly invisible. For me, this new phenomenon was as though someone had left on the lightning, as I experienced half an hour of sustained supervivid hearing and supervivid seeing, from a spacious interior state of consciousness.

I can still enter the state by recalling the moment the event first transpired, but I can't hold it for any length of time and I am not even sure it *should* be held for any length of time. I do know it certainly trampled my belief about what was and what was not possible within the ranges of sight and sound, and I was reminded that at any moment, all I have experienced heretofore about reality may be only a light brush against all the possibilities available to Life and to Beinghood.

We can understand, then, that not only do we perceive visual data indirectly via electrochemical transforms, but the Unconscious can also project certain inner images onto the screen of reality so we experience those images as real, though there is no external stimulus to account for what we see. While we are dreaming, we don't question the reality of what we are dreaming or the fact that we respond to that reality. While dreaming, we certainly don't sense the dream images as a conjuring of our Unconscious. We sense them as real. When we appreciate the power of the psyche to create dream images, we should not be surprised that the Unconscious can cause objects to appear to exist in our external reality.

This capacity of the mind to project and not just to be a receiver of stimuli from the outside is very important to consider when one is evaluating evidence of unusual sightings, whether of flying saucers, aliens, or religious figures, such as the Madonnas that are seen by small numbers of children in Eastern Europe today. Indeed, if an experience, whether physical or metaphysical, seems to contradict our conventional understanding, we should approach it with healthy skepticism. But we should also be cautious not to dismiss such things just because they happen not to meet our personal criteria for what's real.

All of this points to the necessity of beginning the exploration of consciousness *with the unconscious aspects in mind*. We in the West have gone about as far in the exploration of consciousness—its conscious aspects and its unconscious aspects—as we have in the manned exploration of the universe. We are only to the moon! Likewise, I feel we are in the very early stages of sensing the Self and the possible realities we can engage.

Because dream images can be generated from dimensions of consciousness that are not primarily influenced by outer reality, anyone who has gained the ability to interpret dreams knows the awesome advantage they provide when Self-Realization and wisdom are desired. Dreams are like looking at an incredibly detailed and often complex blueprint of one's individual makeup, with emphasis on patterns that are presently active or are going to be activated. Dreams reveal the selves that dance our lives at both the unconscious and conscious levels. Dreams are a threshold to understanding universal principles of Life in general, and they have collective as well as individual significance.

Dreams present to us, in image form, an awareness of the forces that make up a dimension of our being larger than just the outer mind. To really fathom the importance of dreams, a major shift in consciousness is required. We must cease regarding the outer mind and our usual day-to-day states of consciousness as primary and begin to experience the outer mind and outer reality as only a small part of who and what we are in our total Beingness. From this perspective, all experiences—whether dreams, fantasies, visions, feelings, thoughts, or sensory impressions (sight, sound, taste, smell, and touch)—seem to reflect the deeper nature of our Self and its aspects.

In approaching dream interpretation, then, we want to become familiar with the forces *behind* the images, since the images themselves are only vehicles that carry the deeper intention of the dream material.

It is important to understand clearly that the images are not a literal/rational representation of reality. They are symbolic of forces in tension, in relationship . . . forces that make up the vaster aspects of the individual and the collective to which he or she belongs. Dream images may represent organ systems dialoguing with one another. They may represent one part of the psyche expressing and experiencing another part. They may be revealing ancient/future patterns that Life requires us to dance for its purposes, in regard to which no personal gain to the dreamer may be involved. Dream images may be interacting with no other purpose than for creative expression, or they may be expressing an attempt to balance the overall makeup of forces within the individual and have little to do with the outer sense of self. As Carl Jung suggested, dreams may be the conscious mind of the Unconscious.

Every force can be represented in the conscious mind as an image, though what we are calling forces are not things in and of themselves. They represent *intentions* and *inclinations* of an underlying Mystery. The image, then, is related to the intention or the inclination behind the force and is not an exact equivalent of the force. *The effects we see as images are not the generating forces themselves.* What these forces actually are is unknown.

The action of forces can be experienced in a number of ways—as needles moving on a gauge, numbers flashing on machines . . . or images in our minds. For example, whenever forces that intend healing or harmonizing in an individual come forth, the dreamer may experience them in any and all objects that could represent healing to that individual or to the collective to which he or she belongs. The healing intention may take the form of a flower, a green grassy meadow, a tender and compassionate woman, a circular shape (regardless of what the actual object is, such as a hat, a Frisbee, a circular rainbow, a round dish on a table, the sun, a magic circle, etc.), a Christ figure, an East Indian Guru, chicken soup, or the mending of a fence. The possibilities are unlimited. The intention remains the same and is eternal, while its expression may take myriad forms.

This is why one cannot learn the art of dream interpretation as if it were a cooking lesson. One must be able to read the *intention of the images* and not get lost in the many ways the Unconscious can represent its inclinations and intentions.

Witnessing Our Dreams

While I am discussing dreams and their importance, I want to stress that the deep psyche, which produces the dreams, is a master of balance and integration. If we recognize that we are much more than we understand at the outer levels of consciousness, then we can see that the forces experienced in dreams may reflect healing and balancing processes that never need reach the outer levels of our awareness, yet are profoundly important to the overall Beingness.

I remind the reader of this again because some dreamwork tends to go back into the dream awareness and change the forces of the dream so the outcome is more satisfactory to the outer mind. But I believe no one should change a dream image or pattern, no matter what the implication of the dream to the outer mind may be. "Lucid dreaming," a state of consciousness wherein one can have some volitional control over dream states, is a specific example of such ego-controlled activity. However, if the ego is not primary or even close to being the most important aspect of our Beingness, then we certainly don't want to give it access to arenas in regard to which it knows nothing and where it may actually do harm to our whole Beingness.

Just as the body seeks to maintain itself for the purposes the body serves in Life, so does the psyche do the same. Just as the body is in relationship to a larger environment and to other bodies, so, too, is the deep psyche or larger consciousness in relationship to a larger environment, to forces beyond the individual in both space and time.

We must recognize this and not attempt to be manipulative or controlling in areas about which we have virtually no knowledge.

Learning to appreciate the Unconscious and its solutions to problems—its way of handling circumstances and events, particularly as revealed through dreams—is a part of spiritual maturation. This appreciation cannot be based in the value system of the outer mind or egoistic aspects. It must be based in a transpersonal realization that the Mystery Play of Life unfolds in ways beyond the understanding of our ego and, in fact, may call for our particular combination of forces to serve Life in a manner that is not ego-enhancing. The Mystery Play may even call for self-sacrifice and personal death.

The best example of this was presented by my friend David Spangler during a dialogue he and I were having in front of the participants at one of our annual five-day year-end residential retreats. As we were discussing the subject of surrendering to Spirit, surrendering to the Force that directs the Unfoldment of life, David pointed out that when we do so to serve Spirit, we may be asked to become the blade of grass on which the storm troopers' boots walk!

In dreams, we are interacting with forces that only partially reflect the personal aspects of the individual, and to an even lesser degree the outer senses of individual self. Thus, dream analysis involves an appreciation of the deeper inclination of the psyche as it creatively attempts to handle the many selves and their forces within the individual, as well as the forces of the external world and all that implies. One can best deal with the Unconscious, as it is reflected in dreams, by taking the perspective of *an impersonal witness* to a most profound Play, wherein the purpose of the observer is only to appreciate the psyche as it creatively dances the immortal patterns of human existence.

Because the psyche does not operate entirely in time and space, dreams can also be precognitive as to the outcome of conflicts engaged by the outer mind and by the body. Thus, dreams are not only illuminating but also predictive, and we can gain value from them if we have the courage to see dreams—and ourselves—with impartiality.

In every residential Conference I conduct, we devote nearly two hours of each day to the exploration of dream material. This process is so fundamental and revealing, such a truly honest and candid revelation about any individual, that I could not even consider approaching psychological and spiritual development in my work with the persons who study with me without assessing their dreams.

How to Fuse with a Dreamer

Another major aspect of my approach to dream interpretation is more difficult for most people to appreciate and to acquire as a technique. It is *the capacity to begin a fusion with the person who is dreaming*. This calls on the intuitive ranges of consciousness and requires a change in vehicles of consciousness. If I don't change aspects of awareness when someone is telling me a dream, the dream is often perplexing and confusing . . . and may seem to border on gibberish. My ordinary sense of self cannot interpret dreams and certainly cannot "fuse" psychically nor psychologically with another individual. The Dream Interpreter self can.

This ability cannot be taught through words or techniques. It can, however, be inducted in others by a Teacher who is in that state of consciousness. This is how the skill is passed on in all Mystery Training. The Teacher enters the state of consciousness with which the student wishes to become familiar. Then, through being in a quiet, meditative, open, receptive state of consciousness, the student soon begins to find that he or she can enter the same state. This experience, of course, transcends any conventional learning techniques in which dream interpretation might be taught through an intellectual association of images with their presumed meanings.

What most beginners fail to understand is that *an image is only the representation of a force, which itself is the vehicle of an intention*. When that same image appears in another person's dream or in another dream by the same person, the beginner who depends on image-meaning associations will recall the previous interpretation and erroneously assume that the image in the new dream has the same meaning it did before.

These brief comments about approaching the Unconscious

through working with the meaning of dreams will, at the very least, help prepare the individual for a deep, rich, lifelong encounter with his or her own unconscious aspects. If, at this stage, the meaning of a dream eludes the dreamer, he or she should write down or voice-record the dream for later consideration. The dreams should be recorded in one form or another anyway, as there is a tendency to forget or to distort material that is dreamed. As the experience I recounted in Chapter 1 suggests, there are some dreams I wrote down as many as forty-one years ago that have only recently taken on meaning and significance for me.

Projections onto the Screen of Reality

A most illuminating technique for discovering some of the nonego-enhancing aspects of the Unconscious in oneself involves observing one's reactivity to people, events, and other aspects of the outer world. The principle is simple . . . the amount of *reactivity* that is psychologically experienced by any individual reflects the degree to which the reactive material, thought to be external to self, exists and is active at the unconscious level within the reacting individual.

Through the unconscious mechanism of projection, the deep psyche causes aspects of our larger Beingness (which are often unacceptable to the ego) to appear to be either subjective truths or to be features of what we call the outer world, the "real" world. We are not aware that the projection of our own inner material has taken place. We think the outer events *are as we sense them to be*, not realizing that we have distorted the appearance of outer reality through unconscious forces that influence our perception of the events.

This phenomenon is actually an example of the operation of the principle of correspondence. When a pattern of forces is active in the Unconscious of an individual, and outer reality contains an event, person, or action that even remotely resembles that pattern, the individual will "project" the unconscious pattern onto the outer reality. This can obviously create a distortion in the perception of outer reality of which the individual is unaware, which explains why different people often describe the same event in very different ways.

Attorneys take great advantage of individual subjective interpretation of outer events when they construe reality in a way that is most advantageous to their clients. When presenting arguments in favor of a client, a defense attorney knows the client's innocence or guilt is not at issue. What matters is whether a jury's reality system and the witness's reality system can be influenced to favor acquittal. The opposite holds true for the prosecuting attorney. What is experienced as reality by the jury and by the witnesses is not necessarily what happened in actual reality.

The pointing finger is a great way to remind the outer self that an unconscious projection is operating. It is an Oriental insight, thousands of years old. Whenever you catch yourself pointing an accusing finger at anything or anyone—whether it be the apartheid government of South Africa, the issues of nuclear power or weaponry, the way someone dresses or behaves, or how you feel about an adult who sexually abuses children—the hand that is pointing has only one finger pointing *out there*, while it has three fingers pointing *back at you!* This awareness is most appropriate, as the real struggle with the material is predominantly at the unconscious levels of your very own nature . . . and thus beneath your conscious awareness. The reactivity is a consequence of your defending against your unconscious knowledge that the very thing you are pointing at, what you think is so terrible *out there*, is, in fact, a powerful characteristic, impulse, or pattern *in you*, which will most likely display itself from time to time in your own life. And while you remain unaware of what is really going on, the psychic energy you expend for defense and for projection is unavailable for psychological and spiritual transformation.

When developing Self-Realization through withdrawing projected material off the screen of life, we appreciate why Sages refer to outer reality as the mirror of the interior. Everything that is experienced as *out there* has equivalents interiorly. However, once we can catch ourselves in the act of doing the very thing or taking the very action for which we criticize others, we begin to acquire a quality of consciousness that allows us to see reality in a way that is relatively free of distortion. Doing this is often not easy, however, and significant psychological maturity is required for us to take on the knowledge of the rejected aspects of ourselves. Friends, family, lovers, and co-workers are usually more aware of some of our nonego-enhancing aspects than we are.

Most people who seek to hasten the processes of Self-Realization by becoming aware of reactive feelings—of how they respond to projections onto the world of their unresolved and disowned aspects—are shocked to discover that the degree of their projection is far greater than they initially thought. Again, Life mirrors our interior realities.

Rage and Compassion: The Flaw in the Doctor's Facade

To give an example of projection and the importance of understanding its unconscious dynamics, I offer the following personal experience. When I was Director of Medical Education at the Hospital of the Good Samaritan in Los Angeles, my task involved helping to organize and conduct training programs for medical interns and residents. Having had impeccable training as a physician, I had very high standards and expected each physician-in-training to be similarly dedicated to quality care and to the well-being of every patient.

Early one morning, I received a call at home from an intern who said a twenty-three-year-old woman had been admitted to the hospital bleeding rapidly from the rectum. He had fluids pouring into her and had ordered ample blood to be typed and cross-matched. The surgeons had been alerted. I told him I would be at the hospital in half an hour.

When I met the young physician at the hospital, he began the training ritual outside the patient's room. That ritual involves the presentation of the history and the physical findings, and an indication of the working diagnosis as well as the plan of the diagnostic workup and treatment. Nothing in the history gave us an indication as to the cause of the bleeding, and his report of the physical findings was essentially negative, including a negative pelvic and rectal examination. My job was to verify what he had reported.

We entered the room, where two nurses were pumping in fluids and blood. The young patient was ashen, frightened . . . bordering on shock. I began my physical examination while verifying the history, which was essentially as the intern had reported. There had been a sudden onset of rapid bleeding of bright red blood via the rectum over the previous three to four hours.

The physical examination was normal except for evidence of blood loss and the consequent changes in blood pressure, heartbeat, and respiration. At this point I told the patient that since the intern had reported the pelvic and rectal examinations to be negative, I wouldn't put her through those two procedures again. Her eyes widened and she said weakly. "He didn't do a pelvic and rectal examination."

I felt a welling up of anger . . . the deep, smoldering kind. *The intern had lied to me.* He had actually breached the trust that two physicians must have when dealing with life-and-death situations. I could already see the "discussion" the two of us were going to have when we left the room. I called for the speculum and rectal glove.

The pelvic examination was negative, but when I performed the rectal examination, my finger encountered an abnormality in the rectum. The diagnosis was evident. The woman had a rectal tumor, most likely malignant, which was bleeding profusely. Now I was really mad. It was the kind of righteous anger you experience when you have caught someone red-handed. Not only had the intern lied to me, but he had also neglected to perform the most basic physical examination procedure required on a gastrointestinal bleeder. He had risked the life of a critically ill young woman, and I was going to annihilate him! I felt he didn't deserve to have the title of physician. A letter from me in his file would preclude his ever getting any appointments to the staff of a good hospital. In a very shaky voice, as I was attempting to control my rage, I asked him to meet me in my office in forty-five minutes. The woman was rushed to surgery.

I was so angry that I decided to take the stairs rather than the elevator so I could ventilate some of the energy I was feeling. On the stairs, a calmer inner voice entered my mind, saying the situation was not all that bad, but it was countered by an almost delicious rage and anger that was going to destroy the career of the intern. After all, ranted my very, very reactive self, he had broken a sacred covenant and jeopardized the life of a young woman.

My reputation was that of a fair-haired, golden boy of medicine. Not only were my credentials impeccable, but so also was my handling of patients, which left little doubt as to how I—the Medical Director of Education—should handle this intern. I should simply make sure he didn't ever get too close to patients and recommend that he go into research.

After about fifteen minutes of fuming, I decided my reaction was excessive and not warranted by the events, despite the undeniable and obvious errors committed by the intern. I calmed myself through meditative techniques and began to analyze the pattern that had been configurated in the patient's room. It involved an emergency, jeopardizing the life of an individual, deceit, deception, and the breaking of the trust between physicians. Over and over again I examined the pattern, trying to discover the hidden material in my own Unconscious that was being mirrored back to me by these events. Just when I thought I was getting to a wisp of a feeling to which the events might be related, I would experience the rage and anger and want to pick up the Dictaphone and destroy the intern.

Then suddenly I exclaimed, "Oh my God!" . . . for I knew where this material was inside of me. I remembered an evening during my training as a fourth-year medical student in the emergency room of the Los Angeles County Hospital, when I had been overwhelmed with the evaluation and disposition of eleven horrific cases. The requirements were that I do complete histories and physicals and write up the cases for the records. Being in a situation beyond my capacities, I simply invented most of the patient responses, made up diagnoses, and shipped the patients to whatever department seemed most likely to be able to handle them. God only knows whether the patients survived these evaluations and dispositions.

The next morning I presented the cases I had "evaluated," using the information I invented. Because I was one of the top students in my class, no one questioned me closely, and my evaluation was accepted at face value. In other words, *I was not caught.* Such a transgression of medical ethics was incompatible with the image I presented to my professors and to my peers. But, most important in terms of this example, *it was incompatible with the image I presented to myself and defended as being my self!* Flaw, deceit, and the jeopardizing of life were not parts of the ideal physician mask I was wearing.

As I recalled this incident, my anger and rage dissolved. I realized that the real issue lay inside of me and involved my confronting and accepting the material that had lurked in my deeper awareness for over a decade. What lurked there, however, was not guilt. Rather, it was an awareness of my deception and irresponsibility, an awareness I had disowned. Although being deceptive and irresponsible had rescued me from losing face during a time of development when I was not mature enough to handle the overwhelming circumstances, I had not dealt with the humiliation that accompanied them . . . until the intern's behavior triggered my excessive reactivity. I could now appreciate how to handle him without feeling the need to do to him what I had unconsciously wanted to do to myself. I heard a quiet knock at my office door. The forty-five minutes had passed.

I am sure the intern thought I had a multiple personality, for I welcomed him into my office warmly, with an attitude that was the equivalent of throwing a friendly arm over his shoulder. I asked him to sit down. We began to chat about the circumstances that occurred, as I assured him I knew how he must feel and said I doubted he would ever again forget to perform a rectal or pelvic examination on a gastrointestinal bleeder.

Everything was moving smoothly and competently when I began to observe that I was still protecting my mask of the flawless physician. The intern was vulnerable to me and, for the rest of his life, would have to handle the consequences of knowing I was aware of his deception and flaws as a physician. He would, for a long time, be intensely self-critical because he couldn't or didn't meet the standard I held before him—deceptively.

It was then that the true healing of my own immaturity took place. I revealed to the intern that I had been involved with the same kind of deception and breach of medical ethics as a fourth-year medical student, when many more critical patients than just one were involved. I just hadn't been caught. I was now as vulnerable to him as he was to me.

In the forty-five minutes it took me to come to a deeper self-understanding, the courses of two individuals' lives were permanently altered. He went on to be an excellent clinical physician. I was maturing.

I present this story as an example of how unconsciously held material can cause eruptive and even destructive action to be taken—all under the guise of right and moral action. Actually, the real culprit is the hidden material about oneself and the fact that a conscious vehicle is not capable of accepting what has been revealed.

De-struction, Con-struction

The present concern about whales, gorillas, rain forests, elephants, and so on all bespeaks of unresolved material surrounding death. I am not suggesting that the personal levels do not have the right to feel as they do about the plight of anything. The real issue is that the personal level rarely, if ever, fully understands the contribution of the Unconscious to the outer concerns. As David Spangler once said, "Maybe the whales have a yearning to die at this time." Being able to deal with the Mystery of coming into existence and of releasing life into death is a maturational development that our society, still acting out childhood naïveté, refuses to encompass. When the issue of death is integrated, we might have a better chance to make wisdom choices rather than only partially informed rational choices about whatever may be troubling us.

Several billion years ago, an event took place on earth that is reported to have destroyed over 90 percent of all life forms then present. It was so devastating as to have made the contemporary destructive potentials of humanity seem tame and quite manageable by comparison. The event was the appearance of plant life that produced oxygen. Prior to that time, almost no life on earth used oxygen as a source of energy. In fact, oxygen was (and still is) a very toxic substance. Most people don't realize that breathing 100 percent oxygen for more than a few hours can injure the lung tissue and actually destroy it if prolonged for a few days.

Although the production of oxygen destroyed most of the world's life forms, new forms appeared that could handle the oxygen production of the plants. Our life form is one that developed because of the "tragedy."

In fact, most authorities generally agree that only about 2 percent of all life forms that have ever been present on the earth survived the creative processes of the planet. Ninety-eight percent have entirely vanished, and some of them were here for hundreds of millions of years before becoming extinct. In every Ice Age, of which we have passed through at least seven, with the last one ending approximately twenty thousand years ago, all of the oxygen-producing forests of the more northern and more southern latitudes, as well as billions upon billions of life forms, were destroyed as ice accumulated and spread toward the tropical zones, yet the oxygen concentration did not seem to change significantly. Why? And is the attempted preservation of the rain forests of Brazil either necessary or altruistic? Are there unconscious motives to parent so-called primitive human cultures rather than encouraging them to creatively adapt to the evolving world? We are a creation of Life. And it has certainly happened before that Life has created a life form that sets the stage for mass destruction and for what lies beyond such destruction.

Love, Light, and Rage: Fury at Findhorn

Returning now to the phenomenon of projection, we are confronted by a profound question: What *is* out there if the projection is removed? The question becomes even more important if we are engaged in an attempt to change the world before we have a deeper appreciation of what the world may actually be. Discovering the answer requires decades of inner work, for we must learn to see outside of ourselves and our own material, a process that is accomplished by constantly pulling back projections, whether we are experiencing great beauty and great good or great ugliness. In the meantime, we must realize that if unconscious forces and dynamics are controlling the way we view the world, our parents, our children, our boss, the government, nuclear bombs, and war (to cite only a few significant areas of concern), perhaps the view we are taking of what we wish to change is not accurate. Perhaps it is distorted due to unresolved and conflicted value systems at the unconscious level in ourselves. Perhaps what we see is a function of a psychological set or habitual way of viewing reality and doesn't reflect what is actually present. This is true at the individual level, and it is true at the collective cultural level. If we don't recognize that our sense of reality is skewed, we are simply blind people leading other blind people, unaware that the basic issues which disturb us so profoundly are those of *our own inner people* and *our own inner world!*

Finally, then, we shall see that what is "out there," rather than being what we thought it was, or feared it was, is really the mysterious dance of Life, and that the world and the people in it are no different from that which exists in the Unconscious of every person and every collective.

With all of this in mind, I would like to relate an experience I had on a return visit to Findhorn, in Northern Scotland, the New Age community I first visited on my initial journey into the world following my leaving the practice of orthodox medicine.

After I wrote *Joy's Way*, I worked intensely for two more years conducting Conferences before I permanently left Sky Hi Ranch in California to begin a year of spiritual retreat. To hold the final Conference of that period, I returned to Scotland, near Findhorn. The Conference participants were a group of Americans who had traveled there with me.

When I first visited the community in 1975, I was just beginning to explore the possibility of training individuals to feel the energies that radiate from the body and to be able, themselves, to transfer energy into another person's body for purposes of physical healing and psychological balance.

The Findhorn community at that time was youthful and very much under the influence of the Divine Parent/Divine Child energetics. When I was asked to give an impression of what I felt was to transpire in the immediate future for the community as a whole, I said I sensed that a forthcoming vast influx of people would bring with them the danger that the innate "soul" of the community might be diluted, by their numbers and by the business concerns to which they would have to attend. I was a welcome guest. The community generally loved my talk.

Five years later, I was again asked to talk to them about what I sensed was ahead for the community as a whole. This talk followed the two-week Conference, subsequent to which each participant was to enter the communal life of Findhorn, and to do so with heightened awareness. The participants were not tourists or just visitors. They had been prepared to experience the full range of the community's life, including what is not ordinarily seen upon the first approach: its dark side.

When I shared my then current impressions at one of the community's evening gatherings, I presented a different picture from before . . . and a difficult one. I said that the forthcoming period was to be a time for contraction and for the release of physical assets. The community had enjoyed a phase of increase and abundance, but the counterphase of that cycle was approaching. Best to prepare for it ahead of time, I said.

I talked about the consequences of feeling "special" and how doing battle against the "evils of the world" not only creates the "enemy," but is actually a projection of the darker aspects of the community onto the world screen. Needless to say, the talk was not popular and I was fast falling into the "unwelcome guest" category. I would soon be seen as whatever was unresolved in the community at the unconscious level. In other words, I would be viewed as carrying the shadow-side of the community, and I knew it!

When we attempt to deny what *is*, to deny such things as the natural cycles of time and space, enormous energy is required. That energy is then not available as a resource for other activities. In this case, the denial by the vast majority of the members of the community of anything that threatened their external values and beliefs was evident. The wisdom of recognizing both expansion and contraction was not part of the general belief system of the Findhorn community, as it is not part of the New Age thought process in general. Despite assertions by most partisans of the New Age that they are promoting such virtues as selfless service to the world, New Age beliefs in the specialness and innocence of the New Age are, in my opinion, regressive . . . toward the infantile, if not the fetal. Such ideation tends to be self-centered . . . concentrating, for example, on images that ignore the contribution of the destructive.

Near the end of this communal post-Conference living experience with the Findhorn community, an evening of sharing and entertainment was at hand. As I was on my way into the meeting hall, the community poet aggressively approached me. I had already had one brief encounter with him a few days earlier when he asked if I would talk to his students, and I declined. Now he was filled with rage and anger. I thought he was going to hit me, but instead he hissed something about what he was going to present in the hall that evening. I began to center myself.

The first part of the evening's entertainment consisted of amusing skits and some singing. Then the community poet came on. He caught my eye . . . and I knew I was to be his sacrifice. In venomous poetry, powerful and afire with wrathful righteousness, he unleashed the dark feelings and destructive forces of the community. The objects of his rage were the Americans in general and myself in particular. We were portrayed in terms that would make fecal material seem sunny by comparison. His attack centered around money and power . . . the dark side of any endeavor that wears the mask of great good and service. The only thing explicitly missing was sex, except he covered that by using the words "fuck" and "fucking" with an extraordinary frequency.

The function of poets is to give voice to the collective. When the content is infantile rage and resentment that has been disowned—and how natural for such to exist in a community that perceives itself only as manifesting love and light—an object must be found to carry the unconscious forces. Through the mechanism of projection, destructive energies were unleashed that night without the participants' having to accept that the forces of contempt and jealousy were not only within the poet but also within the community itself. By his projecting this material onto me and the other Americans, he was actually promoting a healing or balancing of the unconscious forces of the community. However, it would have been better for all concerned had the community been further along in the process of owning the dark side of its nature . . . but that isn't how things transpired that evening. For me, as long as I recognized that his accusations did, in fact, have their counterpart in me and I owned them consciously, I would be able to remain centered and could also appreciate that an eruption of long-held unconscious shadow content of the community was at hand.

While the poet continued his volcanic outpouring of dark emotions, the community as a whole was displaying a wide range of reactivity. Some people called for him to stop. Some began to cry and leave the room. Others were elated that someone had the courage to state what many were feeling. Some began to defend the Americans and the American way of life. Some were humiliated and embarrassed, looking to me to defend myself or the others, or to do something about what was occurring. I encouraged the poet to continue, thinking he couldn't have too much more to ventilate . . . but he did!

He continued for another fifteen to twenty minutes before Eileen Caddy, one of the founders of the community, asked him to stop. He did, and moved out of the room almost gleefully. The community gathered around those who organized the evening's events to console them and to share an embrace of love and nourishment through touch.

I had never been involved in a public attack of that magnitude. My resources for centering and becoming transparent to the assailing forces—for being able to find that place in consciousness where there is no need to defend from the content of the attack—were nearly depleted.

Becoming transparent to accusations does not mean parts of oneself do not feel hurt, humiliated, angry, and defensive. It means realizing what is actually transpiring and not going unconscious or falling victim to one's own disowned material. I knew the shadow of the community was erupting and I was the mirror. I also recognized that those forces and qualities which were being attacked were parts of myself as well. For me, this was a huge leap in maturation. I was being initiated into those collective arenas of consciousness where one handles the unconscious projections not just of one individual or a few individuals but of a large collective, in this case an entire community.

Projecting onto Leaders

I have often wondered how presidents of the United States handle mass projections, when over 250 million people unconsciously project disowned shadow content onto their leadership. How does a president handle this? A good case in point was the sacrifice of Richard Nixon for the public good. The unconscious forces behind the sacrifice were the disowned individual and collective capacities to deceive, to lie, to cover up. This dark counterpart image of self is too disturbing to individual and collective masks of morality and goodness. In other words, all the reactive accusations against President Nixon were also America's own dark side, which, in the case of a president, were too close to senses of public self-identity for us to tolerate. The social immune mechanism was activated and the perceived threat was disposed of. Few people survive such a collective sacrifice. They die in grief and humiliation or alienation. Richard Nixon did survive, and I admire him for this.

To recognize the capacity of any collective to sacrifice individuals (or other collectives) in order to defend itself against its own unconscious forces is a shocking social insight. For instance, if we want to know what the dark side of America is, all we have to do is to ask what country and what system of government we do not tolerate at all or tolerate the least. Up would pop the Union of South Africa and, until recently, the Soviet Union. To help understand the fact that the projection of collective shadow content is behind these feelings and attitudes, all one needs to do is go to these very same countries and ask the people there what they think of America and Americans. Up pop all the unconscious and disowned aspects of that collective, projected out onto us!

One reason for world travel is to see and hear in new ways what we ourselves may actually be—something that is not possible when we just stay within our own country. But if we are working on collective Self-Realization, we don't need to ask other countries to reveal our dark side. It becomes evident the moment we drop the denials and get uncomfortably honest. Which country carries the dark side for the Soviet Union? We do! Isn't it fascinating? Two unbelievably powerful countries, each capable of total destruction of the planet, unconscious of the Unconscious . . . and each still projecting out disowned aspects and defending against each other when the only real enemy is actually interior. Remarkably, as we are now engaging in warmer relations with the Soviet Union, we are in danger of losing the mirror to our unconscious collective aspects. On second thought, however, no matter. Our collective psyche will find a new enemy to contain the forces the Soviet Union once held for us.

Reading Cards and Clouds

Not only does projection provide a way for us to examine aspects of our personal and collective nature that have been disowned, but it allows us to inquire of the Unconscious for the purpose of embracing expanded viewpoints or acquiring wisdom in our search for personal and collective Self-Realization.

The Tarot is particularly noteworthy as a path to Self-Realization because, after one has explored the personal unconscious aspects of Self as they are revealed by one's projections onto the cards, other amazing insights are seen to be available. Since the Unconscious has access to time and space relationships the outer consciousness does not have, one can use the cards to experience realizations about the deeper psyche of others, the world, and the universe that transcend the relatively narrow space and time limits of the outer mind.

After having explained the material I presented in Chapter 7 involving the cloud-reading capacities of Hawaiian Kahunas, I sometimes ask participants in my workshops to read the clouds themselves, when the weather makes that possible. The approach that seems to work the best involves their entering a quiet, meditative state of consciousness, posing a question to the Unconscious, then opening their eyes and looking at the various clouds until an intuitive "zing" attracts them to a particular cloud or pattern of clouds. The associations around the shape of the cloud or the feelings they have about the cloud pattern either suggest or directly provide the answer to the question they posed. I have been astonished how the Unconscious can use patterns in the external world to reveal information that it, the Unconscious, has gathered from interior resources.

As an example of the diversity of possibilities that can emerge from the projection of inner material, I will conclude this chapter with an example of projected shadow content that would seem positive and enhancing to most Westerners of Christian orientation, yet represented dark, disowned material in the mind of the individual who experienced it. And though we have been speaking about projection of the Unconscious onto outer screens, we can recognize that the same phenomenon takes place when the Unconscious projects onto interior screens, as in dreams, visions, and vivid images that appear during meditation. The following example reflects the latter category.

During one of my one-week residential healing Conferences, a woman who had been extensively involved with Buddhism and the religions of the East, and who had been extremely resentful of her early Christian upbringing (feeling she had been manipulated by her parents and by the Church), was using the Sacred Temple by the Sea meditation to experience images generated by her Unconscious. Following a morning's meditation, she reported that while she was in her Temple, she requested help from her Unconscious in regard to some personal concerns. She was shocked when an angel appeared and announced that her name was Veronica and that she had come to help the woman. If this inner image had been that of a Bodhisattva, a Buddha, a Tibetan monk, Quan Yin, or an East Indian Saint, the woman would neither have been surprised nor so upset. But a Christian angel? This was the very last possibility she would have expected.

Whenever a person reports an experience that is completely opposite from his or her outer preferences, the experience can invariably be trusted as an honest revelation of the person's Unconscious. This is particularly true when the person is reactive to the content, as was the case here. The woman said simply, "I don't believe in angels. Too Christian." But the information Veronica related to her was very helpful and healing, so she was unable to deny the experience completely.

A few days later, this same woman—who had already made it clear through various comments that she did not appreciate Jesus one bit—was doing the Sacred Temple meditation when she became aware that Christ was in her temple. In her imagery during the meditation, she ran from the Temple, upset that a Christian spiritual figure was desecrating her sacred place! But moments later in the same meditation, her angel, Veronica, appeared and reassured her that it was indeed Christ and that the Christian tradition was to be the present and future pathway for her spiritual Unfoldment. At that moment, her defenses to the eruption of her own dark and disowned material dissolved. When this woman shared her meditation experience with the group, she was radiant, uplifted, and spiritually transfigured. We all were moved to tears.

CHAPTER NINE

EXPERIENCING THE UNCONSCIOUS: OTHER PATHWAYS

In the previous chapter we concentrated on approaching the unconscious aspects of Self through the interpretation of dreams and through understanding the psychological process of projection—two great pathways into the Unconscious. This chapter presents other significant pathways that can allow us to access and appreciate material in the Unconscious.

Doing the Opposite of What We Think We Ought to Be Doing

One disturbing way we encounter certain unconscious aspects of our own Beingness is through the experience of having made up our mind that we are not going to do something—overeat, smoke cigarettes, drink alcohol, snort cocaine, watch television, take sleeping medications, drink diet beverages, engage in casual sex ... all of the usual New Year's resolutions, large and small—then observing ourselves do exactly what we said we wouldn't do!

From the perspectives we are exploring in this book, we needn't postulate possession or the influence of some demonlike entity, although we may feel as if there is an unruly demon inside. We simply have to remind ourselves that there are more selves to our Self than just the "self" we know about. When we have not taken these other selves into consideration, particularly those which are not in accord with our "New Year's resolution" self (which can be overly moral and overly disciplined), we begin to find out how powerful they can be.

If the dominant unconscious aspects do not wish to participate in what the conscious mind is undertaking, they will undermine and eventually thwart any attempt, any vow, any resolution, any determination to change. In such a situation, our best course of action is to observe what is being satisfied through the undisciplined and unacceptable activity. It may be nourishment needs, sublimated sexuality, punishment and redemption dynamics, or self-rejection patterns, to mention but a few of the unconscious forces that operate in every individual to some degree. Always, and I do mean always, there will be a Child or an Infant self that seeks immediate emotional, sexual, or physical gratification, and this self—which is far deeper and more powerful than the usual outer sense of self—will be usurping the desires of the conscious self in order to satisfy its own desires.

We should remember that these are *unconscious* aspects, operating independently, having a life of their own, and seeking fulfillment regardless of what the rational, outer areas of consciousness have to say or to recommend. This, then, offers us some idea as to why many of our resolves are, for the most part, destined for failure. We simply have not appreciated nor understood our fuller dynamics. To emphasize this point, I note that we cannot even remember our own name if the Unconscious does not want to deliver up that information.

We also need to remember that the unconscious selves involved in these processes are different from the neurological structures and functions that form the equipment through which both the conscious and the unconscious selves express. In contemporary computer language, the hardware—the neurological system—is not the same as the software—the patterns of the selves. In dealing with the inability to recall one's own name, the problem could indeed be due to a hardware deficit, but the problem I am addressing would be in the software and how the parts of the Self . . . the independent selves . . . are interacting with one another.

There is literally nothing the conscious self can make happen, either in the external world or in the internal world, without support from the larger community existing in the Unconscious. In fact, few of us would want to become aware of how really vulnerable and tenuous the conscious self and its feelings of power, autonomy, and control really are.

From self-observation as well as from observing hundreds and hundreds of individuals struggling with defiant, unconscious, selfdestructive selves, I have come to believe that these selves are usually activated when we fail to take action—when we fail to make necessary changes in our life; when we fail to give birth to a more mature self to handle the stage of life we are currently experiencing; or when we fail to begin appropriate, deeper Unfoldment that might bring us into more profound contact with Spirit and the ultimate Mystery of Beinghood.

Thus, like the demons of war, one's self-destructive aspects can serve to force change. They break up the ordinary life-styles, routing one into eventual chaos, suffering, and new possibilities—if one can survive the initiation. They can also orchestrate reality to bring about the fulfillment of deeply desired ends, even when that involves one's own death.

An anecdote illustrating this point was related to me by a close friend. His father, who was sixty-seven, had an abrupt onset of a hemorrhage from a duodenal ulcer. He was rushed to the hospital, where he was not evaluated by a physician for nearly twelve hours. Over the next week, every complication one could imagine transpired, culminating in fluid overload, cardiac failure, and pulmonary embolus, leading to death. In consideration of the incompetence of the physician and the mismanagement by the hospital, an exceedingly strong case could have been marshaled for suit. This was considered. But the underlying dynamics were all too evident to my friend and his family.

This man's life, following the death of his wife of forty-five years, had been filled with bouts of heavy drinking and near calamitous automobile accidents. He had no substantial positive images about the future. Despite his statements about wanting to enjoy life and to find a new relationship, his behavior reflected the opposite intent. My friend knew his father wanted to die, though he also recognized that his father was not conscious of this intention most of the time. The son could only marvel at how his father managed to pick people and places that "cooperated" so fully in his demise. The Unconscious is extraordinary in its capacity to orchestrate events in outer reality to achieve its ends.

Equally self-destructive inner selves (although not ordinarily sensed as such by either the individual or by the collective) are those which represent perfect models of what, according to religion and/ or society, one's life should be. From an expanded perspective, individuals being lived by these selves are essentially automatons who are deeply comatose and not even close to awakening into the greater possibilities of their Beinghood. They almost always accept society's values without a single reservation or question. As long as the conforming self does not move too far away from the supporting structure of the family and the society that propagate the value system, that individual will never know what has been missed or sacrificed in exchange for his or her being in the esteem of the parental forces— as those forces are reflected through the family, religion, or society itself.

What always lurks under such behavior is the need to be loved and accepted, an immense need to which all other possibilities that might undermine it are sacrificed . . . despite the fact that those other possibilities hold the promise of the person's engaging life in more fulfilling ways. Even if these individuals discover their self-sacrificing behavior and seek to express the fullness of their Beinghood, they are frequently overwhelmed by fears of rejection and loss of esteem. Their sense of interiorly based self-value and Self-value is so atrophic that little chance exists for them to make the needed leaps in development and maturation. They have sold their soul for love and acceptance.

Attempting to resolve the problem of a dominant Infant self through increased discipline of the outer awareness is the least effective course of action we can undertake. What is required, following self-observation to ascertain the needs that are being satisfied by the infantile patterning, is the activation of more mature unconscious aspects of Self to take charge of the psyche. This is different from the activation of a mature-appearing outer sense of self. The latter is superficial, while the former is substantial and transforming. The induction of more mature aspects of one's unconscious psyche is accomplished through applying material we have covered in previous chapters, and includes ritual, role modeling, and crisis.

Repeated Life Experiences

I can't count the number of times I have heard people relate their life story, then, after its basic patterns are called to their attention, discover their life is a constantly repeating sequence of events they are apparently helpless to change. This isn't true just for a few neurotics. It is true for anybody who cares or dares to engage pattern-level consciousness and "read" the material for herself or himself.

This is demonstrated most clearly and commonly when a person has had two or more marriages or long-term intimate relationships. Most people are shocked to find out that, in their first marriage, they married the pattern carried by their countergender parent. They will also *continue* to do so in subsequent marriages until the parent-child relationships in their Unconscious are made conscious, and other more mature aspects of the Self are birthed. These more mature or adult selves have far greater resources to engage the powerful forces manifested through the marital relationship.

My informal impression at this time is that in most, if not all, first marriages, both partners, at unconscious levels, have transferred the necessary incestuous bondings between the infant/child and the countergender parent to the marital partner. There may be other reasons for a relationship between two particular individuals, but if the initial aspects of the relationship included anything closely resembling "falling in love," the incestuous parental/child aspects are surely present.

I therefore call the first marriage the teaching marriage. We can, usually with the help of individuals who are experienced in the dynamics of the Unconscious, learn from the relationship and prepare to enter a richer possibility of marriage, either with the same partner or with a new partner. However, until the infantile aspect that is operating—usually unconsciously seeking the original mother or father—is integrated with a larger and more mature sense of Self (as distinct from a more mature outer sense of self), the forces that may eventually disrupt the first marriage will lead to a second attempt at marriage, with exactly the same infantile patterns operating, then this will be followed by a third marriage, and so on. All the while, the individual who is suffering the pain of these multiple failed relationships is thinking he or she is a mature adult, acting responsibly, and—completely unaware of the revolving-door dynamics—is bewildered by the turn of events in each marriage or relationship. When we realize how ignorant the partners in most marriages are of the unconscious aspects active in them, are we surprised that marriages today stand only a one-in-three chance of survival? In all likelihood, if the unconscious reasons for marriage were ever to be completely revealed, marriage, as we experience it in our culture, would collapse. Of course, whether we recognize it or not, this is what is already happening. A change in family structure is clearly under way, as our collective works creatively to adapt to a changing world and changing values. We may even be reactivating the process of collective child-rearing, doing so in ways beyond those presently being explored in our educational systems.

The pattern in which the child aspect of an adult attempts to marry his or her countergender parent makes sense to the outer mind when we realize how powerful and incestuous the original parent-child bondings are. For instance, the bonding of the mother with the son or of the father with the daughter often transcends the spousal relationship in depth and intensity! I have encountered situations where the true marriage was, psychologically speaking, between the parent and the offspring. When such unconscious incestuous dynamics exist, they are usually very difficult to access because of their forbidden or taboo quality. And so, since this kind of unconscious incestuous relationship is so completely disowned and denied by our society and because of the degree to which we abhor knowledge of it, we might suspect that it constitutes one of the most powerful unconscious individual and collective forces in our psyche. And it does . . . for reasons that are perfectly understandable when we consider the importance of procreation to Life.

When unhappy infantile selves are in charge of selecting a marital partner, the stage is set for the activation of powerful, unconscious, destructive forces within the marriage. For example, although our society tends to view children as innocent of highly destructive impulses, unintegrated childhood rage is probably the most common unconscious factor present in marital violence. There are individuals who, because of unconscious infantile rage usually directed at one parent, marry with the unconscious intention to punish that parent. The person's deeper psyche does not care that the marital partner is not the actual parent. It reads the *pattern* of the marital partner, and if it detects sufficient equivalence, it acts as if the partner is the parent and responds accordingly.

A rare but remarkable and formidable recurrent version of this pattern occurs in marital relationships wherein a partner experiences the death of two or more spouses, either through disease or accident. The statistical odds of an early death in a marital relationship are low, but when the death of a second or even third and fourth spouse occurs, the statistical odds are beyond anything close to mere chance, and an underlying pattern that dominates reality must be considered. In such cases, powerful and destructive unconscious patterns related to the selection of, relationship with, and ultimate demise of a marital partner often reveal themselves either in dreams or through projection. The person unconsciously intends to punish, and actually helps precipitate (at an unconscious level) the death of, the spouse. The deaths may be due to illness or they may be due to accidents. In either case, the dark child lurks in the partner who is unconsciously orchestrating the events surrounding the deaths. And from what I observe in Conference participants, the people who become the "victims" of such dark children are not innocent of what happens to them.

When the unconscious patterns that have produced multiple relationships or marriages are revealed and awareness of them is *accepted*, no matter how humiliating or infantile this material may be, the most miraculous possibility emerges—which is that the individual can begin the deeper journey of integration. He or she experiences a sense of euphoria and relief. The resolution does not come from *healing* the dark child. It lies in the full acceptance by the person of this dark aspect and of the part it plays in his or her life. A dominant, mature self then has the opportunity to appear and take up the mantle of living life, while the immature selves, though still present, become less active in the Unconscious.

This is the critical difference between therapeutic approaches that attempt to heal or to deny the disturbing aspect and those that recognize the importance of the disturbing aspect and integrate it into the larger sense of Self. The task of integrating destructive selves is vastly easier when we realize that these aspects are but patterns of forces, forever struck, eternal, dancing each generation from the distant past through the present and into the distant future ... part of the Mystery of Life ... part of the hand dealt, and they serve Life!

The Problem of the Many Selves in Marriage

In dealing with the larger implications and manifestations of a marital relationship, most of us are naive, still thinking we are but one gender ... the outer gender. But in the crucible of marriage and its crises, we can discover inner selves of both genders and of all ages, constructive and destructive. If we wish to begin to acknowledge which males and females exist within us unconsciously, all we have to do is look around and note those males and females who surround us in the outer world, for the outer conscious reality reflects the inner unconscious reality. This correspondence holds true everywhere, and will be especially noticeable in the family and in the workplace. Further, if we wish to see some of the less ego-enhancing male selves or female selves that exist in us at unconscious levels, all we have to do is describe the kind of men or women we simply cannot stand to be around. Doing this exercise is especially revealing, as we are able to see parts of the Self that are particularly difficult to associate with our ordinary, conscious sense of self.

While we are discussing marriage, we should examine the mechanism of falling in love and recognize that it is actually a projection of a beloved, unconscious *inner* countergender self. What appears to happen is that the individual who comes closest to this unconscious aspect of the Self suddenly becomes the One and Only, the Soul Mate, the Beloved, without whom one can scarcely consider living.

An unsettling revelation is that the countergender beloved carries a pattern of forces that any one of many, many individuals could also have matched. In other words, when the time comes to fall in love, the unconsciously held internal beloved is activated, and literally anybody who even remotely resembles this highly charged inner figure becomes the screen onto which we project the Beloved. No wonder we can wake up six weeks later, confused.

When we are in the grips of projecting a countergender beloved, there is no talking us out of our feelings. We feel as if the world has suddenly become magical and meaningful. We have a purpose and we feel alive! The mysterious process of the attraction and union of opposites is powerfully weaving its forces. And the potential resolution to the tension is to create a new life . . . in the form of a child and/or a sense of Adult wholeness centered in the marital relationship.

Adult is an interesting word. Although it has its roots in a Latin word that means "coming to maturity," I like thinking of it as a combination of *ad* (meaning "motion toward" or "nearness to") and *ult* (from the same root as the word "ultimate"). Thus: "near to or toward the ultimate." The mature or Adult self in a relationship, such as in a marriage, is capable of sacrificing the sense of independent self and the earlier Child and Adolescent selves in order to blend with the partner to form a union that transcends either partner's sense of self, a union that moves "toward the ultimate." One partner does not sacrifice to the other partner. Rather, in their experience together of life through the marital relationship, both give up their sense of independence to become something greater than either could be alone.

To compound our insights into the marital relationship, we must recognize that there are also aspects or selves in both partners that can, will, and ought to act independently of the marriage. What has come into being through the marriage is the added experience of oneness through shared creativity. What has not been brought about by the marriage is the loss of those selves in either partner that do not and cannot experience life through the marital blending. As we come to understand the unconscious and multitudinous aspects of Self in each person, I believe we will no longer attempt to control the destiny of individuals through requiring that marriage somehow be an avenue to total Self-expression and Self-fulfillment. From this perspective, we can appreciate how exceedingly unlikely it is for one man or one woman to find relationship fulfillment through the marriage partner alone.

I used to believe marriage had to be defined in terms of, among other things, sexual commitment to a single individual. If the sexual experience was not contained in the relationship, it wasn't a marriage. It was another kind of relationship, but it was not a marriage.

Now I have come to doubt that the human being is intrinsically monogamous. Monogamy feels to me like an ideal superimposed on reality or a defense against forces beyond the control of the rational and intellectual selves. Ample evidence exists that the human being functions very well in polygamous social settings. In societies such as those in Italy which have withdrawn civil sanctions against divorce, multiple sexual relationships are freely explored. Of course, these relationships were going on all the time anyway. Our mouths, under the control of the mind, say one thing while our bodies go right ahead and live the suchness of life.

I am further deepening my understanding of the mystery of marriage to the point of recognizing that a mature marriage may not have its basis in procreative sexuality at all. The sine qua non of a mature marriage is that the relationship be one wherein both partners surrender personal identity to the Beinghood that ensues from the blending of the two individuals. This is the outer form of the mystical marriage and is not contingent on the procreative aspect of either individual. Neither, in fact, is it contingent on the gender of the individuals.

This means that two men, two women, or a group of men or a group of women can enter a true marriage of the Spirit, one that may transcend the genital marriage ordinarily sanctioned by society. Any combination is possible. And within same-gender marriages, sexuality may or may not be part of the commitment toward a transcending union.

If this shocks people, they simply do not understand such things as the mystical marriage to Christ that both men and women enter into with the vows that are taken in nunhoods and priesthoods. Nor do they really fathom the mystical writings about the Beloved in either the Sufi tradition or in the Christian tradition. Similar situations are encountered in Brotherhoods and Sisterhoods, where a transcendental union of souls is experienced without the requirement for the explicit expression of the procreative forces at the genital level. Contemplating this entire phenomenon truly leads to one of the deepest mysteries a human being can encounter . . . the inner mystical marriage, or the union of the masculine and feminine forces of the Unconscious to produce a new transcendent Being . . . a single whole.

Other reasons for marriage may be those which involve the procreation of children . . . and nothing more. Or they may involve security needs and have little to do with children or sexuality. I know people who only wanted to beget children, to bear children, or to rear children, and who married the person who was nearest or most available for that purpose. Or other relationships, external to the legally sanctioned marriage, may actually involve the exploration of a mature experience of marriage, while the marriage itself satisfies unconscious infantile or adolescent patterns.

All the issues about loyalty in a marriage seem to me to be nothing more than mechanisms of control. It is often easier to "behave" than to assume the responsibility for one's greater Beinghood. Any time we find ourselves taking a special vow of total commitment, the Unconscious is certain to erupt at some later time in an attempt to balance what can never be balanced through such a vow. As powerful as guilt and sanctions are, the Unconscious will not tolerate those limitations to the expression of Life. All is well if the marriage actually does contain the patterns for fulfillment, but if the relationship is only one of several stagings, marriage can act as a trap rather than a threshold to later relationships. People die of cancer from such traps! This is particularly true when the individual lacks the maturity to move against the outer containment, if and when such containment becomes evident.

Obviously it is possible to have a genital relationship and a mature marriage with but one individual. This still does not mean that even a majority of the needs of both partners can be fulfilled within the marriage. It is also possible to have a mature marriage with one individual and, simultaneously, a genital relationship with another individual. What profound unhappiness occurs when we try to force our greater Beingness into little definitions of relationship and marriage.

Marriage *Is* a Spiritual Path

In great contrast to the perception I held but a few years ago—that marriage was an encumbrance to spiritual development—I now believe marriage to be one of the great paths to spiritual development and Self-Realization. At that time, I felt all individuals could and should access transcendental awakening along the lines followed by Spiritual Teachers, Gurus, Priests, and Priestesses. I felt that a person could not reach Spiritual Enlightenment while in a marriage. One would either not marry or would wait until the children had been raised before any degree of spiritualization could come about. This perspective represented an unconscious spiritual bias on my part . . . one embedded in esoteric teachings that defended against sexuality, emotionality, and physicalness. The moment I apprenticed myself to a most heretical teacher, Life, I recognized my previous position as having been a prejudice of the masculine psyche, the Illumined Mind.

I then considered the fact that advanced Teachers and Saints have been influencing the populations of India, China, the Middle East, and Europe for millennia. Still, despite the incessant turning of prayer wheels for thousands of years, the collective prayers of the faithful chanted at Easter and Christmas, and the arrival and departure of those held to be God . . . the fundamental patterns of life have renewed themselves from generation to generation. Little if any change in the basic nature of humanity has come about as a result of people being exposed to these heightened beings. Chaos comes and chaos goes. The Priestess/Priest-hoods maintain the same relative position and influence in the human social order they always have. The gods, the litanies, the chants, and the garments may change, but the relationship and significance of the Priestess/Priest-hoods to the totality of Life does not.

This is because the eternal spiritual aspects of Life lie behind all manifestation and all action. The unawakened and the awakened are both part of a larger Wholeness that cannot be seen through the separating filters of the rational, logical, intellectual consciousness. Those who don't spin the prayer wheels and those who do are both immortal aspects of the choreography of life. Together they reflect the Mystery . . . and neither are apart from it.

The idea that spiritual fulfillment must be achieved as the Spiritual Teacher has achieved it may simply not be valid. The perspective I am currently exploring is that all aspects of Life are pathways to spiritual fulfillment and that the Spiritual Teacher and the Teacher's attributes merely reflect one particular path and not *the path*. The Spiritual Teacher is only one very small part of the entity called the collective Self.

Just as the body contains the crucially important central nervous system, with its brain and spinal cord, it also contains other vital parts: heart, lungs, kidneys, skin, digestive tract, and so on. Were these parts to be given voice, the central nervous system would not declare its particular way of functioning and style of being to be the full and only pathway to proper physical functioning. Nor would the anal cells claim to be waiting around to become central nervous system cells in another lifetime. Anal cells would know they are part of the miracle of Life and have just as important a task as do the central nervous system cells . . . as anybody knows when something goes wrong with an anal cell.

We would be in definite trouble if an anal cell tried to become a brain cell or if a brain cell tried to become an anal cell. All the organ systems and all the cells of every organ system of the entire body must carry out their particular function, and do so in harmony with every other system for the full potential of the physical body to be realized. Likewise, the entire psyche, with all of its vehicles of consciousness—from the most deplored to the most revered—is required for the Self to Realize Itself. (This very concept is reflected in the Bible in 1 Cor. 12:14–27, as John Niendorff noted in his editorial review of the manuscript.) And remember that this Self to which I am referring is not to be equated with the Illumined Mind or with the heightened awareness of Spiritual Teachers, so when I refer to the Self realizing Itself, I do not mean that the outer senses of self, even the Illumined Mind, realize the Self. They do not and cannot.

The Whole in Each Part

Fully and experientially becoming what one fundamentally is—and I have come to believe "what one is" is determined during the moment of conception, when the Mystery underlying Life and Matter exerts its most profound influence and expresses its needs with each individual—is the most natural mode by which each of us will come into our portion of Spiritual Realization. And that does not mean each of us is to be a central nervous system cell and attain this realization through the brain cell pathway. Rather, each of us contributes a part to the Realization, with no single aspect, by itself and through its own filter, being capable of the realization of the full Mystery. Full Realization of the Mystery requires the fullest incarnation of all its parts. This means that all the various life patterns that have been dancing the human being since its emergence from the void will continue to dance the human being until the life cycle of our species concludes. Each individual reaches Relative Realization by being fully what each is.

One contemporary viewpoint, for example, holds that the entire world is a conscious, living Being—called Gaia—and that its constituent parts are all aspects of it, including the basic chemical elements, viruses, bacteria, insects, trees, plants, sea life, animals, and human beings. From this perspective, we see a profound example of how humanity is only one aspect of the Wholeness and the Mystery of Life. Humanity may represent the central nervous system of Gaia, but humanity is not the totality. With this understanding, that humanity is only one aspect of Life, we can better understand why each individual within humanity represents only *a* path and not *the* path to Wholeness. For instance, only those individuals who are struck at conception to carry the attributes of the Spiritual Teacher are destined to reflect the Teacher aspect of Life and undergo training to receive the appropriate empowerment. Others will be initiated into those myriad other aspects of Life that are required for Life to fulfill itself. This means that everything we see, everywhere, is actually a part of the Totality—with purpose, a part to play, and a right to be here . . . to exist. This includes individuals who haven't the *slightest* intention of awakening to a vaster Beinghood, who will never question who they are or why they are.

Indeed, everyone does have a part to play. You can see this most strikingly in certain individuals who, through the simplicity of their presence and action, achieve a transcendence through just being fully what they are. They may be rare, but when you run across such a person, you can never forget the moment. This first came powerfully to my attention when I was having lunch at a hotel in Kona, on the big island of Hawaii. I looked over the shoulder of my luncheon guest and into a large, spacious garden, and was suddenly overwhelmed by what I saw there.

I saw a Japanese gardener watering the plants. But I didn't just see a man watering some plants, performing his duty to earn a living. I saw a most incredible fusion of the man, the watering, and the plants. It was a harmonious symphony of interrelationship, which I had never experienced prior to that time. The man, the water, and the plants were in perfect accord . . . each a part of Spiritual Realization. The man was fulfilling his Beinghood by being fully what he was.

The essence of such an experience is hard to communicate, as it is more than merely objective. Rather, one's intuition senses when such an action is transpiring, when each part of a process is being fully what it is meant to be. One's heart pounds with delight and one's eyes fill with tears upon the recognition of a person who has fully realized and accepted the part he or she plays in the Mystery of Life.

I have been privileged to experience this phenomenon at other times. The second such encounter occurred when I was observing a local guide who was revealing the mysteries of the ancient city of Monte Albán near Oaxaca, Mexico. He considered himself a guardian of the ruins and had the most amazing depth of knowledge about the structures and the people whose civilization created them. His whole life was fulfilled in the protection and care of this sacred site. When he spoke, a listener was transported out of time and into the inner experience behind the guide's words. He wasn't talking about ruins; he was the Spirit of the ruins!

The third such encounter was in Japan, while I was visiting a Zen temple. I was traveling with eleven other men, and we were appreciating what it was to travel as a band of spiritual brothers, pilgrims on a spiritual journey to remote and exotic religious centers in Asia.

The abbot of the Zendo was rotund and boyish. He laughed as he motioned us to step over large, ornately braided ropes that defined the territory of the sacred altar, and he encouraged us to touch and hold the ancient statuary, brass bowls, and drums in that area of the temple.

"Just objects!" he exclaimed. My heart melted into liquid light.

The fourth time was while Hannah Veary, the Hawaiian Elder, was teaching me about the various uses for certain of Hawaii's indigenous plants. I recognized that when Nana, as she is called by her friends and family, walks in nature, she is indistinguishable from nature. There is about her a naturalness and reverence for life that cannot be put into words. She responds to nature, and nature responds to her. To state it simply: her consciousness is not localized in her body.

The fifth occasion was while I was experiencing a Catholic priest celebrate Communion at a Benedictine monastery near Lucerne Valley, California. His name was Brother Luke. He didn't know me and I didn't know him. I later learned from a television interview that he had been raised as a Lutheran, received his medical degree from the University of Southern California, was attracted to this high desert monastery near the community of Pearblossom, and in a very short time embraced the Catholic religion and took the vows of monasticism. His reason for conversion was that he was spiritually moved by the rituals of this religion.

As I am not a Catholic, I was not able to take Communion the day he psychospiritually changed the bread and wine into the symbolic body and blood of Christ. But I didn't need to be Catholic to experience what Brother Luke invoked during that most remarkable ritual. Though I had observed Mass many times, never had I experienced a priest transubstantiate as well as transfigurate as did Brother Luke.

I also recognized this fusion of an individual with his or her essence while sharing an early morning walk in the fall-leafed woods in the Cotswolds of southern England with Sir George Trevelyan.

Sir George, who was in his eighties, was transfixed by an ancient and sacred tree, its vast roots, the sweeping upsurge of a massive gnarled trunk, and the cathedral-like arching branches. In that moment, I couldn't tell where Sir George left off and the tree began.

Finally, to bring this discussion full circle, I make note of two individuals I know who are so merged in their marriage that the transcendental qualities to which I have just been referring are overwhelmingly reflected in their day-to-day interaction with each other and with their friends. Their marriage is their spiritual path.

In the kinds of situations I have cited here, an individual is fully and completely in accord with the way he or she truly is. An intuitional or psychic impression would reveal complete equivalence between the person's innermost self and his or her outer nature. There is no mask. The psyche of the individual is completely at peace, aligned with its parts. The individual fulfills his or her destiny and obligation to Life through the simplicity of being who and what he or she is.

One experiences a most wondrous inner appreciation for individuals who are reflecting to the fullest what they have to express. It makes no difference whether they are ditch diggers, automobile mechanics, computer whizzes, book editors, short-order cooks, prostitutes, mercenaries, nuns or monks, physicians, hit men for the Mafia, Gurus, or television evangelists.

One doesn't have to experience one's life in the same way someone else does, even if one feels inspired and lifted by that person. One can continue to discover one's own unique combination of resources, which helps to bring the Mystery Itself into Realization.

CHAPTER TEN

NONORDINARY STATES OF CONSCIOUSNESS AND THE UNCONSCIOUS

The previous two chapters dealt with approaches to the Unconscious through ordinary states of awareness. This chapter explores approaches to the Unconscious through nonordinary states of awareness.

These nonordinary states are aspects of augmented or expanded consciousness, of sensitive awareness or heightened intuition. They are usually referred to as psi, psychic, transcendental, sacred, or transformational, and are generated through the use of hallucinogenics and/or activities that force extreme imbalances in the biochemistry of the body, such as those produced through prolonged fasting, hyperventilation, sensory deprivation, flagellation and other forms of mortification of the flesh, near-death events, the crises of illness, formal initiations and inductions conducted by Teachers, and the augmented states of consciousness that occur during times of extreme collective crisis such as those involving natural catastrophe or war.

The important point is that expanded states cannot be experienced while one is in ordinary consciousness. Ordinary consciousness must be left behind and one must enter a completely different vehicle of awareness. The situations mentioned above seem somehow to thin the veil that separates the conscious and the ordinary from the unconscious and the nonordinary.

One must remember that these experiences do not *cause* the realms of nonordinary consciousness to exist. They merely make entry into them easier. One often hears that an illness was the cause of an unusual state of consciousness or that a drug was responsible for an expanded experience. This misses the crucial point. The Unconscious exists and functions whether we are consciously aware of its existence or not. Chemical substances and unusual events do not create the Unconscious!

I believe all psi (or psychic) experiences are products of transcendental states of consciousness, though not all transcendental states of consciousness produce psi experiences. There are transcendental, or expanded, states of awareness in which no unusual power or psychic phenomenon is evoked. Entering the Silence—a state of pure Being—is a good example of this. But whether or not a transcendental state includes an experience of psi abilities, it does always call for a total revision of one's opinion of what *is* and what is *not* when it is experienced for the first time.

Most of us have a peculiar value system about reality. If we don't know about something ... anything ... we assume it probably doesn't exist. For example, most people don't believe the Unconscious exists, simply because they don't experience it. This changes radically when the expanded aspects actually are experienced. The usual response is, "I don't believe it." The next most common response is, "You're going to think I'm nuts but ... " It is interesting to observe how people attempt to defend themselves from the experience of a psi awareness or a transcendental breakthrough.

Although nonordinary states of consciousness do often frighten and overwhelm an individual when they are first encountered, the same individual may ultimately learn to be quite comfortable with them, discovering how to enter and to leave them volitionally through simple shifts in focus of attention. Most people, however repress such experiences unless they are under the guidance of a teacher who is familiar with the phenomena of the Unconscious.

In our society, I have found very few individuals who are able to present unencumbered pathways into the unconscious realms of Self. Most spiritual teachers are heavily biased with moralistic or cultural dogma, a tendency to seduce students into exclusively mental or intellectual dimensions (particularly those that tend to demean the body), or the teaching of womb-state escapist propaganda and misinformation that can enmesh rather than liberate the individual who seeks awakening. Teachers who carry a Divine Mother and/or a Divine Father pattern are examples of those who are prone to create this kind of enmeshment. A student may feel wonderful around them, but there is little hope of mature development.

Years of guided practice are usually required for one to learn to handle the raw unconscious forces . . . if one survives the entry into the Unconscious in the first place. There is always the probability of death or permanent psychological injury when ordinary awareness encounters the forces of the transcendent. The sacrifice can be enormous in many ways, not the least of which involves the permanent loss of one's conscious innocence.

The psychic phenomena that are encountered take many forms. They might involve a shaman commanding the elements, the Oracle of Tibet prognosticating in regard to future events, St. John receiving the visions in the Book of Revelation, psychics channeling material for individuals and collectives, healers effecting the miraculous through touch, martial artists manipulating physical and psychological forces, individuals performing telekinesis, intuitive analysts interpreting dreams, Hitler moving the masses, Jesus transfiguring on the mountain top, Gurus teaching pathways into Beinghood, or a priest psychospiritually transubstantiating bread and wine into the body and blood of Christ. Regardless of what the particular phenomenon may be, *all* of the people who do these things are operating from states of awareness beyond the ordinary, though well within areas known to be aspects of the unconscious Self.

I repeat, the outer mind, the ordinary self, is incapable of performing such feats. It will never be able to perform such feats. Only through initiation into the unconscious—the expanded—aspects of the Self can we begin to explore and to experience the powers, realizations, wisdoms, and revelations that are ours through spiritual inheritance and by right of initiation.

Who's Doing What? Shifting into Other Selves

When I am in a state of consciousness in which I am somehow accessing information about people, events, or places that is not coming from my usual awareness, there is a part of me that is always surprised and amazed. I don't know how it actually happens. I do know I am not in an ordinary state of consciousness. I feel hyperalert as the information flows to me either as sudden insights, flashes of images, or a voice that tells me about a person, event, or place. At such times my awareness seems to tune in to general information. Rarely do I have access to detailed telepathic material. Similarly, in the feeling ranges, the general, underlying emotional patterning of an individual is more accessible to me than is specific knowledge of physical, mental, or sexual material.

It turns out that the same techniques for intuiting things about a single individual also work when one is psychically exploring a group of people, a community, or a nation. One reads and senses the group forces. It is like reading a vector force in physics. And interestingly, when I am reading a group, the action of the whole group becomes predictable, while the actions of the individuals in the group become impossible to predict. When I am reading an individual, I lose track of the collective energy.

Often, observers believe a person who is demonstrating these dynamics is somehow going inside the heads of others or, in the case of shamans, is entering a plant or animal to gain understanding and information. I do not experience such to be the case. A most profound realization is this: When these events occur, one enters dimensions *of one's own Unconscious*, wherein an equivalence of all that is or ever shall be "exists." This must operate similarly to the way holographic principles operate.

My involvement with psychic phenomena has come to me gradually, and usually in the most unexpected of ways ... most often when I have had a need for guidance or help. Rather than presenting an elaborate account of my experiences with these phenomena, I will simply and briefly describe the outstanding features of some of the encounters I have had.

The first time I really knew I could tune in to nature for guidance in healing was while I was living on the island of Kauai. I had sustained a very painful knee injury, and an extremely unusual thought came to me. Perhaps I could let my intuition guide me to a tree that would heal my knee. I allowed myself to be guided by how my knee felt when I pressed it against several different types of trees. With some trees, the pain increased. With others, it stayed the same. But with one kind of banana tree, the knee felt as if someone had incised it and drained all the pain and injury out. My knee was fully restored to normal in less than an hour. I didn't, however, bother trying to figure out what did what.

I also allow extended ranges of awareness to take over when I am searching for sacred sites by quieting and entering my Heart Center and waiting for inner direction. I may meander for a while until, suddenly, a knowing strikes my awareness, and the direction I need to take becomes evident.

While I was with a group on the Colorado River, rafting and camping in the spectacular Grand Canyon, a dental surgeon who was with us became excited about his ability to make clouds dissolve. I validated his discovery by telling him about Hannah Veary, the Hawaiian Elder, who taught me that one could ask the rain clouds to go away when the sun was needed, as long as one welcomed the clouds back afterward. The trick was to form a personal relationship with the clouds. One simply chanted to the clouds and expected them to leave! When that worked for me, I had not tried to figure out what was doing what.

I also told the dental surgeon that when I do such a thing with a cloud, I often simply imagine I am seeing through it, then I envision it disappearing. I feel an unusual energy swirling about my head, and a strange, heightened mental activity. When this process works, I am always astonished. When he did it himself, the dental surgeon was intoxicated by the experience, though we both forgot to welcome the clouds back after we finished. We had a terrible rain that evening. I didn't try to figure out what was doing what.

One particularly interesting experience of psi phenomena occurred during a powerful ritual ceremony in the Gobi Desert of Outer Mongolia in which I participated with twelve other men. The ritual required that we leave an isolated desert yurt compound and walk out into the open desert. After opening my intuition for direction, I recognized what seemed obvious ... that the site for the ritual was one where the ground reflected an unusual radiance—a kind of glow. The night sky was heavily overcast. Two hours later, nearing the end of the ritual, I looked up and saw a vast circular opening in the heavy overcast, an opening into the starry sky directly above us. It was as if an eye had opened ... through which we might peer into the Infinite, or the Infinite might peer at us. The moment we concluded the ritual, the opening began to disappear, and in twenty minutes the heavy overcast had returned to its preritual condition. I didn't bother trying to figure out what was doing what.

Then, in *Joy's Way*, I described my initial experiences with healing, with becoming able to feel subtle energies radiating from the body, and with radiating energies into another person's body. Unfortunately, in regard to that, I have spent years trying to figure out what is doing what!

Exploring the Unconscious through Individual and Collective Crisis

What may appear to the outer mind to be destructive may appear to the Unconscious to be rectifying and healing. This is particularly true for individuals and societies that maintain excessively rigid controls on human expression. With that in mind, I will present in this section some insights and perspectives that may be unpalatable, unpopular, or even forbidden to many people, viewpoints related to the use of drugs and to collective crisis, both of which can unleash the rich ranges of forces of the Unconscious, whether individual or collective, whether constructive or destructive.

I have been impressed with certain individuals who have survived the ravages of chaos, whether the black pit of alcoholism and drug abuse or the extreme trauma of war. They seem to have gained a depth of maturity, a compassion, and a rich spirituality that is completely absent in people who are naive and untraumatized. It is as though such chaos is a contemporary rite of passage, an initiation, one that was previously handled through sacred rites and vision quests and that selects out those individuals who have the interior resources to become the great Teachers, Priests, Healers, and Sages for a clan or a collective. When that happens, it isn't the first time Life, through an eruption of Unconscious forces, has sacrificed the many for the few.

Rarely do we ever have an overview of our own personal unconscious forces, and even more rarely do we ever see the unconscious dynamics of society. But a powerful way to observe the unconscious forces that dance any individual or any collective is to see how a person or a group actually lives life, as opposed to how each thinks life ought to be lived. In taking this view, however, we must remember that it is a transpersonal one and therefore impersonal. It does not involve our feelings at the personal level.

When we observe life from this sort of impersonal viewpoint, we can appreciate that in every major culture, all human experiences, from the most constructive and stable to the most destructive and unstable, regenerate themselves. Life has had billions of years to rid itself of that which does not function or which does not support it to some degree. It has also had time to nurture and enhance that which is functional and adaptable. Most of us have an easy time appreciating the constructive aspects, but what about the destructive and chaotic aspects? With the latter part of that inquiry in mind, I have found immense value in asking another version of the forbidden question: "How do these disowned societal elements serve us collectively, in terms of the full rhythms of Life?" When I ask that, I begin to understand collective social dynamics from a very different viewpoint than when I do not ask the forbidden question.

One such understanding is that a person whose existence has been overly protected and overly controlled—tending toward abstraction and sterilization—is actually balanced by chaos. The same holds true when war or social chaos erupts in a collective. War is a transcendent event which ushers in great change and invariably brings individuals and groups into a greater creative Unfoldment, whether a particular individual or group is the victor or the victim.

The Warrior/General energetics are incarnated, either consciously or unconsciously, in every generation in certain individuals, whether biologically male or female. They are on call, so to speak, ready to serve the collective in times of chaos and change. They may also be called to initiate chaos and change and not just to protect a society. Not every generation will use the resources contained in these great patterns, and the individuals carrying such forces will experience a lack of fulfillment of destiny during times of prolonged peace or when a society scorns this particular aspect of itself.

Much of the current undermining of the Warrior/General patterning is involved with the collapse of sacred values that once gave meaning to death and destruction during times of upheaval. The collapse of this aspect of the Masculine may well have to do with the emergence of attitudes and values reflecting the positive aspect of the Feminine/Great Mother patterns, patterns that serve to modulate the intellectual and impersonal power of the Masculine. But when they are overvalued, they can also cause emasculation and the collapse of a society. This is a strong contemporary possibility.

Women, in general, are currently too invested in the Masculine to be able to fully activate the Feminine complement at its transcendental, collective level in order to effect a healing reconnection of the mind to the body and of the human being to the earth. Things will probably have to get much worse before the collective Feminine can break the entrancement of the daughter for the Father and thereafter rebirth the Mature Woman.

The Power of Peace/The Power of War

The current wave of sentiment against war and chaos and against the use of power for the maintenance of peace through defensive strength denies aspects of both the personal Self and the collective Self—aspects that have served and will continue to serve Life, ourselves, and all collectives, whether we have the maturity to accept them as part of our view of Wholeness or not. Denial or diminishment do not rid us of the aspects of Self that defend, conquer, or destroy.

In our culture, which generally perceives itself as peaceful and law-abiding, look at how the ghettos and the huge numbers of individuals utilizing drugs and alcohol maintain the environments of war and destruction! In fact, denial, individually and collectively, only increases the destructive potential inherent in the immortal Warrior/ General patterning. It can, and it has, turned upon its own people in the past. It can destroy a civilization when it is not properly inte- grated as an aspect of the societal Self.

As an exercise in maturation, I have often asked individuals to consider embracing viewpoints about war and peace that are diamet- rically opposite from their actual beliefs. For instance, I have asked that they contemplate ten reasons why war serves a collective and ten reasons why peace does not serve a collective. Upon doing this they usually begin to feel the power of shifts in perspectives. Forbid- den thoughts lead to the most amazing realizations if one has the courage to think forbidden thoughts.

We can expect, in fact, that whenever we as a society or as an aspect of society publicly deny an attribute of our natural Self, there will be—in our private lives—an eruption of that which has been denied. Child abuse, in its sexual form, is a particularly good example of this very principle. It is not that child sexual abuse is right. It is that the conscious denial of our incestuous nature is wrong!

The presence of street gangs, violence, drug addiction, and un- bridled sex in every great city of the world must also point to a larger mystery, something more than just "bad" or "evil" persons doing "bad" and "evil" things. When we see these powerful forces sweep- ing through large numbers of people—such as those who are using street drugs and those who are involved with the associated violence, crime, chaos, sex, and death—some deep, profound, and Ultimately transforming, Life-enhancing action by the collective Unconscious is being released, an action that ultimately benefits Life, although indi- viduals and collectives may be the short-term sacrifices.

Some Unexpected Benefits of Television

One very interesting possibility I am considering is that the increase in violence, sex, and drug use depicted on television—a screen into our unconscious nature—may be coming about because large num- bers of people are being prepared for life-threatening changes in the earth's atmosphere, disruption in the world's economic markets, political revolutions, or nuclear chaos, and Life is taking out insurance, assuring that sufficient numbers of people will know how to survive disruption and calamity and will be able to transmit the seeds of future life.

Television programming, along with what is available through home video technology, may be providing the balancing, and therefore healing, experiences necessary for our survival. The level of our consciousness that reads patterns experiences screen images as real, no matter what the intellect has to say about it. With this in mind, I find it most revealing that everywhere in the United States, the films most people prefer to view in the privacy of their own homes present hard-core pornography. But this should not really be unexpected given the general societal repression of sexuality and the fundamental importance of sexuality to human existence. And what films are sure money-makers in the fundamentalist Christian areas of the United States? Horror movies! All of this makes sense when we appreciate how the Unconscious balances and protects itself from forces that may produce limitation or sterilization. Life seeks to be fully expressed. Motion pictures which carry male violence, whether in the form of war, cops-and-robbers conflicts, or shoot-outs in the Old West, are male initiation experiences which, in my opinion, are necessary to the deeper well-being of the collective. Far better and cheaper for males, collectively, to experience these rites and rituals on television than to enact them in the outer realities. And I do understand the feminine perspective which abhors such rites and rituals. Of course, an aspect of the Feminine defends against such activities, as they represent the collapse of the maternal, with the loss of the son to the father and the loss of the boy to the masculine principle. (There are feminine aspects that do celebrate war, though ... for instance the Whores and the Amazons.)

Living through Catastrophic Change—The Dance of Survival

Rites of passage, initiations, chaos, and the forces of change are regularly being experienced by the very individuals we seek to cast out of our societal embrace. If a major calamity were to suddenly present itself, my money would be on the ghetto people, the criminals, the homeless, and the outcasts of society as the ones who would seed the future. Most of us who are completely dependent on the food and water supplies of a large, complex society would have little chance of surviving a complete civil collapse. The parts of an individual or a society that survive chaos and carry Life forward are always very different from the parts that survive only during peacetime or relative calm.

So whether it be world wars, limited revolutions, or gangs in central urban areas, the collective Unconscious is dancing the patterns of chaos and survival, perhaps foreshadowing some future disaster. Maybe we should read the signs and omens of potential collective collapse and appreciate how the Unconscious moves to insure the survival of the collective seed, even though individuals and personal values are always sacrificed in these situations. And if we need confirmation of these statements, we should simply examine the sacred texts of any great religion or the histories of the rise and fall of civilizations.

The Collapse of the Sacred Father

I alluded earlier to another pattern that can be discerned in contemporary Western society, which is that of the collapse of the Sacred Father image. If this were happening in just the military area of our culture, for example, it could be viewed as an isolated peculiarity. But the collapse of the great Paternal pattern as a source of stability and guidance is evident everywhere—in religion, law, politics, medicine, the family, and science.

Something awesome is transpiring in our culture at the family, social, political, scientific, and religious levels. The only thing that can account for such a pandemic of collapsing father figures is an eruption from the collective Unconscious. Are we preparing for the birth of a new God(dess)? Is the Great Feminine awakening from Her long sleep? Can we trust that, when collapse and/or change become more evident, the Unconscious is initiating new possibilities? Are the chaos and pain centered around the birth process somehow reflected in any great change ... almost as if the wisdom of matter recognizes the value of struggle and crisis as ways to activate resources not ordinarily available?

The terrifying, godlike forces that can be unshackled during times of extreme devastation confront the conscious mind with its own mortality and insignificance. Yet, paradoxically, in the very same havoc, the Immortal and Transcendental are more easily accessed and experienced. Individuals are swept up in forces far beyond anything they could have imagined, as the gods and goddesses dance them with wild abandon. The degree to which the great Demon and its Dragons are released is the same degree to which the great Redeemer and its Angels are also released into the world of man and woman. It is High Theater ... the Mystery Play undiluted!

During times of catastrophic change, each individual has the opportunity to feel fully alive and resource-filled—awake far beyond the daily soporific states of consciousness in which most of us reside. Initiations that take us beyond the innocent and the naive are evoked. We can appreciate how individuals are fulfilled through such life-styles as those that involve gangs, drugs, violence, crime, and unfettered sexuality ... why these aspects have been worshiped by so many people in so many different times and so many different places, and why violent films are favored by the masses, and why the masses may deify war or major crises.

We must understand that taking governmental action against such so-called deviant behavior only serves the underlying patterning. It constellates the enemy, for both sides, and empowers the dark and the light Warrior/General patterns. We may consciously declare that we oppose war, yet we unconsciously precipitate forms of war to serve the unconscious and disowned destructive elements of our collective.

The best and the worst of the human being are demonstrated during these times. They are so important to us that we even establish clubs and organizations to celebrate and to recall the events of great dishevelment or chaos. Much of religion celebrates times of chaos, nurturing images of future collapse through an ultimate and concluding Divine act of world destruction.

Is the situation much different in our ghettos and slums? Physicality, sensuality, sexuality, and emotionality are all powerfully experienced there, and often in much more healthy ways than the majority of our population experiences these primary forces. Male and female initiations and vital, often traumatic, social strife are encountered daily. Are individuals in these settings not seeking meaning and significance, too, although through values and behaviors that resist the herd consciousness of the rest of society? Do they not therefore act as seedbeds of new potential, a creative crucible of human life?

Living in ghettos or slums is a very real and powerful mode of existence from Life's standpoint. There is no getting rid of it; it is too successful. When I say this, I am not insensitive to the chaos, destruction, suffering, and pain that accompany such expressions of Life. But I am also aware that there is an aliveness in people who are living life and not merely observing or intellectualizing it. They are real, their world is real; life is real, death is real. Living on an edge heightens the human awareness. It does not dull it. A lot of psychiatrists and therapists would be out of work if we allowed social outcasts to conduct seminars on how to vitalize our life.

Although it is true that the life-styles of these inner-city individuals are often stressful, if not traumatic, and a number will not survive the challenges, either physically or psychologically, this doesn't imply that their lives will have been in vain. Meaning in life and fulfillment of destiny are not functions of life's duration, its quality, or its relationship to consensual standards of morality. Meaning is a function of an inner, personal, psychological sense of whether one's role in relationship to the larger forces of Life, as one perceives them, has been completed.

When we give physicians the right to drug the greater proportion of the population with Valium, yet we react powerfully against other drugs that stimulate and excite and give a sense of heightened awareness, someone or something is actually controlling and calming life and not allowing its fuller, more balanced expression.

The explosive impact of the drug culture in the 1960s was probably the single most important event in recent Western history in terms of opening the partition between the unconscious and the conscious aspects of Self, allowing dimensions of Being previously inaccessible to the masses to be more easily accessed via dreams, meditation, vision quests, prayer, and other nondrug-induced states of awareness. The sacrifice, however, was enormous. Just as it has been with war, the loss in life that occurs whenever the dark side of the Unconscious breaks through into the outer realities is staggering, frightening, and very, very impersonal. Pain and suffering, neurosis, psychosis, and other awesome impersonal forces that shake the human psyche to its core were experienced in both instances—during the height of the drug culture and during the world wars. Had we been trained to be aware of the Unconscious and its power, we might have handled these experiences with greater awareness and less loss of life and psychological injury. As I noted before, however, decades are required to master the techniques necessary for dealing with the forces encountered in an exploration of the Unconscious. We are yet a young life form, and our consciousness is in its infancy.

If we seek to journey into the Unconscious and engage its range of forces, we are wise to remember the immense value of a centering image—an image that helps the psyche orient to a focal point of integration and well-being, no matter what forces may be encountered. Memorizing and contemplating sacred centering images is fundamental to the teachings of most esoteric schools. Without such images, the psyche is blown on the winds of the Unconscious, with little hope of integration or maturation and with the great possibility of psychological injury or death.

In more traditional cultures, the stabilizing images—the sacred images—of the collective were held and protected by the religious traditions, but in our contemporary society, religious institutions do not have the influence over the masses they did in the past. People regularly express life in ways that are different from what the religious dogmas hold to be appropriate or right, and sacred images have been diluted and eclipsed by technological and monetary values. Even within religious organizations, the dollar sign has greater power than the cross. But we would still find much value in having a centering image available—and using it.

I do not mean to suggest that I support a return to what served us in the past. That is exactly what we must not do. The tendency of the human psyche to regress under stress is one of the most tragic components of our nature. It leads either to mass hysteria or to infantile behavior that has few creative resources with which to deal with the new situations. What *is* called for is the ability to allow Life to live through us and present to us the sacred image of the future, one that will stabilize the new order of our existence. The view of the planet Earth and our moon from hundreds of thousands of miles in space might be a good image to consider for that purpose.

Mortification of the Flesh

Morphinelike and hallucinogenic substances are endogenously produced and/or released by the body during times of major stress, trauma, illness, and deprivation. Some of the world's celebrated mystical experiences, evoked when spiritual aspirants flagellated, starved, hyperventilated, or powerfully abused their bodies, may have been due, in part anyway, to this biochemical phenomenon. It was precisely that experience I wished to explore in the Sinai Desert in September 1988. I wanted in some way to touch upon the redemption of painful, personal guilt through sacrifice of the body. The dramatic, powerful, elemental uplifts of massive granite in the parched desert seemed like an ideal place to take on such a task.

For those who are out of condition, the trail to the top of Moses Mountain, as the peak is called, is very difficult if one walks the entire distance from the Monastery of St. Catherine to the temple dedicated to Moses. The first two-thirds of the route involves a slow, meandering camel path with gentle switchbacks, while the concluding one-third is a very steep sixty- to seventy-degree climb up ancient carved stone stairs maintained by dedicated pilgrims. To preserve their strength for the final push to the top, most people ride camels to the bottom of the stairs and then proceed on foot, but whether one rides a camel part of the way or walks the entire trail, the trek to the top is definitely not easy for the average person. As penitence for the guilt I felt over various life experiences, I elected to walk the entire distance as a conscious act of contrition.

As I approached the last third of the hike and the steep staircase,

I was already exhausted and dehydrated, feeling faint, weak, and very vulnerable. My heart was pounding and skipping beats. My breathing was impaired by the altitude. I had been on a modified fast for a week before the journey into the Sinai, so not only was I undertaking an inherently punishing experience, but I was also doing so at a time I was physically weak. Thus, several forces were coming together at once that could easily culminate in a crisis as I trudged up Moses Mountain. The worst of the climb, I knew, was yet ahead.

I had so involved myself with this task that I now realized I might even die in the act of penitence! I stopped innumerable times. My legs were aching and wobbly. The steps and niches carved out by the devout over thousands of years faded in and out of my awareness as one single focus, to reach the top to free myself from the burden of my shame, took me completely. The pain was intense, yet during this amazing experience, I began to see pain from an entirely different perspective. I welcomed it. I savored it. Completely exhausted, I reached the top and collapsed on the steps leading into the temple.

Within a minute or two, I felt a gradual transformation of my mind and body. I felt myself move from a state of viscous density into one of lightness. And I not only felt the burden of shame slowly dissolve, but I also felt a state of supreme ecstasy begin to manifest. The world was changed from being form and matter into a sea of infinite color and light, and I had the impression that my body was being transformed and transfigured. An inner choir sang repetitively in a simple melody . . . *Forgiven . . . you are forgiven*. I bathed in a pool of tears and appreciation. The experience lasted thirty minutes, and only after that time did I finally begin to recognize how extraordinary was the top of Moses Mountain . . . and how moving were its great vistas.

There is no doubt in my mind that this was a mystical ordeal. But I also have a Skeptic and a Scientist inside who constantly offer their opinions as to what happens. Was the experience generated solely by endogenous hallucinogenics augmented by a dangerously low blood sugar and an unstable cardiovascular system, or was the crisis a threshold to the healing power of the unconscious resources of Spirit through penitence? Perhaps it was both, and on the deepest level, perhaps it doesn't really matter. I always had but little regard for individuals who sought redemption, self-healing, or the healing of a family member through acts of mortification of the flesh. But now I feel different. Maybe those people had insight into something I am just beginning to appreciate.

Part of the Work Is to Play

Through accessing some of the unconscious aspects of Self, one has the rights and privileges of gods and goddesses. These rights and privileges are limited only by each individual's capacity to leave the ego awarenesses and to enter collective vehicles of consciousness that can interact creatively with the Unconscious. However, it is a dictum—an inviolate dictum—that the outer mind or ego awareness is not the vehicle of consciousness that can or should handle such forces.

I was swimming from shore to a beautiful coral reef off the coast of Kenya in the fall of 1987. The day was spectacularly sunlit, with an amazing array of tropical fish schooling around the coral. The sandy bottom was a pristine white. Suddenly, as I swam between two coral outcroppings, I found myself facing a vertical drop into an absolute blackness of ocean. Psychologically I was at the edge of my known ego universe, confronted with the infinite and the unknown ... my Unconscious, at the very least ... and maybe even THE UNCONSCIOUS.

I didn't bother to center. Simple Brugh, who was in charge of the morning's excursion, was not equipped to handle this projection of the infinite. I swam as fast as my arms and legs would carry me—back to the safety of the known and the sane. It was, after all, Simple Brugh's morning to play.

CHAPTER ELEVEN

SPIRITUALITY AND SEXUALITY

One of the most difficult challenges I have faced while unfolding into greater ranges of Being is that of integrating sexuality and spirituality.

In the earlier stages of my spiritual development, my perspectives reflected beliefs, opinions, and dogmas that were popularly held among spiritual aspirants. I believed in the separation of sexuality and spirituality. I advocated celibacy, moving beyond marriage and child-rearing, and celebrating the hero's journey and the Arthurian knights' vow to remain chaste and to love unconditionally from afar. I believed in practicing meditative exercises that promoted development of the upper chakras (the higher states of consciousness)—those which involve the transpersonal love associated with the Heart Chakra; the higher creative, intuitive areas; and expanded mental and cosmic states. I, along with a whole host of traditional esoteric seekers of the spiritual life, past and present, vastly preferred such viewpoints to those which involved the lower chakras . . . the instinctual and the animal areas . . . physicalness, sexuality, and emotionalism.

Most individuals who came to my Conferences seemed also to assume that highly developed spirituality and nearly all forms of sexual expression were mutually exclusive. Initially I did not challenge that assumption. It seemed simply to be a cardinal rule of spiritual development. Except for my very superficial awareness of the Tantric practices of Tibetan Buddhism, I was very naive and unfamiliar with any spiritual path that included sexuality as fundamental to spirituality.

I was aware that the vast majority of religious models regard sexuality either as such a sacred act that its expression needs extraordinary control or as a necessary and awkward inconvenience ... a low-level stage of development which must be overcome through discipline of the body by the mind. These same models often regard sexuality and sensuality outside the sacrament of marriage as the product of animalistic or satanic elements.

Although I didn't believe those latter viewpoints, I had not bothered to consider any alternatives. What I did not recognize was that all of the reactivity and hoopla about sexuality might point to some kind of massive, unconscious individual and collective psychological split between the mind and the body, lurking under the guise of refinement, evolution, and elevated spiritual demeanor.

My first full glimpse of this possibility occurred when I was atop the Great Pyramid of Cheops, undergoing the experience I recounted in the Prologue of this book, during which all my spiritual values collapsed in four minutes. At that time I had asked myself several forbidden questions. Why do Western religions place so much emphasis on the spirit as distinguished from the body? Why is heaven celebrated and earth diminished? Why do men hold the power of the traditional Church? Why are sexuality and procreation not central to the Mystery?

Although I intellectually recognized the existence of a fundamental cultural bias in matters addressed by these questions, I had not yet developed sufficient understanding as to the psychodynamics of sexuality and spirituality to tackle them at any depth. But with my breakthrough into the recognition of the multiple selves of the Unconscious ... with my reading some of the seminal works of Carl Jung ... and with my having listened to firsthand reports of hundreds of dreams revealing unconscious psychodynamics in individuals attending my Conferences, I had become more thoroughly prepared to have powerful new insights into the unconscious forces that underlie the separation of sexuality and spirituality.

———

In seeking to appreciate the antecedents of the contemporary forces related to sexuality and spirituality, both in myself and in our Western culture, I decided to review their roots, as those roots are presented in certain biblical stories. I chose the Bible because so many of our cultural biases are a function of religious viewpoints, particularly Judeo-Christian viewpoints. I selected four stories. The first is from the Old Testament book Genesis (the creation of Adam and Eve and their expulsion from the Garden of Eden), the second is from Exodus (Moses and the Golden Calf), and the third and fourth are from the books of Matthew and Luke (the Virgin Birth of Jesus).

It is remarkable that we have such ancient documents so well preserved and so well translated from which to draw creative insights about the unconscious dynamics of the ancient storytellers. Much is revealed by which particular material they chose to represent in stories and how they chose to represent it. Even more remarkable is the fact that the storytellers, all of whom were male, were undoubtedly unaware of the powerful influence the Unconscious has in the construction of story-patterns and in the selection of symbols—whether oral or written—that are used to communicate a story. This is especially significant since the stories were carrying material presumably considered by the conscious awareness of the storytellers to be sacred.

Before I began to read these stories, I decided to approach each story as if it were a dream that was being told to me. I was overwhelmed by the creative insights that poured into my awareness, as I am sure you will understand when you approach these stories the same way. Using this approach to the biblical material, I soon discovered, shimmering beneath the traditional interpretations, answers to many of the questions I had posed on top of the pyramid.

As with the interpretation of dreams, the reader will find that the biblical stories have a very different meaning when they are analyzed from a psychological viewpoint. I feel confident in approaching the interpretation of these religious stories as I would approach dreams because of my basic realization that the unconscious patterns behind any story presented in words or seen in dreams—or, for that matter, behind what happens to us in so-called ordinary life—are of the same source, generated out of the deep human psyche ... and, ultimately, matter itself. No one can open his or her mouth to describe any event or make up any story without revealing fundamental unconscious patterns active in his or her psyche. Thus, this psychodynamic approach dives past the concrete or literal interpretation and directly approaches the hidden patterns ... the less obvious, unconscious messages in the stories. With sacred material, I also assume that the material is reflecting more than the individual storyteller's personal unconscious viewpoint. I assume that the images and patterns reflect a collective unconscious and therefore a culture as a whole.

Because this material has the potential to be emotionally charged, it is important for me to remind the reader that the insights generated through this approach are creative and tentative ... like making rough sketches for consideration before developing an end result. In the analytic sections, I have let the stream of consciousness remain essentially as it came through, to give the sense of its intuitive flow, a sense which is often lost when material is reworked by the intellectual levels of the psyche. And because repetition helps to stabilize the information, I have frequently repeated the key insights in summary form before moving to the next major realization.

It is always possible that I have projected my own unconscious content onto these stories. If such proves to be true, I am then the only beneficiary and I apologize to the reader. But I feel these realizations reflect far more than just my personal unconscious material. I hope you will be as stimulated as I was when these interpretive viewpoints erupted into my awareness.

To inspect these biblical stories, I'll present each one just as it has been translated, so, as with the dreams I presented earlier, you, the reader, will have an opportunity to begin the psychodynamic interpretation without being influenced by my analysis. Next I will present my current, major realizations about the psychological dynamics underlying that particular story. Finally, in some cases, I'll offer a deeper exposition regarding how I reached these realizations.

The original languages of the Bible are Hebrew, Aramaic, and Greek, and experts agree that all translations, including the King James Version, have problems reflecting the original intent of the writers. I prefer the New International Version because of its clarity and comprehensiveness. A relatively recent translation, it is held to be excellent in terms of scholarship and as true to the biblical writers' original intention as current expertise can produce. I am thus satisfied that there should be no question as to the suitability of the source I am using. Nevertheless, I reviewed these stories in three other English translations—the New American Standard Bible, the Amplified Bible, and the King James Version—and found no significant difference in the patterns of the stories.

As you read this material, I invite you to place yourself in a frame of mind that experiences the material as if you were reading an account of someone's dream. A review of the salient points of dream analysis earlier in this book will be helpful if you do not yet feel comfortable with your skill in dream interpretation.

Adam and Eve in the Garden of Eden
(Gen. 2:4-25, Gen. 3:1-24, Gen. 4:1-2)

Gen. 2:4-25

[4]This is the account of the heavens and the earth when they were created.

When the Lord God made the earth and the heavens—[5]and no shrub of the field had yet appeared on the earth and no plant of the field had yet sprung up, for the Lord God had not sent rain on the earth and there was no man to work the ground, [6]but streams came up from the earth and watered the whole surface of the ground—[7]the Lord God formed the man from the dust of the ground and breathed into his nostrils the breath of life, and the man became a living being.

[8]Now the Lord God had planted a garden in the east, in Eden; and there he put the man he had formed. [9]And the Lord God made all kinds of trees grow out of the ground—trees that were pleasing to the eye and good for food. In the middle of the garden were the tree of life and the tree of the knowledge of good and evil.

[10]A river watering the garden flowed from Eden; from there it was separated into four headwaters. [11]The name of the first is the Pishon; it winds through the entire land of Havilah, where there is

gold. [12](The gold of that land is good; aromatic resin and onyx are also there.) [13]The name of the second river is the Gihon; it winds through the entire land of Cush. [14]The name of the third river is the Tigris; it runs along the east side of Asshur. And the fourth river is the Euphrates.

[15]The Lord God took the man and put him in the Garden of Eden to work it and take care of it. [16]And the Lord God commanded the man, "You are free to eat from any tree in the garden; [17]but you must not eat from the tree of the knowledge of good and evil, for when you eat of it you will surely die."

[18]The Lord God said, "It is not good for the man to be alone. I will make a helper suitable for him."

[19]Now the Lord God had formed out of the ground all the beasts of the field and all the birds of the air. He brought them to the man to see what he would name them; and whatever the man called each living creature, that was its name. [20]So the man gave names to all the livestock, the birds of the air and all the beasts of the field.

But for Adam no suitable helper was found. [21]So the Lord God caused the man to fall into a deep sleep; and while he was sleeping, he took one of the man's ribs and closed up the place with flesh. [22]Then the Lord God made a woman from the rib he had taken out of the man, and he brought her to the man.

[23]The man said,

"This is now bone of my bones
    and flesh of my flesh;
she shall be called 'woman,'
    for she was taken out of man."

[24]For this reason a man will leave his father and mother and be united to his wife, and they will become one flesh.

[25]The man and his wife were both naked, and they felt no shame.

Gen. 3:1–24

[1]Now the serpent was more crafty than any of the wild animals the Lord God had made. He said to the woman, "Did God really say, 'You must not eat from any tree in the garden'?"

[2]The woman said to the serpent, "We may eat fruit from the trees in the garden, [3]but God did say, 'You must not eat fruit from the tree that is in the middle of the garden, and you must not touch it, or you will die.' "

[4]"You will not surely die," the serpent said to the woman. [5]"For God knows that when you eat of it your eyes will be opened, and you will be like God, knowing good and evil."

[6]When the woman saw that the fruit of the tree was good for food and pleasing to the eye, and also desirable for gaining wisdom, she took some and ate it. She also gave some to her husband, who was with her, and he ate it. [7]Then the eyes of both of them were opened, and they realized they were naked; so they sewed fig leaves together and made coverings for themselves.

[8]Then the man and his wife heard the sound of the Lord God as he was walking in the garden in the cool of the day, and they hid from the Lord God among the trees of the garden. [9]But the Lord God called to the man, "Where are you?"

[10]He answered, "I heard you in the garden, and I was afraid because I was naked; so I hid."

[11]And he said, "Who told you that you were naked? Have you eaten from the tree that I commanded you not to eat from?"

[12]The man said, "The woman you put here with me—she gave me some fruit from the tree, and I ate it."

[13]Then the Lord God said to the woman, "What is this you have done?"

The woman said, "The serpent deceived me, and I ate."

[14]So the Lord God said to the serpent, "Because you have done this,

"Cursed are you above all the livestock
    and all the wild animals!
You will crawl on your belly
    and you will eat dust
    all the days of your life.
[15]And I will put enmity
    between you and the woman,
    and between your offspring and hers;

He will crush your head,
　　and you will strike his heel."

16To the woman he said,

"I will greatly increase your pains in childbearing;
　　with pain you will give birth to children.
Your desire will be for your husband,
　　and he will rule over you."

17To Adam he said, "Because you listened to your wife and ate from the tree about which I commanded you, 'You must not eat of it,'

"Cursed is the ground because of you;
　　through painful toil you will eat of it
　　all the days of your life.
18It will produce thorns and thistles for you,
　　and you will eat the plants of the field.
19By the sweat of your brow
　　you will eat your food
until you return to the ground,
　　since from it you were taken;
for dust you are
　　and to dust you will return."

20Adam named his wife Eve, because she would become the mother of all the living.
21The Lord God made garments of skin for Adam and his wife and clothed them. 22And the Lord God said, "The man has now become like one of us, knowing good and evil. He must not be allowed to reach out his hand and take also from the tree of life and eat, and live forever." 23So the Lord God banished him from the Garden of Eden to work the ground from which he had been taken. 24After he drove the man out, he placed on the east side of the Garden of Eden cherubim and a flaming sword flashing back and forth to guard the way to the tree of life.

Gen. 4:1–2

[1]Adam lay with his wife Eve, and she became pregnant and gave birth to Cain. She said, "With the help of the Lord I have brought forth a man." [2]Later she gave birth to his brother Abel.

Now Abel kept flocks, and Cain worked the soil.

Analysis of the Story of Adam and Eve

Near the beginning of the story, the creation of Adam occurs as the "Lord God formed the man from the dust of the ground and breathed into his nostrils the breath of life, and the man became a living being." Before this happens, we find that the earth was barren and not yet filled with life. Here, even as my interpretation commenced, I was faced with the first of many startling insights. Since the earth and the body are one and the same thing to the deep psyche, to my surprise, I saw this story, also as an account of the development of the fetus. specifically the male fetus! As I read further, that impression appeared to be supported.

With this in mind. I realized that the earth's being barren and not yet filled with life indicates symbolically that the body, although in the process of forming in the womb, is not yet under the animating influence of the brain and will not be significantly influenced by the brain until the head area is developed, at least to the degree that nostrils are differentiated. (The nostrils are a late embryonic development and require that the components that make up the nose have fused.)

Water was not initially present, reflecting that the dust of which Adam is formed is germinal, or a seed. Water then does spring forth and covers the whole surface of the earth. These two statements— that water was not initially present and then water was present— reflect the development of the amniotic fluid, which is not initially present around the fertilized egg. This helps to substantiate the hypothesis that this creation story is related to the earliest sequences of human embryonic development. The appearance of water may also symbolize the awakening of the primitive feeling and emotional dimensions, but as yet, there is no awakening of the head (brain) area, where consciousness is capable of sensing itself.

When God breathes the breath of life into Adam's nostrils, we see the basic human creation pattern being repeated, but instead of the male penetrating the vagina of a woman, God penetrates the nostrils of Adam with air and makes man a living being "to work the ground." There must be some special symbolic meaning intended here, a meaning symbolized by air entering the head area ... one that allows the tending of the ground. And there is, for this creative action, involving the head, nostrils, and air, implies that the part of Adam which is awakened by God is not the body but the brain, which is now to take dominion over the body, referred to in the dream/story as the ground.

Air (breath) has usually been associated with the Masculine ... just as the earth is associated with the Feminine. Thus, the God who is directing this creation story, utilizing not sperm but air and penetrating the head of Adam, must be a God of the brain or Illumined Mind area, and is undoubtedly masculine. Therefore, we recognize we are witnessing a creation story, but not that of man and woman. It is, rather, a creation story solely of the human male and of the masculinization of the brain functions.

The mouth area is perceived by pattern-level consciousness as vaginalike. The image of the juxtaposition of God's mouth to Adam's nostrils is a fertilizing image. Because the nostrils are the first to receive the creative awakening, the early and primal importance of scent and the sense of smell to the discerning and differentiating functions of human consciousness is being emphasized. The sense of smell, after the sense of touch, is considered to be the oldest sensory modality in the human being. Here, then, in the image of God breathing life into the nostrils of Adam, is symbolized the initiating division between the mind and the body ... between Heaven and Earth ... between Male and Female ... between intellect and feeling ... between Apollo and Dionysus.

The brain (with its innate need to control the body) and the masculine psyche (with its need to control life through conceptualization, idealization, and nominalization, by using images, music, and words) are inextricably interwoven with each other here. The brain takes charge of the body, and the mind prepares to take charge of the world. At this stage of the embryonic development, consciousness is differentiating just as matter is differentiating. The philosophical distinctions between idealism and materialism, between conceptualism and realism, are formulating.

Since there is no reference to the genitals in this particular process, the creative aspect of the brain/head area is apparently regarded as independent of the body's mysterious creative potential. The masculine God of the early Hebrews does not, in fact, seem to need either the genitals or the body. It is, therefore, a God representing deified mind (or Illumined Mind) and associated with the brain and the masculine mental functions. This represents a potentially dangerous situation, as an important part of the whole has conceived of itself as independent of the whole and has forgotten that it is only a part that helps to organize and to direct the whole. There are vast repercussions when a part, in this case the brain and the masculine mental functions, perceives itself separate and superior to the whole, to the body, and to the earth. One consequence is that part of the unconscious masculine mind perceives the world, the body, woman, emotions, feelings, and sexuality as subordinate to itself. This translates into an unconscious rejection of anything that is not of the mind or under the power of the mind. This unconscious attitude supports the assault to the body, to earth, and to women in general. Any spirituality exclusively based in this separated mental arena rejects the world (and the body) and holds to a heaven (and a mind) of its own making.

The lack of reference to the genitals at this stage of development also suggests that the biological genital center has not yet awakened and does not awaken until after the development of the brain center. It is tempting to consider another simultaneous possibility ... that the lack of any mention of the genitals (in fact, genitals are never mentioned throughout this entire creation story) is a blatant yet unconscious defense against genital creativity and the competitive struggle of the genitals with the brain. The brain can do without male and female, but the genitals cannot! For natural procreation, the penis needs the vagina, and the vagina needs the penis ... fortunately. The author reveals his masculine bias and unconscious defenses against the body, woman, and the phallus in this aspect of the story by describing the creation of Adam only as occurring through the penetration of the head area with air. Certainly immortality and creation

through the mind *protect* the mind from the power of the genitals
... which is very convenient if the intent is to deify the mind and
to establish the superiority of the brain over the body.

In Eastern spiritual traditions, the mouth and nose are related to
the fifth chakra, the creative states of consciousness associated with
the throat area. The opening and concavity of the mouth and the
erectilelike aspects of the tongue (which can protrude and penetrate)
have obvious sexual connotations. Symbolically, words coming out
of the mouth are the same as life forms emerging through the vagina.
Words, reflecting intellectual thought and created through the exha-
lation of air, can easily be seen as both powerful and as a profound
mystery, since they are intimately connected not only to breathing
but also to life, wind, air, heaven, and to this God of Genesis whose
power derives from the creative potential of the brain.

As the story unfolds, God puts Adam into a Garden "in the east, in
Eden." East symbolizes the awakening mind ... the rising sun as
well as the beginning of life and the beginning of development. The
Garden is a special place, symbolizing a utopian or unconscious
womb-state existence.

In the Garden, God caused to grow out of the ground "trees that
were pleasing to the eye and good for food." Here, trees may symbolize the formation of the separate organs, life forms unto themselves yet parts of the whole. The introduction of sight and
nourishment signals the development of the sensory organs, with
special emphasis on vision, and on the development of the digestive
organ system.

In the midst of the Garden, God further caused to grow "the
tree of life ... and the tree of the knowledge of good and evil." A
garden symbolizes unconscious fertility and creativity ... in other
words, the mystery of sexuality. One meaning of Eden is "soft and
pleasurable," implying the unacknowledged womb of the mother.
The central position of these two trees gives emphasis to them, while
making the fruit of the tree of knowledge of good and evil unavailable
puts even greater emphasis on that particular tree.

To the deep psyche, trees and the phallus are in natural psychological association, as are the ground and the woman's body. The whole pattern of plant sexuality ... of the seed, ground, new tree, fruit, and the seed again ... is basically the same as the pattern of human sexuality, with its phallus, semen, womb, fruit of the womb, and the creation of a new human, with its capacity to seed new life. That there are two trees central to the mystery of creativity brings to light a formidable realization ... *there are two sources of creativity ... two gods ... in the human being!* (No wonder the Hebrew God insisted on the worship of no other gods and declared himself to be the one and only true God.)

This single revelation devastates the dogma of monotheism. I had often wondered why Western theology defended against the idea of polytheism, and now I realize why. The tree of eternal life symbolizes the brain, with its power to create, and the tree of the knowledge of good and evil symbolizes the genitals, with their power to create. By making *only* the fruit of the tree of knowlege of good and evil unavailable to Adam and implying that Adam would die if he should eat it, a classic example of unconscious defense exists. The God of Genesis projects his own unconscious fear of genital creative forces onto the act of Adam eating the fruit of the tree of good and evil. This commandment—to not eat of the tree of the knowledge of good and evil—in the context of a story reflecting the awakening of the pattern of human procreation, gives us the first hint of the Oedipal conflict ... the one forbidden fruit.

The existence of two creative centers in a single life form presents a dynamic conflict and represents the source of the struggle to integrate the spirituality of the mind and the sexuality of the body. Creativity, in fact, always involves the principles disclosed in sexuality ... the coming together of two different aspects, with a resultant new product. This is the pattern of psychological creativity, and it is the pattern of biological creativity. The spirituality of the brain or mind, in effect, reflects the mystery of sexuality in terms of psychological equivalents. The tree of eternal life symbolizes the mind's experience of sexuality and immortality through idealism, conceptualism, and nominalism. The immortal patterns of matter, reflecting through images in the brain ... the fundamental archetypes ... animate the mind's dreams, visions, and perceptions.

Since the experience of eating the fruit of this tree involves dimensions of the mind, God presents no initial barrier to Adam in regard to this tree. By contrast, the second tree, the tree of knowledge of good and evil, representing sexuality through the genital creative forces, generates immortality through the life cycle of birth, procreation, and death, and does represent a profound threat to Adam's God. The existence of genital sexuality forces the brain, with its mind, to confront its own mortality—and thus the basis of the mind's defenses against the body and sexuality becomes clearer. Of the two centers, the genitals are the more primary, as they create new life with a new brain, while the brain's creative forces, as awesome as they are, cannot create new life and a new brain . . . yet. Of course, the masculinized brain is trying hard to accomplish this very task through such of its inventions as computers and robots. No wonder these machines seem, at times, to be antithetical to life!

The death if one eats of the fruit of the knowledge of good and evil must be referring to some aspect of a fundamental realization that death and sex are unconsciously related. To procreate is to give life to a new order, and it simultaneously implies the onset of the death of the procreator. Life will move its energy into the protection and nurturing of the new, and the old will lose more and more energy, and eventually die. The children carry the wave of new life . . . not the parents. The children *are* the parents' immortality.

Innate to sexuality, then, are two apparently opposite dynamics, the two most basic attributes of matter—matter yearning for duality, with its resultant sexuality and new life, and matter yearning for unity, with its resultant sexuality and death. So, central to the creation story of Adam and Eve is the pattern of human sexuality, though in a metaphorical format . . . through the symbols of the serpent and the tree of knowledge of good and evil.

We recall now that the English words "good" and "god" are essentially equivalent in meaning. Therefore, whatever the experience of eating of the fruit of the tree of the knowledge of good and evil is, it must be that which involves the ability to distinguish between what is God (good) and that which is not-God (not-good, or evil). From a psychodynamic standpoint, we can imagine that anything which could undermine or threaten a God based in the brain and its intellectual and Illumined Mind functions might be considered evil or not of God. Thus the body, with its emotional and sexual responses, which may easily overwhelm and even intimidate certain aspects of the brain/mind, would cause the brain/mind to defend against the emotions and sexuality. Actually, from the standpoint of a "jealous God," *anything* that threatens its power and pleasure would be troublesome, wrong, or evil and cause excessive control over the threatening circumstance (in this case the fruit of the tree of knowledge of good and evil, representing sexuality and the creative genital forces).

The symbols of the story so far, then, point to unconscious masculine development in the brain of the embryo, signaling the beginning of the brain's taking charge of the body and the conflict the brain feels in regard to genital sexuality, and its mysteries of sex, death, and procreation.

The Creation of Eve

The next major development occurs when God decides "it is not good for the man to be alone," and he determines to make a helper for Adam. It is psychologically revealing that after God creates "all the beasts of the field and all the birds of the air" and brings them to Adam to name, a helper still has not been found, so the last thing God decides to do is to create Woman as that helper. (Even the reference to Woman as a "helper" is a form of psychological defense against the power of the Feminine and the mystery of sexuality.) As we are still in utero and in the unconscious masculine developmental sequence, the story indicates that only after the brain takes charge of the body, and the unconscious masculine discriminating capacities are developed, does the masculine psyche have enough strength to become aware of its unconscious counterpart ... its feminine.

When God causes Adam to fall into a deep sleep and takes part of Adam's side (translated questionably as Adam's rib), fashions woman, and brings her to Adam, we can appreciate one of the great dynamics of brain/mind function ... the capacity to project an unconscious aspect of self onto the closest screen that most nearly resembles the counterpart. Adam's deep sleep is symbolic of his vast Unconscious, and God's fashioning "Woman" from a part of Adam refers to the brain's capacity to call forth and to project the feminine counterpart into apparent existence, whether in the actual world or, as I propose is occurring in this case, into the dream reality of the fetus. Adam is dreaming his feminine counterpart. Although I am unaware of any work being done on dreaming that occurs during the fetal stages of development, this story, representing disguised psychological and physical development of the embryo and the fetus, strongly suggests that dreaming does take place in utero ... before the physical eyes ever see images, and the ears ever hear unmuffled sounds. This story acts as a reminder that projection occurs in dreams, in storytelling, and in what is called ordinary life.

Adam then proclaims that the woman is bone of his bones and flesh of his flesh, and is to be called Woman because she "was taken out of man." They are both naked, yet feel no shame. This passage confirms that the Woman being described is a dream projection from his deep psyche. At the physical level, no Woman is present! The psychological pattern displayed in this passage is the same psychodynamic that will occur when any adult male meets his unconscious feminine counterpart in the form of a lover or spouse. It also sets the stage for the incestuous infant/child relationship with the mother.

At this point, keeping in mind that we are exploring the psychological and physical changes occurring in utero to a male fetus, the story states that the woman (the future Eve) has been psychologically distinguished (created) and is, at the unconscious level, psychologically separate from Adam's psychological sense of self. Yet we have good reason to believe that neither Woman nor Adam is sexually awakened (neither the symbolic genitals of Woman nor the physical genitals of the male fetus are yet awakened), as the story states that Adam and Woman are naked and "they felt no shame." Shame is a way of defending against overpowering impulses centered around certain feelings, which, in this case, would be those of sexuality, if it were active. Thus we may assume that, due to the absence of shame, a psychological knowledge of sexuality and sexual distinction is still in its immature form. Just as with children who are gender-distinct yet can be naked and completely unashamed until conscious sexual awakening occurs, Adam and Woman are distinct yet not sexually awakened. The power of the masculinized brain still dominates.

Interestingly, individuals who revere and live predominantly in the mind experience exactly the same asexuality as is now apparent between Adam and Woman. The mind is capable of cutting off any sexual implication and of rendering men and women sexless. This is exactly what occurs in most professions that emphasize intellectual prowess.

The Serpent

Now comes the most significant part of the story. The serpent, who is "more crafty than any of the wild animals the Lord God had made," makes his appearance. We note immediately that the snake is male. The serpent symbolizes many aspects of life, such as death and rebirth (through the shedding of its skin), lowliness (because it crawls on its belly in the dirt), and severe illness or even death (as through the bite of a poisonous snake), but its most fundamental and therefore primary symbolic aspect involves its shape. It is basically phallic. There is no getting around this fact. One can rationalize until the end of time, but the similarity of the serpent to the penis is too obvious and unambiguous to be dismissed. Genital awakening is occurring in utero!

We now can appreciate that a formidable contender for power over the body has made its appearance. The genitals have come alive in the form of Adam's phallus in relation to his projected Woman. The one body part that now has enough vitality to rebel against the tyranny of the brain is activated and dominant. And not only can it rebel against control of the brain, but it can also seduce other organs to rebel against control of the brain. (No wonder the God of the Old Testament frequently ignores the sinfulness of the serpent/Lucifer, since ignoring it is a form of intellectual denial, which, in turn, is a defense.)

Symbolizing the male genital organ in the form of a snake ... a dismembered aspect of the body ... further emphasizes the brain's disownment of the phallus. His jealous rages in regard to not having any other gods before him strongly suggest that the Hebrew God is aware of other gods that *can* overthrow him. Indeed, there are now two active godlike creative forces present in the fetus: the awakening brain and the awakening genitals.

The serpent and the tree of the knowledge of good and evil, then, are symbols of active sexual/genital consciousness, the serpent representing the male sexual organ and the tree of the knowlege of good and evil representing the full procreative cycle.

To summarize . . . in utero, sexuality is at last awakened. The genitals have become alive and are momentarily dominant over the brain/mind. The Feminine in Adam, projected out as Woman in the fetal dream state, is attracted to and seduced by the phallus, which in turn overthrows Adam's mental activity and renders his mental defenses powerless. Adam is having a sexual dream! His feminine, derived from his dream psyche, is encountering his penis, and both Adam and Woman partake of the experience of sexuality.

One of the ways the mind can begin a defense against anything it perceives as powerful or overwhelming is to cover the threatening object. The covering of the genitals with fig leaves is therefore a primitive and powerful way to deny and to defend against the power of the genitals. (It is interesting to note that figs tend to look like testicles.) Thus, shame has made its appearance. At the superficial level this shame can be regarded as being caused by disobedience to God, but the deeper psychological implication is that shame is a defense against a threatening circumstance, and awakened sexuality is certainly a threatening circumstance to the mind. There is an axiom: "An erect penis has no conscience."

So, as the uterine part of the story comes to its conclusion, Adam and his dream-projected anima, Woman, are sexually awakened by the phallus and are hiding from God. This must reflect the moments when consciousness is centered in the body and is away from the brain or head area. God confronts Adam, asking if he has eaten the fruit of the tree. Adam does not answer the question directly but immediately blames the woman, who subsequently blames the serpent. God's creations—the masculinized brain in the form of Adam, and his female projection, both derived from the creative and projective power of the brain—have fallen under the momentary spell of the god of the genitals. Needless to say, the brain-God is angry and proceeds to curse (another psychological defense) the serpent—the male genitals and, by association, the female genitals—and to outline the many difficulties that shall befall Adam and Woman. (Again, disempowering and punishing are forms of immature psychological defense.)

The timing of the activation of the genital consciousness in relationship to the brain's rejection of the genitals may contain the pattern of the sequence of events that sets actual physical birth into motion. Since what causes birth to transpire is not scientifically known, perhaps the hints from the ancient story of Adam and Eve will give researchers a clue. (It is worthy of note that physical sexual maturation births the adolescent from the parents. Thus, genital activation—whether psychological or biological—may initiate three major stages of life: birth, adolescence, and parenthood.)

We can now appreciate that procreation and sexuality are clearly fundamental to the Hebrew/Christian religious Mysteries, though they are presented only in symbolic form. If nothing else, we can recognize that the account of Adam and Eve in the Garden symbolizes, among other things, the eternal struggle between two centers of creative consciousness, the brain and the genitals.

Interestingly, in terms of biology, the physical basis for the brain/genital conflict was reflected dramatically in the later developmental stages of the reptilian line, when a sacral brain evolved near the lower end of the spinal cord. This sacral brain controlled the reflex activity of the lower portion of the body and the organs of generation. In certain instances, it was as large as or larger than the forward brain. This might only be an intriguing bit of evidence supporting the existence of a brain-genital conflict, except that a remnant of the sacral brain is present in every human spinal cord today and accounts for some of the reflex activity of the genitourinary tract. There are few adult humans who are not aware that the genitals have a mind of their own. This is apparently what so upset the God of the Old Testament.

The emphasis on the male's development, with little or no direct references to female sexuality, reveals the Old Testament's staggering psychological defense against the Feminine. This reaches its full force through the Judaic male prayer of thanking God that one was born male instead of female.

A great attribute of the masculine mind is its capacity to discern, to define, and to distinguish ... yet it does so at the cost of unity and wholeness. We may simply say the intellect is divisive, capable of creating a heaven of its own, with a tendency to ignore or to deny the existence of the body or the world as it is. A wonderful Jules Feiffer cartoon shows a portly man, well-dressed, with a finely tailored overcoat and a bowler hat, looking down at his body and saying, "It's a good thing you carry my head around or out you would go!"

In view of all we have just seen, we can now have far more compassion for the Hebrew God, who knows about the existence of the serpent but can't control it or even get rid of it other than through banishment, diminishment, or denial.

Adam and Eve: The Symbolic Drama

We can also look at these biblical symbols from another viewpoint, one that is slightly different yet profoundly important. First we identify the characters of the Mystery Play:

Adam ... a male, mind, a nonbegotten son of God, usually associated with the intellectual functions of the brain and modeling on the Father.

Woman ... a female, body, Mother figure, symbolic of unawakened feminine procreation and bodily pleasure, nourishment, and sustenance. She is a mysterious product of Adam's rib, reflecting that she is of the marrow or inner structure of Adam.

The Tree of Knowledge of Good and Evil ... Symbolic of biological procreation.

The Serpent ... symbolic of the independent masculine genitals, which can overpower the masculine intellect. Here, the serpent, therefore, symbolizes the awakened masculine genital consciousness.

God ... in the tradition of the Bible, deified mind with masculine attributes. Brain, Father figure.

We now have all the ingredients of the classic psychosexual conflict in the male called the Oedipus complex, the struggle between the son (Adam), the mother (Woman), the father (God), and the awakened sexuality (the serpent and the forbidden fruit). (The aspect of the psyche that generates our dreams, visions, and stories often interchanges images of the mother/wife/daughter, so the fact that Eve was Adam's wife and not his mother is irrelevant symbolically.)

Thus, and perhaps to our surprise, we discover that the story of Adam and Eve in the Garden represents not only the initiation of archetypal masculine sexuality but also symbolizes the pattern of the future unconscious and fundamentally incestuous dynamics between the mother and the male child. The pattern for the Oedipal conflict is established in utero! Further, the extreme reactivity of the Father figure to disobedience, when this reactivity is understood to be centered around the brain/genital conflict, is much more comprehensible. Unconscious sexuality is the only mystery with which I am familiar that has the intrinsic power to create all the circumstances that are portrayed in the biblical accounts of Adam and Eve.

Whether one acts out the genital awakening or it remains an unconscious event doesn't seem to matter in terms of the Oedipus complex. What utterly overwhelms the young male child is the powerful sexual attraction he feels toward the mother, with subsequent unconscious defenses against such powerful impulses manifesting as guilt and shame and repression of any conscious knowlege of those impulses. Psychologically, when Adam's sexuality is awakened through exposure to Eve, who is also a Mother figure and who represents the threshold of the sexual mystery of birth and death, he falls under the spell of the penis. Having done so, he must now deal with the tyranny of the brain ... the threatened intellect ... the dark, immature side of God. He is confronted by the masculine elements of his own unconscious mind/brain, which, afraid of the overwhelming and autonomous activity of the penis, threatens to cut off the penis ... to cast it out of awareness, to withhold permission for sexual activity, or even to deny sexuality completely through impotence.

I have never been satisfied with the usual rendering of the Oedipal complex as a literal fear of the physical power of the actual father if the child were to imagine or to act out the incestuous relationship with the mother. I can more easily appreciate the real struggle as being completely internal and mostly unconscious.

When the female identifies with the father's values (as do the vast majority of women in the West), she also experiences a fate similar to that of the male ... the unconscious defenses manifesting as shame and guilt and repression of forbidden sexual impulses, but, in her case, directed toward the father. Incestuous dynamics thus exist between the female infant/child and the father, accompanied by an unconscious fear of the reprisals from the mother. What redeems the pain, guilt, and struggle of the incestuous attraction is that this same incestuous attraction becomes the basis of lover/spousal patterns when physical sexual maturity is manifested. The pain and shame in the early stages are usually severe enough to prevent the eruption of actual incest.

Only the most superficial and naive individuals would assume that Western women have taken on masculine values because they were born in a masculine-dominated culture. This is typical victim consciousness ... infantile, to say the least. The issue is far more fundamental and more profound than that, and its source lies in the deep unconscious aspects of our society, where our gods and goddesses are born, live, and die.

To repeat and to emphasize: From these perspectives we discover that one of the basic unconscious struggles of the Western psyche is between two body parts: the genital organs and the masculinized brain. We are also able to appreciate that the unconscious incestuous relationships with the countergender parent are fundamental to spousal selection and to procreation. And we appreciate the overvaluing of masculine perspectives by both men and women in our culture as being a huge defense against the vast, underlying, and powerful Feminine.

Just why the Western psyche, in both men and women, feels it must defend against the Feminine can be grasped through understanding the psychodynamics involved. We can begin by at least appreciating that the Feminine must be very powerful and threatening to individuals and to societal groupings for them to have countered Her influence for such long periods of time. The feminine wisdom transcends the masculine wisdom because the latter is based only in knowledge and the rational and knows nothing of intuition . . . a far greater, interdimensional wisdom which includes the innate wisdoms of the body as well as those of the brain. Or, to say it another way, intuition can include intellect, but intellect cannot include intuition. This very recognition may be what underlies Carl Jung's realization that the masculine tendency is to perceive Unity through exclusivity and perfection, while the Feminine tends to perceive Unity through inclusivity and completeness.

A Summary of Psychological Insights from the Story of Adam and Eve and the Garden

1. The creation of Adam and his placement in the Garden, along with his forced expulsion from the Garden, reflect the pattern of the initiation at the beginning of human life, and the sequences of differentiation of masculine consciousness, at the unconscious level, that occur in utero. It presents the sequence of Unfoldment of the earliest aspects of masculine development, both physically and psychologically.

2. The initial parts of the story/dream reflect the masculinizing of the brain, during the formation of the brain. The development of the masculine mental aspects of the psyche (as distinguished from body consciousness) at the unconscious level are being stressed. The Apollonian/Dionysian split begins here. The Hebrew God is not only masculine but is also a God of the awakened mind, whose base of power is the resources of the brain. This God then represents the initiating forces of male psychological differentiation.

3. The many trees in the Garden reflect the physical development and equivalent psychological development of the various organs of the body. The two trees, central to the Garden, announce a dramatic realization . . . that there are two powerful creative centers in the human form . . . the brain and the genitals! Two creative foci imply two gods, which undermines the dogma of monotheism and sets into activity the dynamic, eternal struggle between the spirituality of the mind and the sexuality of the body. The tree of eternal life represents the creative, immortal forces of the Illumined Mind (which have the capacity to vivify thoughts, wishes, dreams, visions, and perceptions)

and the tree of knowledge of good and evil (which represents the creative, immortal forces of the genitals, as expressed through the physical cycle of new life, procreation, and death).

4. Putting Adam in charge of the garden symbolizes the mind's need to preside over the body, and in this stage of embryonic development, the brain's taking control of the body. In later stages, this symbolizes the mind's taking partial, volitional control over the body and, in even later stages of development, the mind's attempt to control the world.

5. The part of the story where God creates a helper for Adam reflects the fundamental unconscious psychodynamics of projection, whereby the Masculine's feminine counterpart is projected out from the deep masculine psyche. In Jungian terms, this is the projection of one of the unconscious feminine aspects (or anima) by the masculine psyche. Woman, in this case, is not the biological woman but is the Masculine's psychological feminine projection. Adam is *dreaming* his own feminine counterpart for the first time. In this form, Woman is literally derived from Adam's psyche and therefore *is* bone of his bones and flesh of his flesh, and exists strictly at the symbolic, psychological level. We are observing unconscious masculine psychological differentiation . . . in utero.

6. The projection of the male's anima onto a specific female when sexual maturity is reached is what allows that male to transfer the unconscious incestuous Mother/Child relationship to his wife.

7. The serpent in the Garden represents the masculine genital awakening, in utero, which is capable of seducing the creative products of the differentiating masculine mind . . . Woman and Adam . . . into engaging the mystery of sexuality and procreation, as represented by the tree of the knowledge of good and evil. Adam is dreaming a symbolic sexual encounter with his feminine. His penis, in the form of a serpent, has awakened and has seduced his feminine. Significantly, the phallus is seen as being dismembered from the body.

8. The covering of the genitals by Adam and Woman indicates that sexual differentiation, physically and psychologically, may occur in utero and is concealed from the brain through the psychological defense of denial . . . albeit at the level of the Unconscious.

9. The curses of God directed toward the serpent and toward Woman reflect the fear and vulnerability the masculinized brain feels when faced with the loss of control over the body when genital forces are awakened.

10. In English, "god" and "good" are two different spellings of the same word—god—and are associative equivalents. Therefore, anything called Good is, in reality, anything that God recognizes as part of himself. As the Hebrew God is a god of the mind, and resides primarily in the brain or head area or its symbolic equivalents, only that which is recognized as part of the masculinized mind or its symbolic equivalents would be recognized as God or Good, which would not, apparently, include the body. Evil is anything that is not Good, or not God . . . in other words, anything that is not of the dimensions of the masculine mental development. The body (and therefore the world), the masculine phallus (in the form of the serpent), and the projected feminine are all sensed as Evil.

11. That God forces Adam and Eve to leave the Garden indicates that the brain is somehow in charge of initiating the actual birthing process. Psychologically speaking, the casting of Adam and Eve out of the Garden represents the entry of the masculine conscious mind into the awareness of the body and into the world beyond the body.

12. Adam's copulating with Eve after leaving the Garden indicates that conscious (as distinguished from unconscious) masculine sexual identity will not occur until after birth and not until after the impulses to actually physically cover the genitals manifest.

13. The story is saturated with unconscious fear and rejection of the body, with the Masculine's need to control life and the body, the Masculine's deification of the intellect and the Illumined Mind/brain, and the Masculine's fear of the feminine mystery.

14. A modified version of the classic Oedipal conflict is embedded in the story.

Moses and the Golden Calf

During the trip to the Sinai Desert when I experienced a form of redemption through mortification of the flesh, I also had further validation about my insights into the Judeo-Christian separation of sexuality and spirituality. This was stimulated by my being at the site where the famous celebration of the Golden Calf is supposed to have taken place.

It started with an all-day excursion, which included a difficult climb to visit some ancient Egyptian temple ruins rarely seen by tourists. Evidence of the worship of Hathor, the feminine goddess of fertility (usually represented in the form of a cow), could be seen everywhere. That suggested to me that the temple was constructed in the age of Taurus, the bull, which would make it approximately four to six thousand years old.

Hours later, I was still filled with awe and appreciation for these Egyptian ruins as our bus approached the road that led to the Christian Coptic monastery of St. Catherine, near where, according to tradition, Moses experienced his visions of the burning bush. Usually any involvement with a monastery deeply moves an aspect of me, but even as the tour of this monastery was under way, my attention was focused entirely on thoughts and feelings of the Egyptian ruins and the contemplation of Hathor. Then suddenly, and much to my amazement, I found myself attracted to the site where the celebration of the Golden Calf is said to have occurred.

The site is in the middle of an ancient cemetery, on top of a mound, where there is a very small, rectangular, adobelike building containing an altar. Of all of the interesting features in the immediate vicinity of the monastery, this area held the most power for me. Initially that was simply due to the incongruity of having a sacred cemetery in the area where such a rebellious and shameful event as worshiping the Calf is reported to have transpired.

The old wooden door was bolted and locked, which precluded my entering what was apparently a place where Bedouins and certain other tribespeople came to pay homage, in their own fashion, with animal sacrifices to the God of Moses. I sat down on the worn stone threshold step of the small adobe structure and settled into a quiet meditative state. Then I asked myself one of those forbidden kinds of questions. "Why would Moses have reacted so violently to the worship of the Golden Calf?"

A sudden breeze jostled my hair, and as though night had become day, I suddenly could appreciate why the celebration of the Golden Calf had taken place while Moses was receiving the Word of God and why the reactivity of Moses was so violent.

Let us again return to the storytelling of the Bible, and as the material is presented, enter a state of consciousness that appreciates the story as if it were a dream being recounted.

The Golden Calf
(Exodus 32)

¹When the people saw that Moses was so long in coming down from the mountain, they gathered around Aaron and said, "Come, make us gods who will go before us. As for this fellow Moses who brought us up out of Egypt, we don't know what has happened to him."

²Aaron answered them, "Take off the gold earrings that your wives, your sons and your daughters are wearing, and bring them to me." ³So all the people took off their earrings and brought them to Aaron. ⁴He took what they handed him and made it into an idol cast in the shape of a calf, fashioning it with a tool. Then they said, "These are your gods, O Israel, who brought you up out of Egypt."

⁵When Aaron saw this, he built an altar in front of the calf and announced, "Tomorrow there will be a festival to the Lord." ⁶So the next day the people rose early and sacrificed burnt offerings and presented fellowship offerings. Afterward they sat down to eat and drink and got up to indulge in revelry.

⁷Then the Lord said to Moses, "Go down, because your people, whom you brought up out of Egypt, have become corrupt. ⁸They have been quick to turn away from what I commanded them and have made themselves an idol cast in the shape of a calf. They have bowed down to it and sacrificed to it and have said, 'These are your gods, O Israel, who brought you up out of Egypt.'

⁹"I have seen these people," the Lord said to Moses, "and they are a stiff-necked people. ¹⁰Now leave me alone so that my anger may burn against them and that I may destroy them. Then I will make you into a great nation."

¹¹But Moses sought the favor of the Lord his God. "O Lord," he

said, "why should your anger burn against your people, whom you brought out of Egypt with great power and a mighty hand? [12]Why should the Egyptians say, 'It was with evil intent that he brought them out, to kill them in the mountains and to wipe them off the face of the earth'? Turn from your fierce anger; relent and do not bring disaster on your people. [13]Remember your servants Abraham, Isaac and Israel, to whom you swore by your own self: 'I will make your descendants as numerous as the stars in the sky and I will give your descendants all this land I promised them, and it will be their inheritance forever.' " [14]Then the Lord relented and did not bring on his people the disaster he had threatened.

[15]Moses turned and went down the mountain with the two tablets of the Testimony in his hands. They were inscribed on both sides, front and back. [16]The tablets were the work of God; the writing was the writing of God, engraved on the tablets.

[17]When Joshua heard the noise of the people shouting, he said to Moses, "There is the sound of war in the camp."

[18]Moses replied:

"It is not the sound of victory,
it is not the sound of defeat;
it is the sound of singing that I hear."

[19]When Moses approached the camp and saw the calf and the dancing, his anger burned and he threw the tablets out of his hands, breaking them to pieces at the foot of the mountain. [20]And he took the calf they had made and burned it in the fire; then he ground it to powder, scattered it on the water and made the Israelites drink it.

[21]He said to Aaron, "What did these people do to you, that you led them into such great sin?"

[22]"Do not be angry, my lord," Aaron answered. "You know how prone these people are to evil. [23]They said to me, 'Make us gods who will go before us. As for this fellow Moses who brought us up out of Egypt, we don't know what has happened to him.' [24]So I told them, 'Whoever has any gold jewelry, take it off.' Then they gave me the gold, and I threw it into the fire, and out came this calf!"

[25]Moses saw that the people were running wild and that Aaron

had let them get out of control and so become a laughingstock to their enemies. ²⁶So he stood at the entrance to the camp and said, "Whoever is for the Lord, come to me." And all the Levites rallied to him.

²⁷Then he said to them, "This is what the Lord, the God of Israel, says: 'Each man strap a sword to his side. Go back and forth through the camp from one end to the other, each killing his brother and friend and neighbor.' " ²⁸The Levites did as Moses commanded, and that day about three thousand of the people died. ²⁹Then Moses said, "You have been set apart to the Lord today, for you were against your own sons and brothers, and he has blessed you this day."

³⁰The next day Moses said to the people, "You have committed a great sin. But now I will go up to the Lord; perhaps I can make atonement for your sin."

³¹So Moses went back to the Lord and said, "Oh, what a great sin these people have committed! They have made themselves gods of gold. ³²But now, please forgive their sin—but if not, then blot me out of the book you have written."

³³The Lord replied to Moses, "Whoever has sinned against me I will blot out of my book. ³⁴Now go, lead the people to the place I spoke of, and my angel will go before you. However, when the time comes for me to punish, I will punish them for their sin."

³⁵And the Lord struck the people with a plague because of what they did with the calf Aaron had made.

Analysis of the Story of the Golden Calf

Here are classic symbols of the mind/body split, manifesting in what might initially appear to be a very different story from that of Adam and Eve and the serpent/forbidden fruit. Moses—masculine, a Father figure, an extension of the deified mind (represented by a bodyless and faceless God, who reigns through covenants, rules, and regulations)—goes up into the mountains (a symbol of higher mind) to encounter his God. At other times in this same period, God was represented by a column of smoke—a mixture of air and products of fire, which are symbols representing the masculine mind. God appears so rarely in bodily form as to suggest that the higher mind or Illumined Mind does not consider the body as its home and implies that the body is somehow inferior. From a psychological perspective, this avoidance of the body implies that God may unconsciously fear the flesh and therefore denies the body and anything centered in the body.

Through this encounter with God, Moses receives the Ten Commandments . . . or *the Law*. But while the masculine mind, Moses, is involved in the legislation of life, the Feminine (the body) down below (that is, below the area of the head) in the valley (an allusion to the vagina) erupts with eating, drinking, song and dance, and suggestions of fertility, sexuality, and sensuality, symbolized by worship of the calf, or cow, symbolic of a form of the Egyptian Goddess Hathor, which, in turn, is symbolic of the Procreative Feminine . . . the Mother.

Of course, God, as the brain, knows this is going on and threatens to destroy the body, but Moses, now acting as the rational, balanced aspect of the masculine mind, intercedes and convinces God to withhold punishment. When Moses (masculine mind) returns and finds for himself the desires of the flesh being satisfied in full and raucous celebration, which is symbolic of the mind becoming conscious of the body's desires and impulses, he becomes enraged and crushes the tablets (symbolizing the power of the emotions to overwhelm the mental and the rational elements of the masculine psyche). Stone, a cold and impersonal substance, is further symbolic of the mental functions.

The humiliation and vulnerability the Illumined Mind must feel when the emotions and sexuality of the body become dominant must be terrifically threatening, sufficiently so to account for the reprisals Moses inflicts on his people (symbolic of the body, the Feminine, the emotions, and chaotic sexuality) through the slaying of three thousand people who were family, friends, and neighbors! Only an immature, vulnerable, and extremely insecure masculine aspect of the psyche, devoid of any feminine influences, could direct such havoc against people with whom one has had close, personal relationships. Since the Golden Calf represents the genital creative center, we are back to the brain's inordinate reactivity to a contending creative force.

Following the devastation at the hands of Moses and his followers, God himself sends a plague to further punish the Hebrews. The fact that both Moses and God impose awesome punishments symbolizes that both the conscious and the unconscious aspects of the masculine Illumined Mind are defensive and acting in concert. The plague symbolizes the incapacitation and suffering experienced by the body through destructive impulses and thoughts issued from the mind. And all this happened because the body sought balance and relief from the shadow side of the Illumined Mind ... an overcontrolling, insecure, jealous, vengeful, infantile mind.

Do you see the amazing similarity between the story of Adam and Eve, the story of Moses and the Golden Calf, and the fundamental conflict each of us faces in our own psychological maturation? Do you see how primitive and powerful defense mechanisms are evoked by an immature psyche when it encounters an element that has vast unconscious power over it?

When these realizations struck my awareness, I entered a state of near ecstasy. I recalled that fateful sunrise atop the pyramid, when my lifelong beliefs in the Judeo-Christian and the Illumined Mind religious models of the East collapsed, when my feeling was that I should not seek to fill the void with another model but should let Life teach me about spirituality. I now realized why that material came in as a feeling, not a voice. I realized why everything pleasurable, sensual, sexual, fertile, and naturally creative is regarded as unspiritual and is reduced to sin and evil. I now had new eyes through which to see why pagan rites of spring, celebrations of genital fertility, and—most important—women themselves have been condemned by Western religions. It isn't that they deserve condemnation. It is that they are too powerful to be contained and ruled by the intellect.

I saw all of the "thou shalt nots" as the defense of the intellectual Masculine against the "corrupting" influences of the Feminine, as symbolized by the body below the head. With such a God in charge of masculine consciousness, no wonder women were desecrated and diminished, with their status placed beneath that of an animal. No wonder Moses destroyed the Golden Calf by rendering it into powder (or dust, with its obvious correlation to the body returning to dust at death).

The most fundamental mysteries of Life have always been, are now, and shall always be under the influence of the Feminine . . . no matter how upset the Masculine, as mind, becomes.

As I lead workshop after workshop and seminar after seminar, I see—either through the participants' dreams or through their group-alogues—unconscious projections revealing the patterns of the fundamental split between the body (Nature, genital sexuality and sensuality, earth, Artemian, the Feminine) and the brain (Spirit, God, Illumination, heaven, Apollonian, the Masculine). This fundamental dichotomy is referred to by many names, including the mind/body split, the God/Nature split, the heaven/earth split, and the Male/Female split. But I prefer to refer to it as the Apollonian/Artemian split, since that name honors the antiquity of the struggle as well as the gender aspects.

A Summary of Psychological Insights from the Story of the Golden Calf

The story fundamentally represents the conflict in the human male between the two basic centers of creativity and divinity . . . the brain, with its masculine intellectual function, and the genitals, with their association with the Feminine and the desires of the flesh. The degree to which the Masculine reacts against the Feminine and the Body is the degree to which the male is threatened and potentially vulnerable to the female and sexuality. The masculine behavior is immature . . . reactive and overcompensating.

Jesus and the Virgin Birth
(Matt. 1:18–25, Luke 1:26–38)

The two major biblical accounts of the details surrounding the Virgin Birth of Jesus through Mary are contained in Matt. 1:18–25 and in Luke 1:26–38. I will present both as they are given in the New International Version. What deserves special attention are the details around the asexual conception. The birth itself is normal and is of less importance.

Matt. 1:18–25

¹⁸This is how the birth of Jesus Christ came about: His mother Mary was pledged to be married to Joseph, but before they came together, she was found to be with child through the Holy Spirit. ¹⁹Because Joseph her husband was a righteous man and did not want to expose her to public disgrace, he had in mind to divorce her quietly.

²⁰But after he had considered this, an angel of the Lord appeared to him in a dream and said, "Joseph son of David, do not be afraid to take Mary home as your wife, because what is conceived in her is from the Holy Spirit. ²¹She will give birth to a son, and you are to give him the name Jesus, because he will save his people from their sins."

²²All this took place to fulfill what the Lord had said through the prophet: ²³"The virgin will be with child and will give birth to a son, and they will call him Immanuel"—which means, "God with us."

²⁴When Joseph woke up, he did what the angel of the Lord had commanded him and took Mary home as his wife. ²⁵But he had no union with her until she gave birth to a son. And he gave him the name Jesus.

Luke 1:26–38

²⁶In the sixth month, God sent the angel Gabriel to Nazareth, a town in Galilee, ²⁷to a virgin pledged to be married to a man named Joseph, a descendant of David. The virgin's name was Mary. ²⁸The angel went to her and said, "Greetings, you who are highly favored! The Lord is with you."

²⁹Mary was greatly troubled at his words and wondered what kind of greeting this might be. ³⁰But the angel said to her, "Do not be afraid, Mary, you have found favor with God. ³¹You will be with child and give birth to a son, and you are to give him the name Jesus. ³²He will be great and will be called the Son of the Most High. The Lord God will give him the throne of his father David, ³³and he will reign over the house of Jacob forever; his kingdom will never end."

³⁴"How will this be," Mary asked the angel, "since I am a virgin?"

³⁵The angel answered, "The Holy Spirit will come upon you, and

the power of the Most High will overshadow you. So the holy one to be born will be called the Son of God. [36]Even Elizabeth your relative is going to have a child in her old age, and she who was said to be barren is in her sixth month. [37]For nothing is impossible with God."

[38]"I am the Lord's servant," Mary answered. "May it be to me as you have said." Then the angel left her.

Analysis of the Story of the Virgin Birth

The Virgin Birth of Christ represents a major shift in the collective Unconscious of the Western religious psyche, as the two primary creative centers, the brain (in which the God of the Hebrews is based) and the genitals (represented by the Feminine, or Mary) enter a joint venture, with the product being Jesus Christ.

From another, similar perspective, the God of Adam and the God of Moses—if it is the same God—has become more human and more loving. The female is now to be the temple of creation of his son, Jesus, which is a far different circumstance from that of the creation of Adam or of Eve. The feminine mystery of the womb and of pregnancy is now being celebrated and sanctified through this creation/birth pathway. The fact of the missing elements (the male genitals and actual physical intercourse) still reflects a disownment and distancing from the genitals and sexuality. Importantly, however, the lower portion of the body is being acknowledged through pregnancy and birth. As the body simultaneously symbolizes the world, a new relationship with the world is being engaged by the Masculine.

The powerful attitudes, conscious and unconscious, about the purity of a woman who has been untouched by a male phallus also confirm the disownment and demeaning of the genitals and sexuality in general. Whatever God is in the New Testament, God is obviously still insecure about sexuality and the body, because, as we have seen already, sexuality, emotionality, and physicality can easily overthrow and embarrass the mind. Still, the female organs of generation are being utilized . . . which represents a huge leap in the acceptance of the Feminine and the body. The masculine psyche is incarnating into the body and into the world.

The Holy Spirit, which somehow inseminates Mary, is of the air and of heaven and therefore under the influence of the Masculine, but not yet physical ... just as the angels who appear to Mary and Joseph were of the air, of the mind, with its dream dimensions of consciousness. The pattern of the firstborn son as the most important of all the children, a Judaic tradition, is apparent. The fact that God has a son but no daughter is also an overt denial and diminishment of the Feminine. Thus, there is still a strong tendency to exploit the Feminine for masculine ego enhancement and miss the full richness and depth of the Feminine and Her capacities for relationship, nourishment, procreation, and death. The compassion and understanding of Joseph, however, are truly remarkable, signaling a maturational development in the Masculine ... in Joseph's capacity to relate to other than his own progeny.

A Summary of Psychological Insights from the Story of the Virgin Birth

1. The birth of an individual without sexual union (i.e., Adam and Eve, and Athena) symbolizes the operation of the creative forces of the mind as opposed to the creative forces of the body. The Virgin Birth of Jesus Christ represents the product of the blended creative forces of the mind (God) and the body (Mary) ... of the brain and the genitals. The root word from which the name Mary is derived means "the ocean." The ocean is symbolic of the vast Unconscious and the Great Mother, so the asexual conception of Christ has taken place in the collective Unconscious and basically issues from the Great Mother.

2. The vehicle of the virgin—as distinct from the vehicle of the woman who has already conceived children, the mother—suggests underlying defense against the masculine phallus, as the virgin is unpenetrated.

3. The preference that the firstborn child be male and the dedication of the firstborn son to God, as was done with Jesus and is done in all traditional Jewish families, indicates that the God of the Hebrews and the God of the Christians is still psychologically masculine, is still brain-based, and is still fundamentally defended against the Feminine.

4. The announcements of two unusual births—Jesus to Mary and John the Baptist to Elizabeth—by the angel Gabriel symbolize the power of the mind over the body, and the creative power of the masculine psychological elements in relation to the Virgin and the Post-Menopausal woman, or Crone. Gabriel is a psychological projection from the deep feminine psyche and is under the power of the masculine, as he is a being of the air and not of the earth. Gabriel is represented as blowing a long horn, which is phallic and represents the power of insemination by the Masculine through the creative powers of the mouth and head areas . . . through words and thoughts.

5. The emphasis on the house of David and the male line, with no mention of the lineage of Mary, again points to an insecure Masculine, which reflects its vulnerability to the Feminine through denial of the Feminine's importance. This is reflected again in the realization that God has no daughters.

6. The virgin birth transpiring in Bethlehem implies an improving relationship between the mind and the body, as the word Bethlehem means "house of bread or food . . . for man and beast." The Christ child in a manger and in the area of a barn also reflect this same theme, that of the harmony between the human elements of the mind and the animal aspects of the body.

The Many Aspects of Jesus

The emphasis Jesus places on love and relationship clearly reflects that he is Mother-complected or unconsciously under the power of the Feminine, despite his biological gender and his relationship to the God of heaven. I even have some concern when I evaluate Jesus' statements supporting the teaching of love and compassion, for my own experiences with Self-discovery as well as my work with many other individuals confirm that whenever an attribute is overly stressed and overly emphasized, its counterpart—here, that which hates and divides—lurks powerfully in the Unconscious, always ready to spring forth. This shadow side of Love, in the case of Jesus, seems to be mostly handled through stories about his unconscious counterparts . . . Lucifer, Satan, and the Devil.

The Luciferian principle breaks up and divides, destroys and diminishes, while its counterpart relates, creates, augments, and heals. At the human level, Jesus' personality shadow was displayed in his reactivity to the money changers in the temple, in his using his powers for personal reasons when he changed the water into wine at a wedding, and in his cursing the fig tree that had no fruit. To be exposed more directly to the shadow side of the messianic Christ, without projecting Christ's shadow onto Lucifer, all one has to do is read the book of Revelation!

With this foreshadowing in mind, we can inquire as to what Mary's son, Jesus, must reflect from a psychospiritual viewpoint.

Great writers have already acknowledged Christ as reflecting the Cosmic Person or the Christed states of consciousness, the symbol of the integrated Self, the collective sacrifice of the best Western society had to offer for redemption and salvation, a Sun God of the Illumined Mind, the symbol of immortal Life, the symbol of the awakened Heart Center, and God Incarnate, to mention but a few. I can attune to each of these perspectives without hesitation when I approach Christ (in distinction to Jesus) as a Symbol. What I would like to peruse, however, are a few less elevated reflections about Jesus, with the hope of providing a more balanced and deeper appreciation of what is involved in carrying both the human and the divine aspects of Life. From the perspective that all of us—including Jesus—are multidimensional beings and have many selves based predominantly, if not entirely, in the unconscious aspects of Beinghood, I can approach Jesus with far greater awareness than if I conceive of him as a single entity in a single body.

The primary psychological pattern Jesus represents is that of one specially born through heavenly intervention. This pattern includes a special mother (in effect a goddess), absent physical father, precocious childhood, youthful experience as a wisdom teacher and healer, and the achievement of godhood as an object of collective sacrifice and death, followed by resurrection and ascension to heaven. It is not complete, since, in the end, all the forces withdraw into heaven (the mental arenas), to the diminishment of the body or earthly elements. Even the traditional shape of the cross reflects this, as the horizontal bar is not centered between the top and the bottom of the vertical bar but is positioned closer to the top, signifying a skewing toward the Masculine and the mind. Jesus' dying at the age of thirty-three rather than living out a full expression of life also reflects an incomplete incarnation. The Buddha, by contrast, reflected a full life cycle of conscious awakening, as he was the product of human parents, he married and procreated, struggled to reach Illumination, achieved it, and stayed on to live a long life of teaching, finally dying in his eighties.

I find it interesting that many individuals passing through my Conferences have little difficulty perceiving Jesus as an androgynous being—a blend of male and female—yet they have great difficulty imagining him as having feminine selves and masculine selves, human selves, and immortal and divine selves. For instance, Jesus' inner feminine is mostly reflected through his relationships with Mary Magdalene, the former prostitute, and his mother, Mary, who reflects both the Virgin and the Divine Mother. Psychodynamically, those who are important to us and surround us are outward reflections of our inner, unconscious equivalents, and we may learn much about Jesus from understanding what aspects of his inner nature were reflected by those outer persons.

The female Virgin/Prostitute pair refers to Jesus' unconscious feminine split between the feminized brain (the asexual female or Virgin) and the body (the Prostitute). The fact that Jesus, Mary (the Virgin), and Mary Magdalene (the Prostitute) are all worshiped almost interchangeably in Catholicism supports the suggestion that the primary attributes of Jesus that are worshiped are his feminine attributes. I have come to believe, in fact, that Jesus represents the feminization of Judaism.

The Deification of the Parent

The Divine Male Child/Divine Mother and the absent-Father patterns set in motion the male initiation into the Feminine mysteries of relationship, nourishment, healing, intuition, and feminine sexuality. Such a mother-complected circumstance also predisposes the individual to sexual conflict in terms of sexual ego-identity crises and to the Divine Mother/Whore oscillation. The sexual ego-identity crises may resolve as selves reflecting predominantly homosexuality (if only female sexual selves are inducted through the mother), predominantly bisexuality (if both female and male sexual selves are inducted through the mother), or predominantly heterosexuality with a powerful mother fixation (if only male sexual selves are inducted by the mother). The hand dealt by Life to the conceptus determines which aspects of the Self are available for induction by the mother. It is not a matter of child abuse or victimization of the child by the mother. It is a matter of forces operating unconsciously and serving Life, as the Divine Male Child/Divine Mother dynamics are immortal patterns that incarnate in every generation, in every society.

In the oscillation between the Divine Mother and the Whore which a mother-complected male can experience, the male is attracted to the power the Divine Mother bestows on her special Son but is trapped in the split between divinity and sexuality. He can sexually engage the Divine Mother aspect of his wife (which is invariably present, as he projects this aspect onto her) only through permitted and acceptable sexual behavior. He must, through fantasy, masturbation, and/or extramarital affairs, seek either a very uninhibited lover or a prostitute to express the full range of sexuality to which he feels overwhelmingly attracted. The chaotic sexuality balances the overly defended and unconscious incestuous attraction to the Divine Mother.

In both men and women, and regardless of other contributing factors to the development of the parental complexes, the opposite-gender parent is deified by the child at the unconscious level. I feel this occurs primarily as a defense, which protects the child from the fundamental incestuous nature of the parent/child relationship. Somehow the deification cuts off the conscious realization of the genital impulses. Although this is natural at the infant and child levels of development, this same dynamic, when carried over, at the unconscious level, into the marital relationship, creates the potential for "sacred" sex within the marriage and "abandoned" sex outside of the marriage.

A fast way to realize whether one is still operating under the influence of a deified parent to defend against sexual impulses toward that parent is to see if one can easily image one's parents engaging in wild, uninhibited sexual activity, or whether sexual images are forbidden, difficult to consider, or are strictly controlled and limited to what is regarded as "acceptable."

When we approach Jesus as a man and Christ as the messianic, collective overshadowing of Jesus, we can well appreciate that there may be many possible facets to the personal and transpersonal sexuality of Jesus. I am aware of large groupings who claim that Jesus and Mary Magdalene were married and issued children. I am also aware of those who hold that Jesus was predominantly homosexual and that this was reflected in his relationship with John and with some of the other disciples. That he was unmarried is only a minor contributing piece of evidence. That he uses primarily feminine resources and values, is symbolized by a cup containing blood and later referred to as the Holy Grail (a cup containing blood is actually symbolic of the feminine mystery or womb), and that he completely avoids sexuality with women are more substantial indications of his possible feminine sexual disposition. In my mind, the stronger evidence for a sexual Jesus, whether the sexuality be predominantly heterosexual, bisexual, or homosexual, is the anecdotal support for the existence of heightened sexuality, including bisexuality and homosexuality, in those individuals who have experienced the messianic or collective states of consciousness, regardless of what their preference is at their ordinary outer levels of awareness.

For a male, the homosexual attraction activates when the heightened self is predominantly, if not exclusively, feminine. This female aspect is naturally attracted to the masculine and seeks to balance its forces in relationship to a male. When the heightened self is masculine, the heterosexual attraction occurs. If the heightened state is neutral (and there are neuter gods), the sexual energy is apparently neutralized, yet powerful attractive forces seem to be operating. Also, when I stop to consider the deeper feelings I personally have about charismatic individuals, I almost invariably find sexual attraction operating. The attraction to power is present as well, but the deeper primal force operating is sexuality. It is, in fact, impossible to explore the Unconscious without discovering aspects of Self that are manifesting the full ranges of gender and sexuality. For the vast majority of people, however, most if not all of these unconscious aspects will take form only in the dimension of dreams and never emerge as active, outer senses of self.

The struggle with sexuality and spirituality was candidly revealed in a PBS program called "The Monastery." According to that documentary, 80 percent of the priests, within the closed order that was evaluated, reported being homosexually inclined. Yet given that most men attracted into the Western religious life are mother-complected, the revelation was not that surprising.

There is no question that being isolated into single-gender populations—which happens in prisons, in the military, and in priesthoods and nunneries—leads to the expression of homosexuality by usually heterosexual males and females. Are we seeing the power of the Unconscious to induct the countergender in an individual for internal and external balance when the physical countergender is unavailable in the external reality? This certainly raises some interesting questions regarding the multiplicity of the psyche in unusual situations.

Hopefully, through a greater awareness of unconscious dynamics, we may have more compassion for those individuals within the religious traditions who wear the mask of great virtue, yet find themselves forced to engage the Whore/Prostitute counterpart, much to their own moral disgust and humiliation. When we have a greater understanding of the Unconscious and those of its counterbalancing forces which keep us from becoming too rigid, sterile, and abstracted from Life, we won't be so willing to perform personal and collective sacrifices on these people.

Individuals awakening to the larger aspects of Beinghood should be prepared to take on the deeper, natural forces of the psyche as they extend their ranges of interaction and creativity. In regard to sexuality, these include, but are certainly not limited to, a range of homosexual and bisexual expressions that are beyond the infantile and adolescent stages of life. Every individual has masculine and feminine aspects—not just one of each, but many. Upon realizing this, we can have a far greater understanding of unconscious behavior and a deeper appreciation for those who venture beyond the limits imposed by society and religion. We can also recognize that discussions of the sexual experiences that occur on pathways of spiritual development, whether those experiences are expressed outwardly or inwardly, could well serve novitiates in their preparation to handle the service to Life their calling entails . . . which includes the capacity of a single individual to demonstrate heightened masculine *and* feminine states of Being.

The public outrage over *The Last Temptation of Christ*—initially over the book by Kazantzakis and later over the film version—is further evidence that defense against the sexuality of Jesus and Mary Magdalene is still very much a part of our culture today. In the film, for example, there is a dream sequence in which Jesus engages Mary Magdalene sexually, and if ever we wanted psychological proof of how sexually immature our society is, the near riots over the implication that Jesus was sexually involved with her are all too revealing. And the forbidden question remains: Why do we react against any implication concerning the sexuality of Jesus? From the perspective we are exploring, it doesn't matter what the sexual preferences may be, as sexuality of any kind is defended against . . . not a specific type of sexuality. When we appreciate reactivity as a defense against forbidden impulses and disowned selves contained in the one who is reacting, it becomes obvious why the outer awareness would react so violently to Jesus expressing sexually. Jesus as a sexual being makes us too vulnerable to our own disowned senses of sexuality, including incestuous parental/child and sibling sexuality.

CHAPTER TWELVE

CATHEDRALS,
THE PELVIC MYSTERY,
AND A TEACHING DREAM

Most of us who are involved in spiritual exploration have such a need to see only that which meets our expectations or beliefs about people or about Life that we hardly realize how prejudicial most of our viewpoints actually are. An example of this can be seen in the architecture of the great Cathedrals of the world.

To achieve the feeling of great lift, of *upwardness* one senses in cathedrals such as Notre Dame, Chartres in France, and Winchester in England, a building technique called the flying buttress was developed. The buttresses surround the outside of the cathedral, quite literally holding up the high walls. When one is inside these cathedrals, one's eye is inevitably drawn upward. All the forces within the cathedral seem to be lifting and celebrating that which is *rising and above*. In other words, the spiritual path is away from earthliness.

I had this thought in mind recently when I was sharing with a close friend my observation that the main aisle in Winchester Cathedral is an unforgettable experience. He is very well informed about the architecture of most European churches, and he pointed out to me the almost miraculous arrangement of components which gives one the sense of inspiration and elevation. One's senses are constantly raised toward God, which is an inspirational experience itself.

I then suggested that there must be elements reflecting a *down-*

ward thrust. I wondered: Where were they, and why couldn't we see them? He noted that such is the mystery of the Church that the focus is always upward, to which I suggested that that was just the problem. After thinking about the issue, I realized the downward forces *are* represented ... in the aesthetically less pleasing exterior structure, with its flying buttresses and other supporting walls. Nevertheless, an overall deception suddenly became obvious to me. The architecture is geared to lift the state of consciousness into the air ... toward the masculine element and the mind. However, the unrecognized component of the architecture is its denial of the earth, the implication that the earth is less than, or not as good as, the elements of the sky. Since, fundamentally, to the deep psyche, the body and the earth are appreciated as being the same thing, these architectural features symbolize a denial of the body, the earth, the Feminine, and, of course, sexuality.

Subsequently I realized something even more profound about the Church's conscious and unconscious relationship to the Feminine when, to my own astonishment, the thought occurred to me that the physical configuration of churches might intrinsically symbolize the Feminine pelvic mystery. Among the things I considered were that the main entrance and aisle could reflect the vaginal canal, with the altar or more sacred area reflecting the mystery of the uterus. The Holy Water that is sprinkled onto a person upon entering might suggest amniotic fluid. It was a startling possibility, but the more I thought about it, the more credible it became.

Observing the way the Masculine surrounds and attends to the mysteries represented by the Church reminds me of how, in the insemination of the female, many sperm are usually required to penetrate the protective layers of the ovum so one sperm can eventually fertilize the ovum. Perhaps the basic mystery of biological procreation is being unconsciously enacted in terms of the numbers of priests serving the Church. Perhaps this is also one reason why women have not been permitted to serve the Church, since it is basically a *masculine* deification of the mother, the womb, and the ovum!

The fact that the Masculine exclusively controlled the feminine mystery for thousands of years points to unconscious masculine inferiority in relation to the Feminine and to the body. At the outer level, the Church proclaims that it exists to celebrate Jesus and the resurrection, while at the inner, perhaps more unconscious level, the Feminine and the mystery of creativity are being celebrated.

In fact, all temples, magic circles, churches, sacred caves, haeaus (Hawaiian temples), kivas, and other similar places are interpreted by the deep psyche as reflecting the mystery of the womb. No matter what the cognitive overlay may be, that will be true. It is what gives these places such power. Of course, in our outer lives, just as in dreams, we are unconscious of such deeper meanings, and until the unconscious elements are appreciated, we are sleepy souls thinking we know what our lives are about.

With these things in mind, I would like to present some of the insights that came to me in the Cathedral of Notre Dame in Paris. As I sat there, well down the main aisle near the left side, the cathedral as a representative of the feminine mystery was more apparent to me than ever. In my journal, under the title "Ideas to Contemplate while Approaching a Temple," I wrote the following:

> The mystery of the entry . . . the portal into the unknown . . . the labia . . . Death.
>
> Approaching the Temple requires a certain state of awareness to access the deepest mysteries and resources. Whether one visualizes a mysterious temple or is actually seeing one of the great temples of the world, it matters not, for the deep psyche experiences both as being the same. The mystery of returning to one's source of Being is everywhere evident. The womb, the water, the Feminine, the infants in the form of cherubs, the awesome size of the symbols!
>
> The unknown . . . the greater than oneself . . . sets the tone for the inner experiences. It is as if one's deeper beingness appreciates the unstructured, the uncommitted, the unrealized in order to display its inner resources and treasures.
>
> The purification . . . meaning the focus and selection of an unencumbered, clear, more innocent, and therefore fresh presence . . . facilitates the entry into the mystery.
>
> Some of our great temples connote hugeness and grandeur, stimulating states of awareness associated with the

womb consciousness, early infancy, or early childhood wherein the parents are perceived as gods and goddesses. This tendency to regress under the impact of the awesomeness of the architecture risks the precipitation of fetal and infantile resources and parent-child bondings ... empowering the church rather than the individual. These same forces, in a more mature individual, bring the psyche to the threshold of the transcendental.

Enter the Temple without hope that one will exit ... that one will die into the sacred, and should the sacred seek life through one's being, a new incarnation emerges ... fresh and awe-filled. This allows the moment to become fully charged with the Presence of the Temple.

To prepare to die, then, is part of the ritual of entry, just as it is part of the ritual of entry into the woman. It's the loose ends, the incompletions that hang up the psyche and prevent one from entering the mystery completely.

A Teacher's Teaching Dream

This brings me to another life-altering dream I had. It came in 1984, following the dreams of an Easter Death and of the healing performed by an East Indian. It was a werewolf dream.

Although I didn't know it at the time, a werewolf dream is an initiation dream, signaling maturation of the Unconscious and announcing major changes in the outer levels of experience. This one was reflecting the beginning resolution of the split between spirituality and sexuality, between the mind and the body. It was not only the sort of dream that takes a lifetime to integrate fully, but it was also humbling, reminding me where I actually am in my soul's Unfoldment. The dream:

I am exploring a large, beautifully constructed cathedral. I am outside on some sort of scaffolding, which contains a brightly lighted elevator. I am two-thirds of the way to the top of the cathedral. From this scaffolding I can see into the cathedral through large archways and circular windows. An old man and an old woman are with me. Both are in excellent health and have bright blue eyes and white, white hair.

There is a space of about one foot between the scaffolding and the church exterior. We are at a landing where one could step over that space and enter the cathedral, which I do. As I enter, I see a massive, spiral stone staircase that leads down into the cathedral. The old couple, who are still outside, motion for me to join them and go down in the brightly lighted elevator, but I say I want to go down the stone staircase inside the cathedral rather than using the elevator in the scaffolding.

As I gaze into the cathedral, I see that it is immense, spacious, and beautifully but simply decorated. The stone is pinkish red, like the cathedral in Alba, France. The floor is azure blue marble. The staircase itself is gray stone and well crafted.

As I descend the staircase, I realize that I am going to the crypts under the cathedral. I come into a dark passageway deep beneath the church. I can hear two men talking, shoveling dirt, and using a pickax. I follow what little light is available until I see the men in the distance. They have a lighted kerosene lantern and are struggling with some stone slabs at chest level.

I suddenly realize that they are opening the tombs of two werewolves that have been buried there for thousands of years.

The two men are excited about opening the tombs to get the bones of the werewolves. Their intent is to display these remains in a carnival show to exploit their commercial value. The men are raunchy-looking characters, dirty, unshaven . . . basically fitting a criminal stereotype. They are tugging on one of two burlap baglike containers and manage to pull it out of the burial crypt, but they are unable to get the second one out. Something startles them and they flee, taking the one bag of bones, leaving the crypt open and the lantern still in place.

I inch my way to the crypt and look in. To my amazement,

I see a huge wooden beam supporting the whole church. It is lying horizontally across the top of a small cup, like a coffee mug, which is a rich azure blue, and which in turn is pinning down the burlap bag containing the remains of the other were-wolf. The bag is lying on top of an earth foundation. I think, "It's a good thing they didn't get this particular werewolf or the whole church would have collapsed!"

The dream suddenly shifts and I am at a carnival, where there is going to be a contest in which three men will see who can most rapidly eat a three-page handwritten letter sealed in a white envelope. Each man is given one such en-velope. I cannot see two of them, but I can see the third, who is a sweet, white-haired old man, soft-featured, gentle, tooth-less, and benign. He is loved by all, especially the children, who are rooting for him to win.

As the contest starts, I suddenly know that a bone frag-ment of the werewolf that had been taken from the church is in the old man's envelope, and if he eats it, he will turn into a werewolf. I am going to warn him, but he suddenly eats the envelope and all its contents in one swallow. He is smiling a victorious smile and is seemingly unaffected. I think, "Oh, my God, in a few minutes the changes will begin to appear."

Right on schedule the old man suddenly starts to slump to the ground, but already the changes in his body and face are apparent. He is rapidly becoming strong, virile, and youthful. His mouth fills in with new teeth, and his hair turns dark brown and then black. The hair on his head covers the upper half of his face. The lower half of his face remains uncovered and is clean-shaven. A well-formed, smooth black plastic mask/helmet forms over the upper half of his head, so only his eyes can be seen. The hair growth isn't as evident when the mask/helmet covers it.

He stands up and, with hands that have long fingernails, reaches out to the crowd, which hasn't quite realized what happened. He roars powerfully to the women, "I want to eat your breasts!" Needless to say, the crowd and I scatter . . . fast.

Then, I find I am trying to hide in a very large two-story motor home that turns out to be where the two men who took the werewolf remains from the church are living. They are on the second floor, in what seems to be a command post or control room, counting the revenue from the various carnival businesses they run. I imagine that, based on the amount of money I see on the table, they have done well.

I burst into where the men are, to tell them the werewolf is coming to kill us. I know from the noise and motion of the motor home that the werewolf is now inside and coming up the stairs. The two men flee through a side door, as do I . . . just as the werewolf breaks into the control room.

Outside on a narrow shiplike deck with a rope railing, I slip and lie helpless on my back as the werewolf comes out onto the decking. He has a gun and is pointing it at my head. I am begging for my life when this part of the dream ends.

Next, I am watching the werewolf running toward his black vehicle, which is half automobile and half jet airplane. He is warning the children to stay away, as he is not what they think he is. The children are still seeing the kindly old man. When the werewolf reaches his vehicle, he speeds off at low altitude, heading for the North Pole, where there is an airport at which he can change planes and get home.

Upon arriving at the North Pole airport, he gets out of his sleek, black auto/plane and again warns the children who are gathered there to stay away from him if they don't want to get eaten or hurt.

When he enters the airport terminal, the werewolf sees a small group of men and women who seem to be waiting for him. They greet him with eyes that are filled with tears of compassion and understanding. The werewolf removes the mask/helmet to fully expose his face and head. His eyes are also filled with tears. The dream ends.

The following is a beginning interpretation of the highlights of this dream . . . a teacher's teaching dream.

The large, beautifully constructed cathedral is the fully developed Spiritual Feminine, with its inner mysteries. My being on a scaffolding means I am still in the masculine mode of overview, structure, abstraction, and mapping. The gap signifies the separation between the masculine and feminine elements in my psyche. It is not a large gap, but is significant enough in size to indicate that fusing or blending has clearly not yet occurred.

Being two-thirds of the way to the top of the cathedral reveals how far my masculine psyche has taken me from the foundational, elemental, earthy, and sexual aspects of my life. The old couple symbolize wisdom figures. Their blue eyes indicate clarity of seeing, and their white, white hair reflects Elderhood and vintage wisdom. The fact that both the male and the female aspects are present indicates that the balance of the Masculine and Feminine is available and correct. Also, my engaging the greater mysteries of creativity in the later stages of life is foreshadowed by the old couple, who are far beyond the procreative stages and well into Eldership. My separation from them indicates that masculine and feminine Eldership are not part of my personal identity at this stage of my development, although those resources are available. The brightly lighted elevator is the Illuminated Mind aspect. It is safe and attractive but also presents the danger of being womblike and overly protective . . . just as does the Garden of Eden.

My electing to descend the stone staircase inside the cathedral rather than taking the elevator in the scaffolding signals that my experience of the Feminine is going to be direct, vulnerable, and first-hand, rather than indirect or abstract and overly protected, as it might be if I received it through the masculine mind. The wisdom figures are also descending, though via the elevator, signaling the grounding and anchoring that will be available at a later time in my life.

The fact that I can see into the Feminine—the cathedral—indicates that my inner masculine nature is well developed, which allows me to see clearly into many aspects of Life not ordinarily seen by others. The Feminine is open to me and allows me to use Her resources of intuition and feeling. (The archways are thresholds, and the circular windows are like eyes into the soul.) The proportions of the cathedral in relation to my own size may reflect proportions of the Feminine to the Masculine. They indicate, for example, that for Masculine-Feminine balance to exist, only a small amount of the Masculine is required in relation to an enormous amount of the Feminine, perhaps a proportion akin to the size of a sperm relative to the size of an ovum. Balance thus need not be a fifty-fifty proposition.

The beauty and immensity of the cathedral also reflect my deification of the Mother and the degree of influence she has over my psyche. The pinkish-red stone indicates the earthiness of the structure ... perhaps even symbolizing the blending of the red fluid of menstruation and the white fluid of ejaculation. The plain decor signifies a satisfaction with simplicity and the absence of a need to mask inferiority with superiority. The azure marble floor indicates the water element and how water reflects the color of the sky, thus pointing to a deep, clear blending of the elements of air and water ... the masculine and feminine elements. The spiral staircase may speak of the very essence of biological life ... the DNA strands and the double helix. Descent itself implies getting more real or more foundational, while the crypts refer to that which lies buried under the surface content.

As I descend the staircase, I realize that I am going to the crypts under the cathedral. I come into a dark passageway deep beneath the church. I can hear two men talking, shoveling dirt, and using a pickax. I follow what little light is available until I see the men in the distance. They have a lighted kerosene lantern and are struggling with some stone slabs at chest level.

I suddenly realize that they are opening the tombs of two werewolves that have been buried there for thousands of years.

The two men are excited about opening the tombs to get the bones of the werewolves. Their intent is to display these remains in a carnival show to exploit their commercial value. The men are raunchy-looking characters, dirty, unshaven ... basically fitting a criminal stereotype. They are tugging on one of two burlap baglike containers and manage to pull it out of the burial crypt, but they are unable to get the second one out. Something startles them and they flee, taking the one bag of bones, leaving the crypt open and the lantern still in place.

The darkness of the crypt area suggests that whatever is contained in this area of my psyche is unconscious and disowned. Sure enough, the dream presents two shadow elements of my masculine psyche: criminals (those who would exploit the sacred for money and power) and bones of werewolves (the dormant, transitional, half-animal, half-human aspect).

Despite the fact that the two criminals are sleazy, definitely antisocial, and power-driven, they also symbolize those elements of my psyche which are capable of breaking through barriers, mind-sets, and taboos to get at what more acceptable characters might not have the nerve to undertake. My usual conscious self would definitely not be opening crypts beneath a great cathedral to steal the bones of werewolves.

From the perspective of dream symbology, the criminal elements and the werewolf elements are probably two different forms of the same shadow self within me. The fact that there are *two* men and *two* werewolves is a way for the Unconscious to emphasize aspects it feels are important, as well as for it to reveal important simultaneous possibilities regarding the symbols. For example, the presence of two men causes me to acknowledge more completely the criminal-like activity of opening crypts and stealing bones and exploiting the sacred through the carnival show. Two bags of werewolves' bones emphasize the importance of the bones underpinning the superstructure of the cathedral (the Feminine) and also emphasize the importance of the werewolves in my own personal development, something that is soon to be elaborated on in this dream. Twos additionally connote opposites and the attraction of opposites. My having a twin brother may also be referenced.

Clearly the masculine elements (represented by the males who have so far been in the dream) are trying to regain their roots but are having to enter dangerous circumstances involving potential reprisals of the Mother/Church, which is evident when the criminals flee at the first indication they may be caught. (This part of the dream reminds me of the story "Iron John," from *Grimm's Fairy Tales*. Popularized by contemporary poet Robert Bly, it tells symbolically of the awakening of the caged, raw masculine element in a boy and indicates that the key to his freedom to experience the early stages of manhood lies under his mother's pillow. The boy has to cleverly steal the key by slipping into his mother's bedroom when she is away, as she would never willingly give it to him.)

The most dramatic aspect of this part of the dream is not the frightening nature of open crypts or my finding the werewolf bones. It is my seeing the bright azure blue coffee mug that separates the structure above from the earth elements below.

> ... I see a huge wooden beam supporting the whole church. It is lying horizontally across the top of a small cup, like a coffee mug, which is a rich azure blue, and which in turn is pinning down the burlap bag containing the remains of the other werewolf. The bag is lying on top of an earth foundation. I think, "It's a good thing they didn't get this particular werewolf or the whole church would have collapsed!"

From the viewpoint of basic pattern-level consciousness, a cup or mug represents the Feminine, for it is concave and acts as a container ... reflecting the womb. Its circular lip further emphasizes the Feminine. In my interpreting this aspect of the dream, however, the first association I had with the cup was that of the Holy Grail and the masculine spiritual path fundamental to Christian beliefs. It symbolized the blood and body of Christ ... the vital essence.

Then I suddenly realized that the quest for the Grail was really a disguised quest for the ovum, the Feminine, the Mother. If the Masculine doesn't seek out the Mystery and prepare to die for the Mystery, it doesn't fulfill the most fundamental masculine purpose. One of Life's great spiritual intentions, in fact, is to achieve a proximity to God and, hopefully, to be absorbed into God. This resolution of the spiritual quest reminds me of the sperm's arduous journey from the male into the female and, by grace, its reaching and penetrating the ovum. At an unconscious level this may be what the Arthurian knights were doing, and the fact that they deified the Feminine and the Church tends to support this hypothesis.

The basic, unconscious biological yearning for union pervades our religious rituals, but in a manner that is very, very disguised. So, as long as God is conceptualized only as spiritual and therefore non-physical, the body as part of the nature of God can be avoided. (Fortunately, Sir Lancelot—note the wordplay with *lance*, or the penis—experiences the Fall and accepts the seduction, only to find the true Holy Grail in the arms of Guinevere.) Thus, through the image of the Grail we can appreciate Christ's androgyny, if not actual femininity. Any cup with blood symbolizes the womb, with its mystery of menstruation, and through the symbol of the cup we can get to the body and to the blood . . . to the foundations of spirituality.

A blue coffee mug suggests masculine clarity and masculine structure or form, which will allow discernment and conscious realization. Blue is also the color used by the Catholic Church for the robes of Mary, the mother of God, so we may be experiencing an androgynous or blended symbol. In addition, blue is the color associated with the throat chakra state of consciousness, the nonprocreative aspects of creativity. The wisdoms associated with feminine intuition and related psychic abilities are symbolized by the blue of the throat color, as well.

The bones of the werewolves are under the mug and part of the supporting structure, reflecting that they are an earlier developmental aspect, upon which the later aspects (represented by the cup, the cross beam, and the church itself) will rest. The burlap bag—a coarse, womblike container—reflects the more ancient earth mother, which precedes the contemporary mother of heaven, represented in the dream by the cathedral, and, in general, by the corporate Church. That the burlap bag is resting on the earth reflects the connection to the body and to the earthy Feminine.

Examining these elements from the bottom up, we see the unconscious body (the earth), the animal/man (the bones of the werewolf), the transformed vehicle of man/woman (the cup), the huge wooden cross beam (the horizontal aspect of the cross of crucifixion), and finally, the cathedral (the deified Feminine Mystery of creation).

The mug—Christ—is the integrating principle . . . the crossing point between the Unconscious and the Awakened Consciousness, which has the capacity to support the entire Church. Christ integrates divine mind with the body. The unconscious incestuous relationship between the Mother and the Son is being transformed into the creation of a collective adrogynous figure in which the Masculine and the Feminine fuse inwardly to create a larger vehicle of consciousness to handle the dimensions of the collective.

The fact that the crypts are at chest level rather than in the ground or higher than the chest reflects the opening of the Heart Chakra. The Heart state of awareness is the first state of consciousness that is wholly human; it is the level just above the animal/human, the first experience one has of compassion and service to humanity. Christ represents the open Heart Chakra, that which is transpersonal, impersonal, compassionate, feminine, and deeply feeling.

In this dream the Divine Child self, who eventually turns into the Sun God self (Christ), doesn't reflect completed development. Rather, he reflects an intermediate stage, a blending of the masculine body and the feminine consciousness. He is basically in service to the Feminine/Mother. And we also see that the Feminine/Mother is in debt to Christ. She would collapse without him.

The danger in any path of Self-Realization is that of being absorbed into god/goddess patternings, with the resultant loss of one's humanity or soul . . . one's humanness. The Awakened, Self-Realizing individual is able to maintain a position between the animal and the god/goddess, utilizing the resources of all aspects yet not being absorbed into either one of the poles of existence. The seduction into the deified aspects of Self would lead to sterility and loss of connection to the body.

In this section of the dream, the central focus is on the blue cup, the cross beam, and the bones of the werewolves. Thus, my Unconscious is in the process of revealing the relationships between the higher and lower aspects of Self and unleashing important, vital energy into my psyche in the form of what is represented by the criminals and the werewolves. I must have been in danger of losing my connection to the body, as the dream is concentrating on masculine physicality. The dream also indicates that going back to one's roots

provides a new understanding and appreciation of disowned or un-
appreciated selves and their function. It is a path by which seques-
tered energy may be set free.

The dream symbols revealing my commercial, criminal, con man,
exploitative, power-driven, materialistic aspects are simply what they
are. Just that! I have learned the hard way that attempting to deny these
aspects only empowers them. I have also learned that they serve my
deeper Beinghood, as I suggested earlier. In this dream they are helping
the masculine part of me to handle the dark side of the Feminine . . .
her capacity to absorb and to control her creation. They are the "clever"
aspects which enable the boy in the fairy tale "Iron John" to come
forward and steal the key from under his mother's pillow.

The fact that only one sack of werewolf's bones is removed means
to me that the basic pattern of my spiritual development is to remain
intact while I experience the importance of what gives support to the
Christ image and to the Mother. The symbol thus splits into two
simultaneous paths: an exploration of the foundation of the Church
and the revelation of what the werewolves' bones represent.

> The dream suddenly shifts and I am at a carnival, where
> there is going to be a contest in which three men will see
> who can most rapidly eat a three-page handwritten letter
> sealed in a white envelope. Each man is given one such en-
> velope. I cannot see two of them, but I can see the third, who
> is a sweet, white-haired old man, soft-featured, gentle, tooth-
> less, and benign. He is loved by all, especially the children,
> who are rooting for him to win.

The carnival setting to which the dream switches symbolizes a
place where the line between dream and reality fades, and one might
imagine that what lies behind the dreamlike realities of Mardi Gras,
Halloween, Easter, and Christmas may be similar to what will be
revealed in the dream. In addition, the fact that the word *carnival*
is derived from the root words referring to animals, meat, or flesh
suggests that the body and the realms of body consciousness, in contrast to the head realms of consciousness, are to be emphasized. (In

the past, little had I realized what unconscious aspects lie just beneath the surface of our religious holidays, both present and past.)

The three men competing in the letter-eating contest may be masculine equivalents of the feminine developmental stages: the virgin, the mother, the crone. In this case, I see only the white-haired man, signaling that the focus is going to be on the masculine aspect of Eldership. The geometric form of a letter may be related to the basic square or rectangle associated with masculine stability and integration. A handwritten letter is associated with personal communication and expression. Its three pages may be reflecting the same three aspects of masculine development that are represented by the three men.

To eat a letter is to consume, to take in for absorption, to digest, to devour, or to eat . . . words. All are probably operating in this pivotal sequence in the dream. That the pages of the letter are white implies innocence, naïveté, and purity . . . perhaps referring back to the arctic white automobile in the Evil Incarnate dream in Chapter 1. That the letter is sealed in a white envelope also suggests a womb, protection, and isolation from a larger whole.

The old man ingests the letter in one big gulp, indicating that whatever the letter symbolizes, the entirety of it is to be ingested, digested, and assimilated. It may also imply that something I have written before will have to be eaten . . . that I will have to "eat my words." Certainly I have had to eat some of the words I wrote in my first book, *Joy's Way*, as new perspectives and a new vehicle of consciousness have demanded the sacrifice of some of my earlier values and perspectives.

The kindly old man, toothless and loved by the children, represents the end-stage Masculine, strongly influenced by the Feminine. He is almost like a child, harmless and soft. The two sets of polarities of Elder and Child, and Masculine and Feminine, well-known in psychodynamic circles, often transform into each other in dreams as well as in life, for the natural progression of the strong Masculine is to become more and more feminine in the later stages of life, with the older person becoming more and more childlike with further aging. In this case, however, the opposite is happening. The feminized Masculine is reverting to the virile animal/Masculine. I apparently have not expended all my masculine energy, as it is available to the Elder.

> . . . The old man suddenly starts to slump to the ground, but already the changes in his body and face are apparent. He is rapidly becoming strong, virile, and youthful. His mouth fills in with new teeth, and his hair turns dark brown and then black. The hair on his head covers the upper half of his face. The lower half of his face remains uncovered and is clean-shaven. A well-formed, smooth black plastic mask/helmet forms over the upper half of his head, so only his eyes can be seen. The hair growth isn't as evident when the mask/helmet covers it.

That the toothless old man transforms into a werewolf with healthy teeth, capable of biting, wounding, and chewing, reflects a reinvigoration of the oral area as an offensive and a defensive weapon. It also suggests that the verbal areas may be vastly strengthened . . . an augmentation of the spoken word and, by association with the fifth chakra, the written word as well. The strong dentition means that this aspect can really get its teeth into the matter . . . whatever that matter may be.

There is significant emphasis on the Feminine and the Masculine, with the lower part of the werewolf's face being feminine and the upper part masculine. That the lower face is hairless suggests a partial civilization of the animal/Masculine. Undertones of immaturity and youthfulness may also be involved. But the main point of this image is that there is a humanization of the animal. The top half of the head is covered by hair, then by a black mask/helmet. The virility symbolism of hair over the upper half may imply fertility and creativity of the mind, and the mask implies a protective covering or disguise (which is of unconscious origin, since it is black). Perhaps the fertility and creativity of the mind are actually in the unconscious and instinctual levels and are masked by intellectualization and refinement, represented by the smooth black plastic helmet. In other words, under the guise of the rational and intellectual lurks the powerful, virile, creative, instinctual animal/Masculine.

The statement "I want to eat your breasts" is very revealing. The animal/Masculine doesn't just want to suckle or nurse. It wants to eat the breasts ... to ingest and to digest them. It doesn't want to read poetry to the women or talk about Brahms. It wants what it wants, and it wants it now! This voracious animal behavior must have threads of meaning for me in regard to breast-feeding, particularly since I was a twin, and my brother and I were breast-fed only briefly before being bottle-fed. My mother told me I frequently used to take the bottle away from my twin. (I am sure there must be times when women who are breast-feeding feel this ravenous animal aspect of the infant ... that the infant can't get enough of the breast and almost devours it.)

The two-story motor home is a disguised symbol of the Feminine. Home and hearth are traditionally feminine, especially in terms of the feminine symbols that equate home and the womb. The two-storyness of the motor home reflects the sexual components, with their related power drives, as the sexual chakra is the second of the seven major human levels of consciousness. The two men counting the day's take reflect the seedy side of my psyche, which compensates for certain sexual inadequacies through power and money. (Money, power, and sex are all related in the deep psyche.)

With the appearance of the werewolf, my troubles are over—and quite literally so, since the sequence where I am begging for my life concludes with the feeling that the werewolf kills me. The gun pointed to my head area is a sexual symbol of creative insemination of the head area ... representing seeding for creative thought and the cross-fertilization of ideas, causing the death of old forms and the beginning of new ones. It is similar to cross-breeding with wild stock to improve the virility or strength of a strain or species.

Next, I am watching the werewolf running toward his black vehicle, which is half automobile and half jet airplane. He is warning the children to stay away, as he is not what they think he is. The children are still seeing the kindly old man. When the werewolf reaches his vehicle, he speeds off at low altitude, heading for the North Pole, where there is an airport at which he can change planes and get home.

Upon arriving at the North Pole airport, he gets out of his sleek, black auto/plane and again warns the children who are gathered there to stay away from him if they don't want to get eaten or hurt.

The werewolf's warning the children shows the development of the Unconscious. It is reflecting the opening of the Heart and the capacity to maintain appropriate human development as the virile animal/Masculine is reclaimed. The black automobile/aircraft—powerful, sleek, and able to fly just above the ground—symbolizes that which is masculine, sexual, and powerful.

Going to the North Pole suggests that the Unconscious is concerned with the head or the mental polarity of consciousness and is emphasizing the Masculine, which is further indicated, though subtly, by the Pole as a phallic symbol. The North Pole is also a good description of the intellect, which has the tendency to freeze or control or block the emotions, as is reflected in the ice of the north polar region. The werewolf's intention to change planes at the North Pole (the head area) in order to return home implies that the transformation of the animal, instinctual, creative, fertilizing function will complete itself with some change in the mental or mind area, allowing the werewolf to return to the unconscious aspect of the larger Self. An important relationship and balance must be struck between the animal/Masculine and the intellectual/Masculine.

When he enters the airport terminal, the werewolf sees a small group of men and women who seem to be waiting for him. They greet him with eyes that are filled with tears of compassion and understanding. The werewolf removes the mask/helmet to fully expose his face and head. His eyes are also filled with tears. The dream ends.

The compassion of the small group of men and women at the North Pole airport signifies that both masculine and feminine elements appreciate what sacrifice the werewolf has made and support its return home. The awakening of the animal/Masculine has served its purpose ... to humanize the mental aspects of Self. We don't know how the ending sequences are to be worked out, except that the characters are all in place and the conclusion is very hopeful ... the werewolf removes his helmet/mask to reveal the honesty of what he is. Compassion and vulnerability are the predominant feeling tones at the conclusion of the dream.

The Awakening of the Feminine

This dream, then, is a teacher's Teacher. As a result of my understanding its symbolic content, powerful new insights became available to my outer mind regarding the nature of the Church and religious paths purporting to be inclusive and beyond sexuality, as well as new viewpoints that deal with the Grail myths, the importance of the animal/Masculine when the masculine psyche is too close to absorption into the Mother, the vast power of the Feminine, and the heroic struggle the Masculine undergoes when awakening to the deeper forces of the Unconscious. It also emphasized that no matter how high a man or a woman climbs, his or her roots must be respected and appreciated.

As I reflect on this dream, I realize even more profoundly that we are still very early in the development of our particular life form. We are more prototypic than evolved ... still vastly dominated by defensive and abstracted psyches rather than by mature, inclusive ones. Can we come to the mystery of spirituality through sexuality and creativity ... celebrating the world as a unity rather than as an enemy to be attacked and destroyed? The masculine spiritual abstraction from the world, evident in both the East and the West, has unleashed an unconscious destructive force against the Feminine, the body, the earth. There must be a way to heal this most ancient split without either aspect becoming absorbed into the other.

I know a revolution in spiritual thinking and values must transpire. The values and dogmas we are currently living out are simply too anti-Feminine, and therefore too antilife. But it isn't easy for most men and women to admit, in terms of spiritual development reflecting the fullness of Being, that the Feminine purview is vastly superior to that of the Masculine. And considering that the psyche and the body are mostly Feminine, one can hardly blame the Masculine for defending and protecting what vestige of its integrity remains.

What I still do not understand, however, is why women feel the same way as most men about the Feminine at deep and unconscious levels. This was not always the case, as is evident in Egyptian religious practices wherein the celebration of the phallus and the vagina were appreciated as being integrative and wholesome, powerful, magical, and mysterious. Death was also a powerful theme in Egyptian culture—and with the worship of Death comes the worship of Life and sexuality. A balanced Trinity of Osiris, Isis, and Horus—Father, Mother, and Child—was in place for fifty centuries before it was replaced by the Judeo-Christian values we, in the West, hold today.

But those earlier practices are not entirely absent from modern religious expression. In fact, contemporary Western religious structures and rituals rest upon foundations from earlier and less well-known religious practices, in addition to those of Judaic origin. And just because the outer mind does not recognize the significance of the symbols doesn't mean they don't powerfully impact us. Further, in our contemporary society, in the form of the Maypole dance and the celebration of Easter, there are remnants of pagan rituals of the worship of the phallus and of the fertility rites of spring. The names of the gods and goddesses may change, but the forces behind the labels are immortal.

What is the deep Unconscious up to today as it weaves and dances us in its long, long cycles? Is a new god and/or goddess gestating as we become aware of the elements that have animated and empowered religious structures for thousands and thousands of years? Is the feminine mind, with its intuition and inclusivity, preparing to enter our awareness? Is this distinct from the procreative Feminine? Is the serpent going to get connected to the male body? Is the Word (as in "In the beginning was the Word . . .") going to get a body? Following a particularly abstracted, defensive masculine cycle of human development, is our present concern for the planet and emphasis on environmental harmony related to the awakening of some integrative, inclusive deity that reflects a blend of the mind and the body? These are exciting questions, particularly at a time when the overwhelming evidence of what is transpiring in our society points to the collapse of the Father figure.

As I watch all of this going on, I don't feel a need to do anything about it, other than celebrating the change, with its unknown future. This should not be interpreted to mean I don't believe in taking action in appropriate circumstances. It does reflect my belief that in regard to these far-reaching cycles of Life, this is not a stage in my life, or in the life of the collective, when taking action in an attempt to alter their effects is an appropriate response.

I trust the process.

CHAPTER THIRTEEN

ELDERHOOD

Elderhood is the shadow side of incapacitating old age. In the concluding phase of our life cycle, Elderhood brings us to the threshold of a mystery as profound as that of birth and procreation . . . the mystery of death and personal dissolution. Elderhood represents a state of consciousness that can draw upon the fullness of an individual lifetime *and* access a pattern of the Self, that of the Elder, which holds vast collective resources of masculine and feminine wisdoms along with concomitant collective Spiritual Realization and integration. Because Elderhood involves many kinds of experiences—not only change, decay, dying, and death, but also birth, development, and life—it functions as a stabilizing force during times when birth or death are the primary experiences of the individual, family, clan, or cultural grouping. Elders till and prepare the soil of the younger generations, guiding them into a successful relationship with Life and with Death. Elders are the sculptors and the guardians of culture and civilization. They are the great teachers of life, second only to the Master Teacher, which is Life Itself.

The Elderhood to which I am referring is a transcendent, collective dimension of Beinghood which requires that one leave the ordinary sense of self, with its provincialities, and enter the sublimity of a far grander state of being. This Elderhood contains a composite of

human experience—from the past, the present, and all possible fu-
tures. It is a dimension of majestic scope, a wholeness to which each
individual Elder's life contributes a unique measure.

Access to this wondrous state of consciousness, a state that is
eclipsed in the West by our preoccupation with the selves of Youth,
is not easily gained, even if one has lived a long life. An individual
who has lived long but whose wisdoms are confined only to the
narrow range of experience of his or her personal lifetime represents
only the earliest, most superficial stage of Elderhood Awakening. This
point is critical, for a single life is short and limited, no matter how
much one has lived. Experiences and resources based only on a personal lifetime have value, but cannot bring the full benefits that a
more developed Elder, an Elder based in the collective pool of experience, can offer.

Everyone has a certain degree of interior access to Elderhood
states of consciousness. Some individuals, in fact, are destined to live
a life predominantly based in such wisdom, and they assume that role
from the time they are very young. I have already referred to infants
who suddenly give evidence of knowing about life to a degree far
beyond what their age would suggest. Some children are even revered
as Masters Incarnate, as the scope of their wisdom and knowledge
vastly transcends their personal and individual experience. In esoteric
circles the wisdom revealed by Jesus at the age of twelve is held to
be due to his having been overshadowed by an Elder state that eclipsed
his ordinary consciousness.

Although these people are in young to very young bodies, they
present a consciousness based almost exclusively in the Eldership
ranges of being. Our prejudices might tell us that spirituality and
wisdom must be products of lifelong attainment, but those prejudices
may simply not represent truth. Each stage of life has associated with
it a psychological dimension that contains the sum total of all experiences that have ever been encountered by anyone in that stage of
consciousness. For instance, there is the Child dimension, which contains the collective total of all experiences of all children, and which
acts as a reservoir of patterns from which all incarnating individuals
draw their personal patterns of childness. One's allotment seems to
be determined at conception by one's family *and* by collective life

forces. Another example is that of the Feminine, which is the collective total of all experiences of feminine development, from which all women and men draw their individual expressions of feminineness.

So while we usually experience life as a sequence of developments that unfolds from birth to death, we may take an expanded perspective and regard all of the stages—and one's allocated patterns within each stage—as having been struck simultaneously at conception and therefore always present. This allows us to understand how the Elderhood state of consciousness may appear at much earlier biological stages, perhaps during a life-threatening illness or event, or upon the approach of early death. Not everyone, however, is destined to partake of all the psychological stages of life, and only a few individuals are destined to represent the collective Elder. But this does not suggest that those who do not experience this state will somehow be deprived, since from a mature viewpoint, one understands that the mystery of Life makes all of us part of the whole, and the whole is transcendentally part of each one of us. The individual's only task is to live well the personal hand dealt.

Many participants in my Conferences have described experiences in which they encountered the Elder state of consciousness while in an earlier stage of development. Such encounters often take place during a near-death experience and involve touching realms of vast wisdom and understanding. They may also be of a visionary nature that is not precipitated by a crisis, and that involves spontaneous revelations from a great figure such as Buddha or Christ. Most common, however, are encounters with Wisdom figures in dreams who may presage events far into the future.

Experiencing Elderhood states of consciousness during times of need or crisis is not limited only to encounters of personal significance. A family, clan, or even an entire ethnic grouping may need the Elderhood wisdoms. In these cases, someone with a greater access to the collective Elder state of consciousness will bring forth the wisdom for the family, clan, or ethnic grouping.

On such occasions, as with other times when nonordinary states are entered, very different resources of consciousness are brought forward from those which would usually be available. I know that when I enter certain teaching states of consciousness, I have access to knowledge and experience far beyond what I know and experience to be true through my usual vehicles of the self. I don't feel the constraints of chronological age . . . in fact, I feel almost ageless and intimately related to the subject matter, whether I am discussing the esoterics of Mystery Training, specific events in people's lives, or circumstances with sweeping cultural significance.

Cosmic states of consciousness are part of the Elderhood ranges. Young and relatively young individuals report vast wisdom states that last anywhere from a few minutes to many months, only to subside and not recur for the rest of their lives. An excellent example of this is Franklin Merrell-Wolff, the Western Mystic, who experienced a cosmic state of consciousness—an Illumination—at the age of forty-nine. He then spent the remainder of his years contemplating the wisdom he acquired in but half an hour, even though the "current" or "ambrosia" (as he termed it) of the experience lasted many months and he could access it to a small degree throughout the rest of his life. He died at the age of ninety-eight!

Eastern literature contains many stories of individuals who had access to the Elderhood Enlightenments (as I prefer to call them) at early stages of biological development. One example is Shankara, the East Indian Sage and Teacher, whose precociousness—I would call it access to Elderhood Illumination—was present in childhood. Franklin Merrell-Wolff would often speak to me of this most remarkable young Sage and mathematician, who lived in India from A.D. 788 to 820. He told me Shankara realized that the stage of consciousness operating through him was of a supernal order of being, referred to in the East as an intermediate principle of consciousness, or a *Tulku*. When Shankara was sixteen, his access to the Tulku was ending, though he somehow renewed his access to it for another sixteen years, until he reached the age of thirty-two. The Wisdom state was then completely withdrawn. (People often ask me how this withdrawal occurs, and I must acknowledge that I simply don't know.) Shankara, having lived almost his entire life in the Wisdoms, was so overwhelmed with grief when he was left with his ordinary, simple state of individual being-ness that he is said to have taken his own life at the age of thirty-three.

Elderhood consciousness has various degrees of expandedness.

There is the Elderhood of an individual who has simply lived a long life at the ordinary level of consciousness. There is also the historical family Elder, who deals with the richness of the family or clan background at both a personal and a collective level. There are Elders of a community or a culture, with access to the collective pool of the community or the culture. Then there are ranges into the universal collective, carrying the richness of humanity as a whole. This latter state is represented by our great Incarnates or Teachers. It will only rarely and partially manifest in a single individual and has yet to manifest in any individual in its full, universal aspect. It doesn't take much to realize that even Christ and Buddha are but partial incarnations of the universal collective Self. Perhaps the actual universal Self may only be experienced through the whole of the human collective and cannot be embodied in any single individual.

Obviously, the closer one comes to the universal Elder state of consciousness, the deeper and richer are the wisdoms. Again, I don't feel that Adults *develop* into Elders, just as I don't feel that Children *develop* into Adults. That is an illusion based on what appears to be continuity of the physical form. Indeed, the body does pass through stages of development, but the psyche is not restricted to such processes. The development of the body and the development of consciousness are not correlated one to one. Biological age and psychological age are, for the most part, independent of one another.

In the East, the Sage often states that nothing needs to be done to attain Realization. Everyone is already Realized. When we take the perspective I am presenting in this book, one in which the Self is regarded as including a multiplicity of inner beings, we see that the Sage is correct—and we see why. Any individual's equivalent of the Fully Realized state *is already* formed yet unexperienced by his or her conscious sense of self. When we don't know we are fully Realized, it is only because we are in another vehicle of consciousness, which serves a different purpose. Knowledge gained in both places in consciousness is correct: the non-Realized person knows from a non-Realized state that he or she is not Realized, and the Sage knows from the Realized state that he or she *is* Realized. Each is recognizing a relative truth. The mistake made in the former circumstance is to imagine that the non-Realized vehicle of consciousness will develop into the Realized state. This does not happen. The non-Realized state will always be non-Realized. The individual must learn how to move from one interior vehicle to another interior vehicle . . . in this case, from the ordinary to the transordinary vehicle. And this involves a relative death/birth.

The Blinders of Youth

In our contemporary American society, which overly celebrates youthfulness, the Elder and the function of the Elder have been almost totally eclipsed and even rejected. When we so identify with the Child and Youth, there is little for most people to contemplate or to anticipate beyond these two developmental stages. The gods and goddesses of Youth, with their sexual attractiveness, vitality of mind and body, and seeming immortality are cruel and uncompromising, guarding their resources jealously. The loss (actual or threatened) of what is valued in the Child and Youth states of consciousness usually leads to senses of rejection, abandonment, loss of power and prestige, and a dismal or demeaning outlook about the remaining stages of life. The aging individual is cast on a huge dung heap and often isolated and shielded from a society that doesn't care to view that which is physically weak, perhaps decaying, and certainly—from the perspective of Youth and Beauty—nonego-enhancing. And this is the very point that must be made. Our attitudes and beliefs about aging and Elderhood are based in and viewed through the consciousness of the Child, the Youth, and the Youthful Parent vehicles of awareness and are steeped in issues of control. Therefore, our view is invariably biased and prejudicial. Worse yet, in our culture there are very few, if any, good examples of true Elderhood that people might emulate. When no outer example exists to inspire and to induct individuals who are approaching Elderhood consciousness, such individuals tend to regress into childhood, infancy, and fetal states of consciousness or to withdraw from Life completely.

I have begun to wonder if degenerative, debilitating diseases of old age are somehow related to the deep psyche's not wanting to face getting older and yet not being able to die, either. Such a psyche unconsciously manifests its worst fears and attitudes about aging and dying and therefore lives its fears rather than living the resources and experiences that the Elder stage of the life cycle potentially represents.

Our images of getting older are horrific and overwhelming. Even when we are resigned to aging, the process is not without resentment and anxiety at some level. Could it be that such a large number of people die between the ages of forty-five and fifty-four due to the cultural abhorrence of the aging process and the simultaneous inability to surrender the powers and resources of Youth and of the Prime Adult?

When one or several related stages of psychological development are almost exclusively dominant, such as is occurring in our society with the Child and the Youth, one can be sure that we are witnessing but a single stage in a much longer collective cycle. Only when the society is at mature stages of development do all the stages of the cycle blend harmoniously. Times of chaos and rapid change require the facile bodies and minds of the youth of a collective. But the youthful stages must eventually give way to the Elder if the full fruition of any new cycle is to be fully realized.

One concern we might have about returning to an emphasis on Elderhood is the danger of tapping into its dark side. The dark side of the Elder deals with those aspects that seek to *control*, to fixate individuals or society at previously successful but contemporarily inappropriate ways of expressing life. The dark Elder in this form constantly refers to the old days as the better days. It brings forward fundamentalism as the solution to current problems. It seeks stability in terms of past solutions. It does not recognize unconscious motives and their implications ... especially those involving defense against change and a lack of trust that old dilemmas can be resolved by the dance of Life and by the wisdoms of Life's creative potential.

Under the stress of anticipating death and dissolution, an individual approaching Elderhood can easily fall prey to these darker, controlling elements of the Elder state. This, in fact, is exactly what has transpired in our society. We have incarnated the dark Elder into our midst. This is the person who is controlling, critical of the present, angry over the loss of physical power, dreading death, filled with arthritis and chronic pain, losing sight and hearing, and has a bedside table filled with prescription bottles.

How are we to encourage the incarnation of mature Elderhood, with its balanced approaches to life and death and its access to the larger degrees of collective wisdom? How do we, at the same time, prevent ourselves from defending so vigorously against the dark Elder that we unconsciously attract to ourselves only a narrow and contracted manifestation of this stage of life?

My own approach is simple. Whenever my travels bring me near individuals who manifest Elderhood states, I make an effort to visit with them. For me, the best approach is not to engage them from an intellectual or cognitive aspect. Rather, I just hang out with them, rub up against them, so to speak . . . opening myself as fully as possible to the presence of the Elder self in these persons. I am also alert for the other aspects in them that may be similar to, but not truly part of, the Elderhood resource. Elderhood and Childhood, for example, can sometimes resemble each other closely. I have come to believe, in fact, that most of our older populations are more in touch with the Infant and the Child states of consciousness than with any of the stages of Elderhood. But Childhood resources, as rich as they may be, cannot come close to the depth and expanse of those of the transcendent Elder.

A most powerful way to be with Elders is through mutual meditation, whereby a fusion of consciousness . . . of one's own *into* the Elder's . . . occurs. My experience in doing this started with Eunice Hurt, the outer Teacher who awakened me to my Soul's Path. As Eunice would say, it was as though she were "carrying individuals on her back" into the dimensions she was engaging. Although Eunice was only forty-six when I met her, she manifested an Elder state when she entered certain vehicles of consciousness. Meditations with Hannah Veary in Honolulu; with Satya Sai Baba in Bangalore, India; with Sir George Trevelyan in Southern England; and with Franklin Merrell-Wolff in Lone Pine, California, enrich my life and Beinghood through Elderhood inductions.

Throughout this book, I have emphasized that the deep psyche only reads *patterns of forces* and that the personal identity of the individual carrying those patterns is not important. Of course, this continues to be true in regard to the forces of Elderhood. The person's state of consciousness, not his or her outer personality, is what is being attuned to.

The similarity of Presence among all the individuals I mentioned above was truly remarkable. This leads me to believe that transcendental states are collective states, or collective vehicles, to which an individual finds his or her equivalences. The collective, transpersonal realms unite all humans and give us our sense of Soul/Spirit as *Humanity*. I am sure this is why there is so much consensus among developed Elders. Just as there are but a few fundamental patterns of Motherhood to which, in varying degrees and in varying combinations, all individuals attune, there are but a few essential patterns of Elderhood. The Elderhoods meld the personal and the transpersonal in the context of the fullness of life from birth to death. No other vehicle of consciousness can serve this purpose. Thus Elderhood is invaluable—both to the individual and to the collective.

Universal Elderhood, however, can never be completely incarnated in any one individual. Certain people may reflect aspects of it more profoundly than others, but its fullness can only manifest inclusively through the collective itself, through the Elders of many societies, in many places, and of many diverse traditions. Someday, when the Great Elders gather, the face of the Universal Elder may briefly grace us.

New Perceptions of Parenting

An excellent way to begin offering a sense of direction to older individuals within our culture while the true Elderhoods are redeveloping—a meaningful and fulfilling way—can easily be appreciated through some of the work of Laura Huxley. She has advocated the establishment of local community resource centers where older individuals of the community can make themselves available to care for the young children of working parents. Huxley's may be an idea that has arrived too early to be implemented, since so much emphasis today is placed on the idea that each woman should be a full mother to her own children. What is usually not recognized, however, is that few, if any, mothers can actually handle the full range of motherhood responsibilities—from pregnancy through dealing with a child's leaving home.

In this regard, my experience with having heard the feelings of thousands of women is that some women love pregnancy and detest the rest of child-rearing. Some mothers detest pregnancy and love the infancy stages but loathe the later stages. Some mothers hate the earlier stages of raising children and love the teen years. Some women hate the entire experience and wish it had never happened, while others love every moment of the entire cycle. The range of feelings of adequacy and inadequacy that women have over the experience of Motherhood is phenomenal!

Other civilizations have realized that no one mother can be all that any one child might require in its development. Thus, collective child-rearing has been successfully explored by many, many cultures throughout the world, both historically and presently. The extended family approach—either via the clan or the community, including the Elders—could offer a great advantage in child-rearing, as the resources and emotional stability of the collective can dilute out the momentary lapses of individual parents.

Perhaps the disruption of the family unit in our culture is actually in preparation for an era of collective parenting. The children entering life in these times require a much larger perspective on the world and on relationships than can be offered in a single family or even in a single ethnic grouping. The world is rapidly moving past such circumstances. A whole new perception of the individual and collective self/Self is unfolding, and with it are coming radical changes in lifestyles, religion, relationships, and boundaries of possibility.

Our society's self-image is rapidly changing, especially due to the large influxes of people from Asia and the Middle East. A most wonderful opportunity thus exists for creative interaction and cross-fertilization, in terms not only of ideas, cultures, and religions, but also of genetics. The changes have come so fast that collective immune mechanisms may activate and destroy or curtail such creative interactions; the cultural, ethnic, and racial dark Elderhoods could also contribute to regressive possibilities. Yet the hope and inspiration of our incarnating more universally oriented Elders, who can lift our eyes to appreciate the human family and its rhythmic relationship to Life, is powerfully potential in the physical, psychological, and spiritual blendings that are currently manifesting.

Possibilities for the Future

As the masculine focus on exclusivity, deification of the mind, mental abstraction through mathematics and technology, glorification of physical prowess, goal-orientation, and accomplishment begins to soften in dominance, the feeling of the world as an extended family ... of unique friends living in various places ... becomes more and more possible. The earth itself can be perceived as an organic whole again, something to be valued and revered, as feminine elements of healing and relatedness are expressed more openly and widely by men and women as individuals and as collectives. Religious dogmas and other beliefs that demean life, the body, and the world may begin to atrophy. Incarnating beings may once again be able to celebrate the full expression of the Soul/Spirit Mystery ... an inclusive expression of the body, and the mind, and the spirit. The spiritual pathway reflected by the ten ox-herding pictures of Zen may come to prominence, and the rich resources of the Elderhood state may be reflected into Life instead of away from Life.

The simplistic approach in which each individual is regarded as a single, isolated unit could vanish, as new realizations about the unconscious aspects of self/Self spread through the interior and exterior worlds like a smile of recognition. As we have a new basis for our beliefs about reality, vast new possibilities in law, medicine, psychiatry, psychology, sociology, theology, and relationships of all kinds will be set into motion.

We will discover new ways to look at war.

Isn't it intriguing, for example, that the nuclear bomb issue, with its threat of total destruction and annihilation, is basically the same projection from the Unconscious as that of Lucifer, the light bearer, who was also everywhere present to destroy or to annihilate? Only a brief span of seventy-five years separates the Western world's old belief that the earth is a dangerous place because of Lucifer from its new belief that the earth is a dangerous place because of nuclear weaponry. Little children were worried as much about the Devil then as they are now about the nuclear bomb. Both issues, however, are the same: the projection of the unconscious dark masculine intellect onto whichever outer screen comes closest to being able to carry the pattern.

The degree to which our society disowns and therefore rejects the ultimate destructive aspects of the psyche and projects these unintegrated issues onto the nuclear bomb is the degree to which our society is psychologically and spiritually immature. Equally important issues that carry the same societal immaturity are our collective rejection and disownment of sexuality from infancy to old age and our collective rejection and disownment of the Feminine.

Too much alienation, isolation, abstraction, and intellectualization are the very forces that are contributing to the decline of the Masculine in our culture. Behind the exaggerated expression of these masculine elements are vast currents of unconscious fears of intimate relationship to the body, to people, and to life.

The solution to the problem is obvious: getting beyond the regressive and instinctual patterns which are activated by anything that makes us feel powerless and meaningless.

Antiwar demonstrations and peace marches to save the planet or to provide a safe world for our children will not help. They are part of the problem and not mature solutions. They are exactly the same approach that is taken by those who perceive the need to convert everyone to a particular religious viewpoint and rid the world of Satan. Both are unconsciously based in issues of control and feelings of intrinsic inadequacy or powerlessness! You can't uninvent the ultimate weapon and you can't uninvent the dark masculine. They must be integrated into our sense of self.

One great possibility for bringing about a solution is to call upon the maturity, wisdom, and healing power of the universal Elder in its combined male and female form. This combination does not distinguish between cultures and nations and does not need to compete with or for the masculine or the feminine. I emphasize the *universal* Elder because "any old elder" will not do. What is required are the rich resources of the masculine aspect of the Elder self (which values the creative adaptation that is stimulated by disruptive forces for change) and the healing power of the feminine aspect of the Elder self. These two aspects can begin to unite what masculine intelligence has carved into pieces over thousands of years. This statement is not intended to demean all the great contributions to life and to living that the Masculine has brought about over the millennia. It *is* intended to indict the infantile patterning of the human psyche that manifests when vulnerability and loss of control begin to threaten. As I mentioned earlier in this book, only the feminine aspects of the psyche can heal, and for the Masculine to surrender and to receive the benefits of the feminine healing powers, the male must subordinate and surrender himself. But this is not easy, for the only reason the male usually can surrender to God ... in contrast to a Goddess, the void, formlessness, or nonexistence ... is that he instinctively thinks he knows what God is. To surrender to the unknown, the chaotic, the undefined, may be too difficult for the Masculine. After all, we may remind ourselves that both Freud and Jung concluded that the Masculine takes form because of a need to defend against the Feminine.

The Realization of Presence

Then ... finally and ultimately, for an individual to transcend even the Elderhoods, to come into relationship with inner and outer totality, to unify experience at every level of awareness, to bring all the selves, stages, and aspects of life together under an overarching wholeness and inclusivity, a universal, transcendental vehicle of consciousness is required. The term I use to reflect the integration and fullness of this transcendental vehicle is PRESENCE.

People who have this quality are remarkably developed psychospiritually. They are inclusive and at peace within themselves. Their Unconditional Love is palpable. Individuals carrying this sacred form of PRESENCE into the marketplaces of the world cause the flowering of the collective human soul.

I am not of that order at this stage of my own life cycle. I have a deep yearning to be so, but I have still incomplete patterns, mistakes to make, and life experiences to engage in order to have the necessary depth and richness of Being. I touch degrees of the wisdoms, yet almost daily I discover the need for further integration of so many aspects that are still fragmented and isolated.

The most powerful and direct way I have discovered to facilitate the development of PRESENCE—one's full incarnation blended with the vast collective pools of Being—is through a meditation I call *The Realization of Presence*. It is based on the material in this book.

The meditation has six parts, which I present here as I practice them myself. The sequences are logical and, once the essential structure is understood, they are easy to remember. After the presentation of the meditation, I offer some informal comments that may be helpful and can augment your experience. At the conclusion of the chapter, I have included a summary of the meditation for quick reference. For those who might find value in a prerecorded version or who desire a direct experience of the state of consciousness from which I present this material to groups, I have also prepared a professionally recorded audio cassette tape of the meditation. However, that cassette is simply a convenience and is not necessary for successful practice of the meditation.

I suggest that you prepare yourself for this meditation by sitting quietly and comfortably. Place your hands lightly on you Heart Center (the lower front area of your chest), with your left hand on top of your right hand and your thumb tips touching gently. Take a few deep breaths to relax into the meditational state of consciousness, then proceed by giving silent attention to each statement in the following sequence. *Feel* (don't merely think about) the forces working through you. Let the intent of each aspect of the meditation work on you. Let the meditation do you!

Six-Part Meditation on the Realization of Presence

Part I. Psychological Preparation
1. Contemplate the intention of this meditation, which is to enter

a state of consciousness that experiences the full range of your incarnational resources blended with the vast collective pools of Being. The experience of this Realization is called Presence. Seek that aspect of your Being that yearns for the Realization of Presence. This intention must be your single consideration at the outset of the meditation.

2. Next, acknowledge that you desire to blend and fuse consciously with the balanced nature of all forces, known and unknown. This is called the directive of the meditation.

3. Finally, conduct an inner evaluation by asking yourself this question: "Are the personal selves in harmony, ready to release control in order to blend and fuse consciously with the balanced forces of greater and greater arenas of awareness?" If not, use your meditation time to do inner healing and harmonizing work, then continue the meditation itself on another occasion. If so, experience a sphere of protective light around yourself and proceed.

Part II. Stimulation of the Chakras

In this part of the meditation, you may rest your hands comfortably in your lap or gently place them, in turn, over each chakra as it is stimulated by your awareness. Figure 1 (page 318) will assist you in finding the chakras.

1. Now blend and fuse consciously with the balanced forces of the first chakra (root chakra), concentrating your awareness in the area between the anus and either the lower opening of the vagina or the beginning of the scrotum. Breathe into this energy center several times. Continue until you feel a stirring or a sense of aliveness there. Imagine a gradually expanding ball of warm, radiant energy gently developing. When your awareness is well centered in the root chakra, lift your sense of this energy until you . . .

2. . . . blend and fuse consciously with the balanced forces of the second chakra (sexual chakra), concentrating your awareness in the lower central abdomen, just above the pubic bone. Breathe into this energy center several times. Continue until you feel a stirring or a sense of aliveness there. Imagine a gradually expanding ball of warm, radiant energy gently developing. When your awareness is well centered in the second chakra, image or direct your awareness down to restimulate the first chakra . . . breathe into the first chakra . . . then gently direct your

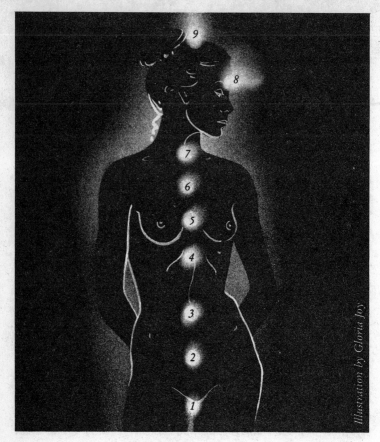

Illustration by Gloria Joy

1. *First Chakra*

2. *Second Chakra*

3. *Mid-abdominal Chakra*

4. *Third Chakra*

5. *Fourth Chakra*

6. *Mid-chest Chakra*

7. *Fifth Chakra*

8. *Sixth Chakra*

9. *Seventh Chakra*

*awareness back up to restimulate the second chakra . . . and breathe into
the second chakra. Now lift this sense of energy awareness until you . . .*

3. *. . . blend and fuse consciously with the balanced forces of the
mid-abdomen chakra, concentrating your awareness in the umbilical
area. Breathe into this energy center several times, until you feel a stirring there. When your awareness is well centered in the mid-abdomen
chakra, image or direct your awareness down to restimulate the second
chakra . . . breathe into the second chakra . . . then image or direct your
awareness down to restimulate the first chakra . . . breathe into the first
chakra . . . then gently direct your awareness back up to restimulate the
second chakra . . . breathe into the second chakra . . . then gently direct
your awareness back up to restimulate the mid-abdomen chakra. Now
lift this sense of energy awareness until you . . .*

4. *. . . blend and fuse consciously with the balanced forces of the
third chakra (solar plexus chakra), concentrating your awareness in the
solar plexus in the central upper abdomen. Breathe into this energy center several times, until you feel a stirring there. When your awareness
is well centered in the third chakra, gently direct your awareness down
to restimulate the mid-abdomen chakra, then the second chakra, then
the first chakra, then the second chakra again, the mid-abdomen chakra
again, and back to restimulate the third chakra, breathing in turn into
each chakra. Now lift this sense of energy awareness until you . . .*

5. *. . . blend and fuse consciously with the balanced forces of the
fourth chakra (the Heart Chakra), concentrating your awareness in the
lower front chest area. Breathe into this energy center several times, until
you feel a stirring there. When your awareness is well centered in the
Heart Chakra, gently image or direct your awareness down to restimulate each successive lower chakra to the first chakra and back up through
each successive chakra to the fourth chakra, breathing in turn into each
chakra. Now lift this sense of energy awareness until you . . .*

6. *. . . blend and fuse consciously with the balanced forces of the
mid-chest chakra, concentrating your awareness in the upper mid-chest
area. Breathe into this energy center several times, until you feel a stirring there. When your awareness is well centered in the mid-chest chakra,
gently image or direct your awareness down to restimulate each successive lower chakra to the first chakra and then back up through each*

successive chakra to the mid-chest chakra, breathing in turn into each chakra. Now lift this sense of energy awareness until you ...

7. *... blend and fuse consciously with the balanced forces of the* fifth chakra *(throat chakra), concentrating your awareness in the lower throat area. Breathe into this energy center several times, until you feel a stirring there. When your awareness is well centered in the throat chakra, gently image or direct your awareness down to restimulate each successive lower chakra to the first chakra and then back up through each successive chakra to the throat chakra, breathing in turn into each chakra. Now lift this sense of energy awareness until you ...*

8. *... blend and fuse consciously with the balanced forces of the* sixth chakra *(forehead chakra), concentrating your awareness in the forehead area, just above where the bridge of the nose connects to the forehead. Breathe into this energy center several times, until you feel a stirring there. When your awareness is well centered in the forehead chakra, gently image or direct your awareness down to restimulate each successive lower chakra to the first chakra and then back up through each successive chakra to the forehead chakra, breathing in turn into each chakra. Now lift this sense of energy awareness until you ...*

9. *... blend and fuse consciously with the balanced forces of the* seventh chakra *(crown chakra), concentrating your awareness in the area at the top of the head. Breathe into this energy center several times, until you feel a stirring there. When your awareness is well centered in the crown chakra, gently image or direct your awareness down to restimulate each successive lower chakra to the first chakra and then back up through each successive chakra to the crown chakra, breathing in turn into each chakra.*

Part III. Purifying, Balancing, and Heightening the Developmental Stages and Their Aspects

1. Now call forth those forces that can CLEAR, CLEANSE, BALANCE, ATTUNE, HARMONIZE, and HEIGHTEN the self/selves at the stage of the Creation/Conceptus, *the product of the union of the sperm with the egg, in the aspects of the:*

> A. Physical
> B. Sexual

C. *Emotional*
D. *Mental*
E. *Intuitive*
F. *Social*
G. *Environmental*
H. *Spiritual*
I. *Cosmic*

2. ... *then call forth those forces that can CLEAR, CLEANSE, BALANCE, ATTUNE, HARMONIZE, and HEIGHTEN the self/selves at the stage of the* Embryonic, *repeating the sequence aspect by aspect, from the Physical through the Cosmic* ...

3. ... *then call forth those forces that can CLEAR, CLEANSE, BALANCE, ATTUNE, HARMONIZE, and HEIGHTEN the self/selves at the stage of the* Fetus, *repeating the sequence aspect by aspect, from the Physical through the Cosmic* ...

4. ... *then call forth those forces that can CLEAR, CLEANSE, BALANCE, ATTUNE, HARMONIZE, and HEIGHTEN the self/selves at the stage of the* Infant, *repeating the sequence aspect by aspect, from the Physical through the Cosmic* ...

5. ... *then call forth those forces that can CLEAR, CLEANSE, BALANCE, ATTUNE, HARMONIZE, and HEIGHTEN the self/selves at the stage of the* Child, *repeating the sequence aspect by aspect, from the Physical through the Cosmic* ...

6. ... *then call forth those forces that can CLEAR, CLEANSE, BALANCE, ATTUNE, HARMONIZE, and HEIGHTEN the self/selves at the stage of the* Pubertal, *repeating the sequence aspect by aspect, from the Physical through the Cosmic* ...

7. ... *then call forth those forces that can CLEAR, CLEANSE, BALANCE, ATTUNE, HARMONIZE, and HEIGHTEN the self/selves at the stage of the* Adolescent, *repeating the sequence aspect by aspect, from the Physical through the Cosmic* ...

8. ... *then call forth those forces that can CLEAR, CLEANSE, BALANCE, ATTUNE, HARMONIZE, and HEIGHTEN the self/selves at the stage of the* Young Adult, *repeating the sequence aspect by aspect, from the Physical through the Cosmic* ...

9. ... *then call forth those forces that can CLEAR, CLEANSE,*

BALANCE, ATTUNE, HARMONIZE, and HEIGHTEN the self/selves at the stage of the Prime Adult, *repeating the sequence aspect by aspect, from the Physical through the Cosmic . . .*

10. *. . . then call forth those forces that can CLEAR, CLEANSE, BALANCE, ATTUNE, HARMONIZE, and HEIGHTEN the self/selves at the stage of the* Early Elder *(the elder of the family/clan), repeating the sequence aspect by aspect, from the Physical through the Cosmic . . .*

11. *. . . then call forth those forces that can CLEAR, CLEANSE, BALANCE, ATTUNE, HARMONIZE, and HEIGHTEN the self/selves at the stage of the* Middle Elder *(the elder of the ethnic group or community), repeating the sequence aspect by aspect, from the Physical through the Cosmic . . .*

12. *. . . then call forth those forces that can CLEAR, CLEANSE, BALANCE, ATTUNE, HARMONIZE, and HEIGHTEN the self/selves at the stage of the* Full Elder *(the Universal Elder, the elder to humanity as a whole), repeating the sequence aspect by aspect, from the Physical through the Cosmic . . .*

13. *. . . then call forth those forces that can CLEAR, CLEANSE, BALANCE, ATTUNE, HARMONIZE, and HEIGHTEN the self/selves at the stage of* Dissolution/Death, *in the aspects of the:*

> A. *Physical*
> B. *Sexual*
> C. *Emotional*
> D. *Mental*
> E. *Intuitive*
> F. *Social*
> G. *Environmental*
> H. *Spiritual*
> I. *Cosmic*

Part IV. Soul/Spirit Blending

1. *Consciously blend and fuse all these stages with the balanced forces of that which comes from the Earth (the collective Soul). Open to a force that penetrates inward through the feet and slowly moves up through the body and out through the top of the head. Blend personal soul with Collective Soul . . .*

2. ... *then consciously blend and fuse all these stages with the balanced forces of that which comes from the Sky (the collective Spirit). Open to a force that penetrates through the top of the head and slowly moves through the body and out throught the feet. Blend personal spirit with Collective Spirit.*

Part V. Acknowledgment of the Center

1. Acknowledge the forces of the cardinal directions: the north, the south, the east, and the west, and the full mystery of their Center ...

2. ... then from the mystery of the Center, consciously blend and fuse with the balanced forces of the collective conscious and the collective Unconscious by imaging a point of awareness in the Heart Chakra that slowly expands, spherically, into the infinite.

Part VI. Final Merging

Consciously blend and fuse your full sense of Being with:

SOURCE

ESSENCE

... surrendering into a state of consciousness that allows the emergence of the desired state of:

PRESENCE.

Upon attaining this state, simply be in it. Allow yourself to flow fully into whatever awareness presents itself to you. You may also wish to make some declaration of purpose in regard to your life. My own practice at this point is to ask that I be made an instrument of Divine intention and a blessing in service to humanity as a whole.

Be PRESENCE.

Then, when you are ready to leave the meditation, find the place in consciousness that yearns to return to the outer levels of awareness ...

*to the personal, to the individual, to the unique senses of Self . . . and
completely release the heightened state to enter the more ordinary states,
refreshed and prepared to open to the unfoldment of your Soul/Spirit.*

Commentary on the Meditation

Part I. Psychological Preparation

Step 1 (the Intention): You want to attain a full experience of yearning for the Realization of Presence before you start the unfoldment of
the meditation.

Step 2 (the Directive): Seeking a balanced experience of the forces is
very important, as the psyche can be thrown into extremes of polarity
if the meditation is not guided from the outset by your desire for centeredness and balance.

Step 3 (Inner Evaluation): Here you want to sense your interior to see
if your known selves are ready to subordinate themselves to a vaster state
of beingness. If there is a self (or selves) unwilling to enter the discipline,
don't try to proceed with the meditation. Rather, spend time in inner
dialogue to ascertain the concern or the resistance. (When I appreciate my
senses of selves from a state of Unconditional Love, they invariably yield
to the overall intention of this meditation, as each discerns the empowerment that comes from being part of a larger wholeness.)

With the Intention, Directive, and Inner Evaluation completed, you
next call for the protective shield of light, which allows you to proceed
without concern into the vulnerable experience of expansion. This shield
can be imagined as a sphere of light or energy that has the qualities of
protection and insulation. It may also be a sacred image that has the
power to induct you into an expansive, protected area of awareness. It
may be the state of consciousness you achieve when you call forth and
enter your Sacred Temple by the Sea through the meditation elaborated
in Chapter 5.

Remember that you want to feel each energy dynamic, each state of
consciousness, each part of Self as deeply and as richly as possible.

Part II. Stimulation of the Chakras

Become deeply aware of the body area where each chakra is located.
To enhance this experience, you may also place your hands gently over

the energy centers while you stimulate them with your awareness. As you focus your awareness on each chakra, breathe into it by slowly inhaling and directing the sense of your breath to that part of your body. See if you can feel a stirring or a sense of radiant energy there. Let this energy sensation build until it gathers strength and can be gently lowered or raised through the body as directed.

As the meditation progresses and you move your attention downward to restimulate the lower chakras, coordinate your breathing with your attention to each different chakra in order to enhance the sense of energy movement. Breathe into the next chakra area as you approach it. Exhale as you focus your attention there, then inhale as you move to the next chakra, directing your breath into that next area. In awakening the energy centers, you may become aware of resources, attributes, or images associated with the individual chakras or you may merely experience an energetic. Either is fine. Both are fine.

If you have not felt the energy of consciousness concentrated in an area of your body or moving as energy currents through your body, you may need to begin slowly, taking the time to feel an aliveness slowly stirring deep inside your body, in the place your awareness is being directed. The possible sensations are actually too varied to permit specific comment but they usually feel like a sphere of warm light or radiance. On rare occasions, they may even have the qualities of an orgasm.

Don't rush any of the experiences or linger too long with them. (It is important not to let any energy run rampant in the body. Rather, maintain a pleasurable control over the focus and movement of the energy.) Soon, you will achieve the most enjoyable rate of energy concentration and energy flow.

Part III. Purifying, Balancing, and Heightening the Developmental Stages and Their Aspects

Here, where you call for forces that can CLEAR, CLEANSE, BAL-ANCE, ATTUNE, HARMONIZE, and HEIGHTEN, feel the forces behind these words and experience as deeply as possible the effect they have on each of the subsequent stages of development. Understand that:

• To clear and to cleanse refers to forces of purification;

• To balance and to attune involves coming to a fulcrum point or a balanced experience of a stage;

• *To harmonize and to heighten* refers to bringing your consciousness to a deeper and more intense experience of the particular stage.

With the six forces activated, you then experience the aspects of each stage, from the Physical through the Cosmic. (It doesn't matter whether you have lived long enough to have expressed all the stages outwardly. The meditation allows for the experience of known and yet-to-be-known stages of development.)

Part IV. Soul/Spirit Blending

These two steps are intended to mend the split between spirit and soul, between mind and body, between Spirit and Soul.

Step 1. After working with all the stages and aspects, your consciousness is blended and fused with the balanced forces of that which comes from the Earth. What you desire is a sense of merging your own soul with the planetary, Collective Soul. (At a deep psychological level, the perception of the body and the perception of the planet are intermixed and may even be regarded as identical.) Here you want to expand your sense of Being from the personal and individual experience of the body/soul to the collective and the universal sense of Planet/ Soul. Feel this!

Step 2. Your intention here is to merge your individual sense of mind/spirit with the Divine Mind/Collective Spirit.

Part V. Acknowledgment of the Center

Step 1. When acknowledging the directional forces, let your personal experience and understanding of the four great directions be augmented by your creative imagination and your capacity to break into ranges of human experience beyond the personal. When you complete the recognition of the cardinal directions you will find yourself in the midst of a great mystery . . . that of being at the Center.

Step 2. From this Center you now can contemplate blending and fusing consciously with the balanced forces of the collective conscious and the collective Unconscious. This brings you once more into relationship with the vast collective pools of consciousness. To stabilize the psyche, you can use the power of an infinitely expanding sphere to bring you into an integrated experience with these forces. Experiencing yourself *as an infinitely expanding sphere also compels the psyche to move to a place of simultaneous awareness.*

Again, remember to sense this meditation deeply ... to feel the Intention and the Directive. Also remember to deeply sense and to feel the forces, stages, and aspects so when you enter the final blending you are as fully and experientially awakened to the parts of the Whole as you can possibly be. Merely thinking about or just repeating the different steps of the meditation from memory is not enough.

MEDITATION SUMMARY

Part I. Psychological Preparation

1. The Intention: The Realization of Presence.

2. The Directive: To blend and fuse consciously with the balanced nature of all forces, known and unknown.

3. Inner Evaluation: Are the personal selves ready to release control in order to blend and fuse consciously with the balanced forces of greater and greater arenas of awareness?

> *a. If not, do inner healing and harmonizing work.*
>
> *b. If so, experience a sphere of protective light around yourself and proceed.*

Part II. Stimulation of the Chakras

Consciously blend and fuse with the balanced forces of each chakra in ascending sequence, augmenting this process by directing your breath to that chakra. Before proceeding to the next chakra, direct your attention to and breathe into each successive lower chakra down to the first chakra then back, chakra by chakra, to the chakra above the one where you began the descent.

> *1. First chakra (root chakra)*
> *2. Second chakra (sexual chakra)*
> *3. Mid-abdomen chakra*
> *4. Third chakra (solar plexus chakra)*
> *5. Fourth chakra (Heart Chakra)*
> *6. Mid-chest chakra*

7. *Fifth chakra (throat chakra)*
8. *Sixth chakra (forehead chakra)*
9. *Seventh chakra (crown chakra)*

Part III. Purifying, Balancing, and Heightening the Developmental Stages and Their Aspects

1. Call forth those forces that can:

> *CLEAR*
> *CLEANSE*
> *BALANCE*
> *ATTUNE*
> *HARMONIZE*
> *HEIGHTEN*

2. At the stage of the:

> A. *Creation/Conceptus*
> B. *Embryonic*
> C. *Fetus*
> D. *Infant*
> E. *Child*
> F. *Pubertal*
> G. *Adolescent*
> H. *Young Adult*
> I. *Prime Adult*
> J. *Early Elder*
> K. *Middle Elder*
> L. *Full Elder*
> M. *Dissolution/Death.*

3. For each stage, do this in each of the following aspects:

> A. *Physical*
> B. *Sexual*
> C. *Emotional*

> D. *Mental*
> E. *Intuitive*
> F. *Social*
> G. *Environmental*
> H. *Spiritual*
> I. *Cosmic*

Part IV. Soul/Spirit Blending

1. Blend and fuse all the stages with the balanced forces of the Earth (collective Soul). Be aware of a force entering the feet and moving slowly through the body to exit out the crown. Blend personal soul with Collective Soul.

2. Blend and fuse all the stages with the balanced forces of the Sky (collective Spirit). Be aware of a force entering the crown and moving slowly through the body to exit out the feet. Blend personal spirit with Collective Spirit.

Part V. Acknowledgment of the Center

1. Acknowledge the forces of the cardinal directions and the full mystery of their Center.

2. Blend and fuse with the balanced forces of the collective conscious and the collective Unconscious by imaging a point of awareness in the Heart Chakra that expands spherically into the infinite.

Part VI. Final Merging

Consciously blend and fuse your full sense of Being with:

SOURCE

ESSENCE

. . . surrendering into a state of consciousness that allows the emergence of the desired state of:

PRESENCE.

When you are ready to leave the meditation, completely release the heightened state and enter the more ordinary states, refreshed and prepared to open to the unfoldment of your Soul/Spirit.

As you practice this meditation on a daily basis, the full empowerment and aliveness of your Beinghood become more and more available to you, more a part of your everyday experience. The ordinary and the transordinary begin to blend until you find no difference between the sacred and the profane, for all is sacred and all is profane.

EPILOGUE

In the foregoing pages, I have endeavored to share with you my intuitions and my skills, my inspiration, concerns, insights, and vision, as well as my nightmares, forbidden thoughts, pain, and loss of innocence. I have sought to show why, as a result of accepting aspects of myself I previously rejected, I experienced an augmentation of my Being and my personal journey has been redirected to include the dark, the chaotic, and that which is not ego-enhancing.

Much to my surprise, I feel more wholesome and real, more grounded and inspired than when my psychospiritual Unfoldment was directed primarily toward perceiving and celebrating only the positive and the Light. I have realized that the richness and vulnerability of inclusively embracing life, the soul, and the spirit can heal distortions that are created when parts of the Self imagine themselves to be separate from and superior to the profound mysteries of Life and Death.

Life Itself teaches dramatically and powerfully through events centered around crisis, loss, and death. When such events are not embraced—when the dark, the demonic, and the destructive are not integrated—the conscious mind partitions itself from total consciousness and creates a reality reflecting only that which is acceptable to one's conscious awareness. That which is unacceptable simply disappears from awareness, though it certainly does not go away. What is created is a remarkable situation in which the right hand (consciousness) does not know what the left hand (unconsciousness) is doing. The left hand may know what the right hand is doing, but such a circumstance does not serve our conscious awareness ... our ordinary sense of reality.

As we discussed in the chapter on spirituality and sexuality, this primary compartmentalization of consciousness, which is a function of the brain, generates the mind/body split. The ego, using a defense to resolve the conflict created by its awareness of mortality, imagines itself to be immortal. In doing so, however, it sacrifices wholeness, the body, and the earth. An unconscious ego-rage against the vulnerability of the body and its mortality follows. This, I believe, is the basis of self-destructive attitudes that reflect both personally as unhealthy life-styles and ecologically as disregard for the physical environment. Certainly the Christian projection of Armageddon reflects this rage against the body. Mortality is, though, a fact of our existence and, in my opinion, until the conflict over this primary issue is resolved—through integration rather than denial—no effort to salvage the body or the planet is possible.

In my experience, an appreciation of physical mortality can immensely illumine the wonder and sacredness of the body. There is a natural appreciation of and urge to care for the sacred matter that has spawned our bodies ... sacred matter that is, in fact, the planet. The body and the planet are inextricably and forever linked in our deep psyches, though a shadow aspect of consciousness itself has obscured this fact and alienated us from our roots.

Obviously, then, I do not subscribe to an infantile idealization of existence and of the planet. Life is a teacher of great intensity and integrity. Its rewards are mostly beyond the ability of ordinary awareness to appreciate. Its lessons are often painful and final. The Awakening individual does not define mature livingness through children's values—those of personal love, nourishment, protection, immediate gratification, pleasure, sensuality, and unconscious sexuality. The Awakening individual is capable of undertaking a painful, dangerous, and arduous task for the experience of expanded development ... just as Life does when chaotic circumstances serve to churn or even to mutate its vast pool of precious genes, generating unexpected and more resourceful options for existence.

Most of life's dramatic moments cannot be handled with the resources of the Child, and adults who do revert to their Child under stress are a profound liability to themselves and to society. The reactions of people to calamitous events such as the San Francisco earthquake of 1989, the Bhopal gas disaster in India, the Valdez oil spill in Alaska, the Chernobyl nuclear rupture in the U.S.S.R., and hurricane Hugo, to mention only some of the most recent catastrophes, present numerous examples of the differences between adult individuals who approach disaster with the resources of their frightened Child (and who, in our society, often require social workers and therapists to help them handle the anxiety and fear) and those who approach disaster with the resources of a Mature Adult. Persons in that latter category are most likely those who have been initiated into Life and who feel awe and respect for nature, inspiration in regard to the capacity of human beings to help one another physically survive crisis, greater appreciation for their own lives, and a heightened understanding of their personal capacity to engage life and death and the responsibilities of existence.

As an Adult, I do not believe in sacrificing maturity to maintain the Child or to maintain the family context in which the Child aspects of the Adult attempt to survive. I need my full resources to enjoy and to appreciate Life—with its unknown destiny and its unknown purposes. And my soul yearns to discover individuals who can join me in exploring the Mystery of Life, who can do so without defense, and with strength, vulnerability, and a sense of inspiration.

The chthonic initiations help individuals incarnate their full inner strength and engage the mystery of Life more powerfully. True, not all individuals will survive and initiate through the horrific challenges to human life. But those who do are immensely capable of contributing to the overall well-being of our planet and its people.

Our brief journey together now draws to a close. To those of you who have found a sense of renovation and wholeness in this book, my wish is that your spiritual journey through Life may be a process of thorough Self-discovery. May an avalanche of your psyche awaken you to the Mystery Play of Life. And as you find your place in that Mystery Play, I say to you and ask you to appreciate the simple, time-honored phrase spoken by the priests and priestesses of the Theater when a fellow performer goes on stage: Break a leg!

Fall Equinox 1990
Moonfire Lodge
Paulden, Arizona

For information about ordering Brugh Joy's audio and video cassette tapes (including the audio tapes mentioned in this book) or to request information about his <u>non-residential</u> conferences and his lecture schedule, please contact:

Brugh Joy, Inc.
P.O. Box 895
Lucerne Valley, California 92356
(800) 523-3569
(619) 240-5472

For information about Brugh's <u>residential</u> conferences and workshops, please contact:

Moonfire Lodge
P.O. Box 730
Paulden, Arizona 86334-0730
(800) 525-7718
(602) 636-5579

INDEX

About the Author

W. Brugh Joy, M.D., conducts year-round residential workshops in the high desert of Northern Arizona at the Moonfire Lodge and weekend workshops throughout the U.S., Europe, and Canada.

Brugh Joy divides his time between Paulden, Arizona, and Lady Moon Lake, Colorado.